W9-BFQ-707

THE TEMPERING OF EUGENE O'NEILL

EUGENE

❄❄❄ *DORIS ALEXANDER*

THE

TEMPERING

OF

O' NEILL

HARCOURT, BRACE & WORLD, INC.   NEW   YORK

Many people have helped me make this book. First and foremost, I wish to thank Carlotta Monterey O'Neill for her overwhelming kindness to me, and for generously allowing me to quote from a number of the unpublished letters of Eugene O'Neill.

I am powerfully indebted to many librarians—those unsung heroes of research—and to many libraries. I want particularly to thank Elizabeth Baughman, Reference Librarian of the Chicago Historical Society, for her wonderfully prompt responses to my written inquiries, and for her personal assistance when I worked at the library. I wish to thank George H. Healey, Curator of the Department of Rare Books at the Cornell University Library, for making available to me the letters of Eugene O'Neill in the George Jean Nathan papers. I also am greatly indebted to Edward Connery Lathem, Director, Division of Special Collections at the Dartmouth College Library, for making available to me the letters and documents in the Landauer Collection. At the Harvard University Library I owe many thanks to both William Van Lennep, Curator of the Theatre Collection, and to William A. Jackson, Curator of the Manuscript Collection. Mr. Van Lennep went far out of his way to help me when I worked at the Theatre Collection. I also want to thank May Seymour, Curator of the Theatre Collection of the Museum of the City of New York, who has been unfailingly wise and kind during all my visits to the museum over a number of years. To the New York Public Library I owe more than I can possibly express. I wish particularly to thank Mr. George Freedley, Curator, as well as all the librarians of the Theatre Collection, and Rutherford D. Rogers, Chief of the Reference Department. I am also indebted to Alexander P. Clark, Curator of Manuscripts at the Princeton University Library, who has assisted me when I have worked with the William Seymour papers, the George Tyler papers, and the O'Neill manuscripts. I also want to thank Neda M. Westlake, Assistant Curator of Rare Books at the University of Pennsylvania, for making available to me the O'Neill manuscripts there. Finally, I owe a gargantuan debt to Donald Gallup, Curator of the American Literature Collection of the

Yale University Library. I wish also to add my thanks to Althea G. Wilson, formerly Librarian of the American Literature Collection, and Dorothy W. Bridgwater, Assistant Reference Librarian, of the Yale University Library.

Many other librarians have assisted me. I wish to thank Elsie M. Ditmars, Medical Records Librarian of the Bellevue Hospital Center; John J. Herzog, Librarian of the Bohemian Club, San Francisco; Frank Di Canio, Executive Librarian, the Chicago Law Institute; J. W. Reginald Scurr and Alfred Kubelsky of the Newspaper Service and Herbert H. Hewitt, Chief of the Reference Department, the Chicago Public Library; Florence M. Gifford, Head, General Reference Division of the Cleveland Public Library; the librarians of the Denver Public Library who assisted me when I was there; Grace Hope Walmsley, Reference Librarian of the Ferguson Library, Stamford, Connecticut (who went out of her way to assist me in finding materials in the library and in the Stamford Historical Society); Kimball C. Elkins, Senior Assistant, the Harvard University Archives; Alice P. Hook, Librarian of the Historical and Philosophical Society of Ohio, Cincinnati; Henry J. Dubester, Chief of the Reference Department of the Library of Congress; Morris Rieger, Archivist of the Industrial Records Branch, National Archives and Records Service, Washington, D.C.; Marjorie Ann Stuff, Chief Reference Librarian of the Omaha Public Library; Ethel L. Hutchins, Head of the Reference Department, the Public Library of Cincinnati and Hamilton County; Thelma C. Jefferies, Assistant in Local History at the Rochester Public Library; Mildred Boatman of the Reference Department of the St. Louis Public Library; L. J. Clarke, City Librarian, and D. Cadell, Reference Librarian, the San Francisco Public Library; Mary E. Freney of the Silas Bronson Library, Waterbury, Connecticut; Robert Rosenthal, Curator of Special Collections, the University of Chicago Library; and Gertrude Hassler, Assistant Librarian, the Western Reserve Historical Society.

I have also had invaluable help from many private persons. I want to thank Croswell Bowen for allowing me to see a number of documents in his possession to which I should otherwise not have had access. I owe very special thanks to Thomas Dorsey, Jr., for his valuable recollections of James and Ellen O'Neill, James O'Neill, Jr., and Eugene O'Neill. I wish to thank Harold Green for his kindness in showing me around the old grounds of Betts Academy and for giving me his recollections of his schoolmate Eugene O'Neill. I am always grateful to Edward Keefe for his recollections, for showing me his O'Neill letters, and for rescuing me from a great rainstorm in New London. I owe special thanks to Corliss Lamont and the John Reed Committee for allowing me to quote extensively from the Reed papers at Harvard. I also want to thank both Mr. and Mrs. Lamont for their kindness to me. I have delightful memories of Sister Mary Florentine, who taught Eugene O'Neill when he was a boy at Mount St. Vincent, and I cannot sufficiently thank Mother Mary, formerly Mother General at Mount St. Vincent, for arranging that I see the cottage where Eugene O'Neill lived and for helping me to trace O'Neill's classmates. I want to thank Marion McCandless, the Alumnae Secretary at St. Mary's College in Notre Dame, Indiana, for her indefatigable assistance in tracing Ellen Quinlan's career there. I have the warmest gratitude to Arthur McGinley (and his wife and daughter) for much kindness and for very valuable recollections of Eugene O'Neill. I have a special gratitude to Nickolas Muray and to Mrs. Muray for the trouble they took, under trying circumstances, to let me see Mr. Muray's fine collection of pictures of O'Neill. I also wish to thank Mrs. Lawrence White, the present owner of the O'Neill home in New London, for showing me through the house and telling me about all the changes that had been made in it. I also want to give particular thanks to Corwin Willson for generously giving me his rich recollections of Eugene O'Neill and for allowing me to quote from them at length.

I am very much indebted to a number of other people who have written me their remembrances of Eugene O'Neill and have very kindly allowed me to quote from their letters. I wish specifically to thank Donald L. Breed, Everett Glass, Charles Hapgood, Mrs. Edward E. McIntyre (Helen Emerson), Mrs. Ewing R. Philbin and her late husband Ewing R. Philbin, Stephen H. Philbin, Wesley D. Sawyer, William Henry Trausneck, and T. G. Treadway.

Many other people have given me valuable information in interviews and letters and have assisted me in discovering other sources of information. I want particularly to thank Mrs. George W. Bellows; Brother Berard, F.S.C., Principal of De La Salle Institute; Francis R. Boyd, formerly instructor in Latin at Betts Academy; the Reverend John Carey of St. Joseph's Rectory, New London, Connecticut; George E. Clapp, Managing Editor, The New London *Day;* Walter Douglass; Roger W. Flagg; Dr. Joseph Ganey, M.D.; the Reverend Bernard Gilpin of Trinity Protestant Episcopal Church, Hoboken, New Jersey; Richard J. Hancock, F.A.C.H.A., Administrator, the Lawrence and Memorial Associated Hospitals, New London, Connecticut; William C. Jenkins; Sargent Kennedy, Registrar, Harvard College; Thomson Kingsford; Bella Landauer; Lingard

Loud; Dr. David R. Lyman, M.D., Superintendent, Gaylord Farm Sanatorium; Dwight C. Lyman, President, the New London Historical Society; Helen Benson Matthews; Benjamin McLyman; the Reverend Michael McVerry, Assistant Pastor, Saint Patrick's Rectory, New Haven, Connecticut; John Myatt, Personnel Manager, United States Lines; John P. Pero, Jr.; Mr. Peterson of Peterson's Restaurant, New London, Connecticut; K. Marie Prindiville, formerly Superintendent of the Lawrence and Memorial Associated Hospitals; W. R. Sayer, Senior Shipping Commissioner, United States Coast Guard; Mrs. Junius C. Scofield; Thomas E. Scofield; Bessie Sheridan; Mr. and Mrs. Philip Sheridan; Howard Stepp, Registrar, Princeton University; Carol J. Thayer, Deputy Clerk, Probate Court of Cuyahoga County, Cleveland, Ohio; Judge Thomas E. Troland; and Mary Heaton Vorse.

I wish also to thank a number of people who have helped me in a variety of ways. I want to thank my father, Dr. A. J. Alexander, for advice on all the medical problems relating to this work. I thank my mother, Marie Alexander, for serving as a kind of informal newspaper clipping service for me on items pertaining to O'Neill. I wish to thank Agnes Boulton for her book *Part of a Long Story*, published by Doubleday (Garden City, 1958). Although I have quoted her in only a few instances, I am indebted to her for material on O'Neill from 1917 to 1919. I thank Professor Edith Link of Brooklyn College for her advice on some of the historical problems in this book. I also thank Robert G. Link, Assistant Vice-President of the Federal Reserve Bank of New York, for computing the present-day equivalent of Eugene O'Neill's allowance in 1914. I wish also to thank Natasha Silberstein for her careful and accurate typing of my manuscript.

I am thoroughly indebted to Professor Oscar Cargill, Chairman of the English Department, Washington Square College, New York University, for his kindness in reading this book in its entirety and for his assistance in getting it published. I wish also to give my eternal thanks to Professors Paul Parnell and Jascha Kessler for the role they played in bringing me together with my publishers, Harcourt, Brace and World, Inc. I want also to thank President Walter Willig and Professor Edward Pessen of the Staten Island Community College for granting me a leave of absence in which to prepare my book for publication.

If I have overlooked any of the many people who have generously assisted me, may I include them in one general but heartfelt "Thank you!"

D.A.

EUGENE O'NEILL became a legend as soon as he became famous. And the legend grew more grotesque as the years went on. Barrett Clark's account of the early years, O'Neill declared, wasn't true. "It isn't I. And the truth would make a much more interesting—and incredible!—legend." The object of this book is to tell, as far as possible, the truth about Eugene O'Neill's early years—to trace the ideas and events that shaped him as an artist and a man.

Eugene O'Neill's early life, as he himself said, "passed through many entirely distinct periods, with complete changes of environment, associates, etc." By dividing the story of O'Neill's developmental years into seven parts, I have tried to convey their dynamic quality—the change and growth of his personality and opinions. Each part is headed by a biographical sketch of the person (or in one case, the place) that influenced the period most strongly, or that typified its emotional and intellectual atmosphere. The story ends in 1920 when Eugene O'Neill was thirty-two years old—the year his father died. O'Neill had then just received his first Pulitzer Prize for *Beyond the Horizon,* and critics were hailing him as the long-awaited "great American playwright." His great works were ahead of him, but most of the experiences that formed them were already behind him. He had come of age as an artist.

Very little has been known about Eugene O'Neill's early years. The first goal of this work was simply to find out what happened—and that took ten years of research. I started with the family background. Very quickly, I learned that the obvious sources of information about Eugene O'Neill's father, James O'Neill, were not only meager but incorrect—and even more quickly I began to uncover a wealth of new information about him. James O'Neill was a great talker. As he traveled from town to town on his theatrical tours, reporters from the local papers would stop by to see him, and he was usually very ready to tell them stories from his colorful theatrical career or to comment on what was going on in the American theater. Literally hundreds of these interviews with James O'Neill appeared in newspapers all over the United States during his fifty years on the American stage. I found many of them in the extensive collections of clippings at Harvard and Yale and particularly in the invaluable Robinson Locke Collection of Dramatic Scrapbooks in the New York Public Library.

I also scanned—page by page—the two great American theatrical weeklies, the New York *Clipper* and the New York *Dramatic Mirror,* from the time James O'Neill went on the stage in 1868 until his death in 1920. I spent many months handling the huge, heavy volumes of crumbling pages. Often, I had to use a magnifying glass to scan the long columns of tiny print. It was very rewarding work. At its end, I knew where James O'Neill was and what he was doing almost every day for over fifty years—information that allowed me to date many events in Eugene's life, where accurate chronology was very important. I also had hundreds of typed index cards containing interviews with James O'Neill, anecdotes about him and his family, and data on Mrs. O'Neill, Jamie, Eugene, and their friends.

The *Clipper* and the *Mirror* also gave me countless clues to further research. From items in their pages, I realized, for instance, that I could learn more about the death of Edmund O'Neill by scanning the Colorado newspapers for the week of March 4, 1885, or about the O'Neill divorce case by scanning the Chicago daily papers from September through December of 1877.

I went through the other theatrical periodicals—the New York *Dramatic News* was particularly rich in interviews with James O'Neill—and through the memoirs and biographies of actors, actresses, and theatrical managers, as well as through those letters of James O'Neill and his friends that I could find. I also interviewed and corresponded with a number of people who remembered James and Ellen O'Neill and James O'Neill, Jr.

For material on Eugene himself—aside from the obvious sources —I consulted the clipping collections at the New York Public Library, Harvard, and Yale. I went through the collections of O'Neill's letters at Dartmouth, Princeton, Cornell, and Yale. I spent much time interviewing people who had known Eugene O'Neill. For instance, I tracked down the records of Betts Academy (which had burned down) and secured a list of O'Neill's schoolmates. By searching telephone directories from all over the United States, I was able to find and interview many of them. I also went through the memoirs, autobiographies, letters, and biographies of anyone who might—even remotely—have known Eugene O'Neill or his friends.

A description of ten years of research would itself fill a book. A chapter would be needed to describe the search for one little fact— like the date for Eugene O'Neill's last sea voyage. More chapters would be needed to describe the fruitless searches—such as my attempt to get the date of Jimmy Byth's suicide by going through the records of deaths in New York City. Suffice it to say that the method of research on this book was scholarly although I have not used documentation. Where I offer new facts—as I usually do—or new dates, particularly dates that go against precedent, they rest on reliable sources. For instance, my date for Eugene O'Neill's first marriage comes from the church records.

Where I could slip in a reference to a source unobtrusively, I have done so. In the many cases where such references would make for clumsy writing, I have omitted them. For instance, I omit the source for James O'Neill's tale of playing Romeo to Adelaide Neilson's Juliet because it is "an unlabeled clipping in the Robinson Locke Collection of Dramatic Scrapbooks in the Theatre Collection of the New York Public Library." In other instances, as I could not insert complete sources, I have omitted awkward abbreviated references since they would be of little help to scholars. A typical source, like the one for the story about James O'Neill's bargain in horses, would read like this: "Mademoiselle Mephisto's Anecdotes, Personalities and Comments Concerning Stage Folk and Sometimes Others," New York *Clipper*, XLVIII (September 29, 1900), 674. Only a system of footnotes would have allowed me to list such sources adequately.

I have not used footnotes because I did not think they would be appropriate for a book designed as a "portrait of the artist as a young man." I intend to follow this book with another on Eugene O'Neill's mature years. For the complete life of O'Neill which these two volumes will form, I shall, perhaps, be able to offer a fully documented edition for scholars.

I also decided that a critical discussion of O'Neill's plays would be out of place in this work. But I do hope the book will be valuable to people who wish to come to their own critical judgment of the plays, for it gives much new information that may be helpful for interpreting them.

It attempts to give, for the first time, a consistent account of Eugene O'Neill's intellectual development—to show the changes in his ideas and the major forces that brought those changes about. I have tried to go beyond an empty listing of book titles and actually pinpoint specific ideas that excited and interested him. I have tried to show just how these ideas affected the plays. Of course, I have been careful to establish correct chronology for these influences. In all, I have tried to show the growth and change in his political viewpoint and philosophy, the development of his concept of tragedy and of his aesthetic creed.

I have also offered a theory of his psychological development which gives meaning and order to the many contradictory actions of his life. Like any theory—the atomic theory, for instance—it is relatively simple and is not meant as a substitute for the complexity of

reality, but rather as a way of seeing meaningful patterns and relationships in reality, which otherwise would appear to be a chaos
of unrelated facts. I have also tried to show how Eugene O'Neill's
emotional experiences are expressed in his plays. Wherever possible,
I have used his own words to describe his psychological problems.
For instance, I use his phrase "mask of the Bad Boy Pan" to represent one part of the split he felt in his personality because the contradictory mixing of "Bad" and "Pan" shows the complexity of the
system of feelings he was indicating by this label.

I have also tried to present important people in Eugene O'Neill's
life, where I could, as personalities, rather than simply as names. In
this way I hoped to recreate the atmosphere of his world. And so,
incidentally, I offer a number of short biographical studies, including the first complete and accurate account of the life of James
O'Neill—who, as one of America's most popular actors, deserves to
be known on his own account, as well as for the important role he
played in his son's life.

But, of course, the main objective of this book has been to depict
the "incredible" story of Eugene O'Neill's developmental years. When
O'Neill looked back at what he was in one or another of those years,
he said, "I simply cannot recognize that person in myself nor understand him nor his acts as mine." So this book does not offer a final
static portrait of O'Neill. It is, instead, a study of constant change
and growth—the story of the making of a playwright.

✖✖✖ PART ONE

MAMA

CHAPTER ONE

Ellen Quinlan O'Neill

"Beautiful" was the word everyone used for her. Her son Eugene would never forget her hair, "partly a copper brown, partly a bronze gold," or her deep brown eyes, "unusually large and beautiful, with black brows and long curling lashes." "Her most appealing quality," Eugene would say, was her "simple, unaffected charm," her "innate unworldly innocence." Others agreed with him. The few people she thoroughly disliked found her cold, even austere, but everyone else called her shy or charming. She rarely smiled, but a gay "Irish lilt" came into her voice when she was happy, an echo of the Tipperary brogue her father, Thomas J. Quinlan, never lost.

Mary Ellen Quinlan was born in New Haven, Connecticut, on August 13, 1857, but shortly afterward her family moved to Cleveland. There she grew up with her brother, William Joseph, in the flat over the store at 174 Ontario Street, where her father dealt in newspapers, books, periodicals, stationery, fancy goods, bread, cakes, and confectionery. By the time Ellen was eleven, her father became city circulator of the Cleveland *Plain Dealer,* so the family moved to a fine house with a grand piano for Ellen and a library full of books. There her father's many friends were always visiting —the Reverend Kelley of Saint Bridget's Church, John Nevins of Nevins Brothers Steam Printing House, James Lavan, the insurance agent, and, when Ellen was just thirteen, the handsome young leading man at Ellsler's Academy of Music, James O'Neill.

Everyone in Cleveland had been talking about him since his first appearance there in September, 1870. Women liked his "manly beauty," men his unassuming sociability. Before long he had friends all over town, particularly among his fellow Irishmen. "We stick together, we O's," said James O'Neill. Thomas J. Quinlan was accessible to all who entered the big liquor and cigar store on Superior Street, Quinlan & Spirnaugle, so it was not surprising that he and James O'Neill quickly became friends. Both were great readers and talkers. Both were interested in real estate and investments. Thomas J. Quinlan already owned a fortune in property, and James O'Neill wanted to.

All through Ellen's thirteenth and fourteenth years, James O'Neill was a constant visitor at the Quinlan home at 208 Woodland Avenue. He talked easily with Ellen, her brother, and her mother, as well as with her father. He must have told them how he persuaded John Ellsler to put on Cleveland's first regular matinees. "From the first the matinees were successful," James O'Neill declared later, "and in a short time the stars who came along, and who were engaged only for evening performances, were furious that they were not allowed to play and take the lion's share of the profits." Here, Ellen could see, was a man after her father's own heart: alert, hard-working, determined to better himself.

By the summer of 1872, Ellen had long since lost her shyness with James O'Neill. He talked with her of his fears at becoming leading man that fall at McVicker's Theatre in Chicago, one of the biggest cities in the United States, after only four years' experience on the stage. In turn, Ellen confided her fears and excitement at the prospect of going away that fall to Saint Mary's College, near South

Bend, Indiana. College was her father's idea. Thomas J. Quinlan
was ambitious for his children. He was a rich man, and he knew
that Ellen and William Joseph would be rich after him, but he
wanted them to be self-reliant and even left directions in his will
that they earn their own "honest, honorable, and independent liveli-
hood." So he was sending Ellen to one of the finest girls' schools in
the Middle West, run by the Sisters of the Holy Cross, in the hope
that she would become an accomplished musician, perhaps a con-
cert pianist.

After the first shock of strangeness at the big, raw brick building,
Ellen liked the nuns and her schoolmates at Saint Mary's. She liked
the ordered existence at school, where the girls marched from class
to class in little lines. She won second premium in her class in vocal
music and third premium in composition. She even liked cultivating
an elegant curled handwriting in the penmanship class. The nuns
praised her schoolwork and her piety. Ellen wore a large cross on
a heavy gold chain around her neck, and she took a grave delight
in praying in the Holy House of Loreto, a replica of the Santa Casa
in Italy, exotically beautiful with its flickering candles. Sometimes
she and her friend Daisy Green talked of becoming nuns like
Mother Elizabeth Lilly, head of the Conservatory of Music.

Ellen almost worshiped Mother Elizabeth, who was descended
from Dr. George Arnold, Queen Elizabeth's organist. Ellen listened
admiringly as Mother Elizabeth talked in her cultured English accent of her musical education on the continent and of great musi-
cians she had known. Like all the girls who studied under Mother
Elizabeth, Ellen was inspired to work hard. Lillie West, Ellen's
seatmate, talked of going on the stage in light opera, and Ellen
herself dreamed of giving concerts.

Ellen returned to Cleveland in the summer of 1873, a poised and
elegant young lady. Lillie West described her as "a tall, superb
creature with a kind of burnt-gold hair in profusion and deep
brown eyes." Certainly James O'Neill, also back in Cleveland for
the summer, thought her superb. After her first smiles and blushes
at seeing him again, Ellen told him all about Saint Mary's and even
of how she had thought of becoming a nun. James O'Neill sympathized entirely. "It was because my father died and I had to go

to work," he often said, "that I am an actor, not a priest." But Ellen knew that he didn't want her to become a nun.

Much later Ellen learned that James O'Neill had gone courting during his first year in Chicago. A Denver man would tell of his first meeting with his rival James O'Neill in a young lady's parlor. "He walked across the floor, shook hands with me and looked so kindly at me that I immediately yielded the parlor, excused myself and never called again. I knew it was of no use." But that was when James O'Neill still thought of Ellen as Tom Quinlan's little girl. Now she was sixteen.

When Ellen went back to Saint Mary's that fall, her schoolmates talked enviously of her romantic association with James O'Neill. The girls from Chicago told her of his popularity there—the critics had said that his Romeo "comes before us with the sunshine of Italy in his eyes; with the glitter of moonlight in his voice." Ellen listened, and talked shyly of what a modest, friendly person James O'Neill was in real life.

Ellen enjoyed her second year at Saint Mary's right up to May, 1874, when she was suddenly plunged into a nightmare of shock and grief. After only a few days' illness, her father, who was only forty-one, had died at three o'clock in the morning of May 25. The rest was a tear-blurred confusion—the mass at Saint Bridget's Church, the burial at the Catholic cemetery on Woodland Avenue, the solemn faces of her father's friends, the wreaths. Everyone was very kind to the Quinlans that summer, especially James O'Neill.

But the world was changed. Quinlan & Spirnaugle vanished from Superior Street, and her father's partner, Ambrose Spirnaugle, opened a saloon. Thomas Lavan and John Nevins, her father's executors, had long conferences with her mother. Her brother, William Joseph, who had just finished high school, took a job as bookkeeper at R. C. Barret's; he wanted to be a businessman like his father. Ellen did as her father had wished and went back to Saint Mary's to finish her musical education. She was sad that he couldn't be present at her graduation in June, when Mother Elizabeth gave her the graduate's gold medal for instrumental music. Only her mother and brother were there to hear her play Chopin's Polonaise, Opus 22.

. . .

Two years later, shortly before her twentieth birthday, Ellen Quinlan was in New York City planning her wedding to James O'Neill. When he had first become her father's friend seven years earlier, he had been only a struggling young actor in the Midwest—a "prairie bird," they called him when he first came to New York—on a small salary, out of which he had to buy his costumes. Now he had soared close to the top of his profession. He had dazzled audiences in Chicago, San Francisco, and New York, and was getting well over a hundred dollars a week. Moreover, he had saved his money, invested it, and had a tidy fortune of his own, so he was in every way a fine match for the heiress of one-third of Thomas J. Quinlan's fortune.

Only one ugly problem had to be faced as Ellen and James planned their marriage. "I got into a scrape when I was a young man, and I find I am not quite out of it," James said. In 1871, during his first summer in Cleveland, he had become interested in a pretty, dark-haired girl named Nettie Walsh, whose mother ran a confectionery store. Although only fifteen, Nettie was by no means chaste when she met him, James said. As a matter of fact, she had left a young man named Zucker to live with James O'Neill. "Once," according to O'Neill's dresser, " . . . Zucker came around blazing mad with a pistol in his hand to shoot Jim. Jim, you see, had stolen his girl. If Zucker had found Jim that night he'd have let him have it, I tell you."

Nettie had lived with James O'Neill throughout his second year in Cleveland although, from her own story, he kept her in "the most rigid seclusion"; and she had visited him twice in Chicago. Then, just as he was trying to break off the affair, Nettie told him she was going to have a baby. James O'Neill knew that there had been other men in her life while he was in Chicago, so he had no way of knowing whether or not he was the father. He kept giving Nettie money, each time hoping to be rid of her for good. Finally, when she came to him in May, 1875, just as he was leaving Chicago for San Francisco, he told her flatly that he wanted nothing more to do with her. He told her he would take the child—if it was his—and bring it up, on condition that she surrender all claim to it and to himself. Nettie had refused, but later she had written him several times trying to get money from him.

James O'Neill had simply ignored her letters, but Nettie had kept on hanging around the theaters, trying to get money from O'Neill's friends, so that there was talk all over Chicago, and the New York *Clipper* had even come out with the rumor that James O'Neill had a wife and child he had deserted in Chicago. If Nettie Walsh learned that he was married, she was likely to make trouble, particularly as he and Ellen would have to go to Chicago right after their honeymoon, for he was scheduled to open there with the Union Square Company in the middle of July. So James decided that they must keep their marriage secret.

Ellen agreed. She refused to let this old affair blur her happiness. On July 14, 1877, the pair went to the rectory of Saint Ann's Church on Twelfth Street, and there, with only Ellen's mother, brother, and uncle present, the Reverend Thomas F. Lynch joined them in holy matrimony. She and James left immediately for three weeks in the mountains. Then and ever afterward, Ellen and James were profoundly happy in one another. The beauty of their marriage became a legend among theater people. Ellen was far too happy to worry over the problem of Nettie Walsh or over the fact that the secret of their marriage couldn't be kept. Almost immediately after their wedding, the *Clipper* reported it. James denied it, but too many friends were in on the secret. In two weeks all the newspapers had the story. The *Clipper* hinted darkly at bigamy.

On their way to Chicago, James and Ellen stopped off in Cleveland to look over William Joseph's new flour and feed business and to receive congratulations from all their old friends. Ellen felt no uneasiness as she and James settled at the Clifton House in Chicago. Even when Nettie Walsh sent them a threatening letter a few days later, Ellen was not really frightened. She and James decided to ignore it.

Then suddenly, on September 7, 1877, the storm broke. James was about to go to Hooley's Theater for the evening performance of *Forbidden Fruit* when he learned that Nettie Walsh had filed suit for divorce against him. She accused him not only of marrying her and then deserting her and her child, but also of committing adultery with a famous actress, now dead. She declared that "being parsimonious" he had amassed a fortune of $15,000. She demanded alimony and support for the child.

"I think the whole thing is a matter of blackmail on the part of this woman, or her friends or her lawyer," James pointed out at once. Nettie Walsh knew perfectly well that James had never married her. She knew, too, that he would settle money on her rather than face the scandal of a court trial, so she made the story as ugly as possible, accusing him of adultery with the actress the newspapers had already identified as Louise Hawthorne.

"Her statements are untrue from beginning to end," James O'Neill told the *Tribune* reporter he found in his dressing room that night. "She was not my wife. There is only one woman in the world that I ever asked to become a wife to me—" Then he broke off, and his eyes filled with tears. But he quickly pulled himself together and parried further questions with polite irony. Finally, as the reporter insisted, James O'Neill declared, "Well, sir, I don't see why I should be required to tell you my private history. Not that I would object, perhaps, to see it in type, because I conceive that I have in the matter endeavored to act squarely and honorably from beginning to end. But I fancy the public have no interest in me beyond what I can do for them in the way of furnishing amusement, and I don't see why anybody should pry into my personal affairs."

That was the beginning. Every day, James O'Neill had to turn away a string of inquisitive reporters who followed him home from the theater. One of the last of them cried, "Then you decline to open your mouth any more?" "Supper is served at the Clifton House about 6," James answered. "I shall open my mouth there. Good day."

Ellen, too, needed all her wit to parry questions from acquaintances. Lillie West called on her immediately, but Ellen, for all her shyness, knew how to handle Lillie. Years later, when Lillie West had become the powerful drama critic of the Chicago *News* under the pen name "Amy Leslie," she wrote the story of the divorce suit. "Ella Quinlan," she recalled, "never seemed to know what it was all about or worth. She had been my seatmate in college for a year and was almost a child when she married O'Neill, but when, kidlike, I blurted out one day: 'Oh, Ella, what on earth can you do about this woman?' Ella looked a little blank and said, sweetly: 'What woman, honey?' and I had to explain to bring it to her mind. She did not care a rap, and, having myself fallen at the feet of James regularly I was allowed a matinee." Ellen always showed her pride in James by taking her friends to see his performances.

During that September, James O'Neill's brilliant acting with Lawrence Barrett in *Othello* was obliterating the effect of the scandal. Indeed, no one who knew the whole story had ever held it against him. The year before, James had become leading man of the Union Square Theatre Company on the very warm recommendation of Clara Morris, although Clara Morris knew all about Nettie Walsh, who was an old schoolmate of hers, and Nettie had come to her for money and to pour out all her grievances against James O'Neill.

By the time Ellen and James returned to New York for his fall engagement at the Union Square Theatre, the scandal had just about blown over. All that remained was for their lawyer, Charles H. Reed, to beat down Nettie's efforts to get alimony from the court, while negotiating with Nettie and her lawyer to see how much she would settle for. By the time the case came up for trial in December, Nettie had settled for a lump sum (later rumors said it was $550 and legal expenses). So Nettie's lawyer submitted no more evidence, and the case was dismissed for lack of evidence of a marriage.

The problem of Nettie Walsh seemed over for good, for she had signed an agreement never to trouble James O'Neill again. But the three-year-old child "Little Alfie" had signed no agreement. He was certainly James O'Neill's son; at the beginning of the scandal, Nettie had hauled him out before a reporter from the Chicago *Post*, crying, "Look, look, if you have ever seen this man, say if this is his child or no," and the reporter had solemnly declared, "The features are identical." Alfie was too young in December, 1877, to know what was going on, but he would live to grow up.

Neither Ellen nor James thought about Alfie. Never in the whole course of their married life would any but this old scandal touch them; James O'Neill never faltered in his love for his wife. Ellen's only problems were those of any actor's wife. She had to get used to the long hours of loneliness when James was rehearsing or performing, or when he went out for "a social glass" with his fellow actors after the show—and this was frequent, for James, like her father, was sociable.

Ellen also had to get used to uncertainty and impermanence. They had been back in New York only a few months when James was sent with the Union Square Company to San Francisco. Ellen went along. By the end of this engagement, Ellen was pregnant. Perhaps this was one reason why James left the Union Square Company to become leading man at Baldwin's Academy of Music in San Francisco, for they were able to spend the next three years in one place. They lived in family-style hotels like Mrs. Louisa Starkweather's Colonnade House, for James couldn't bear to see Ellen work. She had nothing to do before the birth of her baby but dress exquisitely and join her husband on little excursions. James had a passion for exploration, and even long afterward, when he had become a traveling star, he would hire a buggy, or a sleigh in winter, and they would jaunt about the countryside on afternoons when he didn't have to go to the theater. James also liked to try out exotic restaurants. Ellen had no household duties at all, and she longed for the baby she could care for when James was away.

On September 28, 1878, James O'Neill, Jr., was born. "Jamie," they called him. James doted on the baby, but to Ellen he was everything. Throughout the long hours when James was at the theater, Jamie was lord of the household. Ellen devoted herself to Jamie with a love so intense and so protective that Jamie would be bound to her for the rest of his life.

These were years of great happiness. Ellen and James had troubles, of course; there was the frightening time when James faced threats of lynching for playing Christ in the Passion play; there was the time they lost all their money. "I once got a quarter of a million together in California in stock deals," James told some Cleveland friends at dinner in 1882, "but it went again, partly in the same current and partly in other risks." But on the whole the years were good, and when they went to New London, Connecticut, in the summer of 1883 and decided to build a summer home there, it seemed that the future would be pure happiness too. James and

Ellen had spent their summers on Long Island or in the Berkshires, but New London was just right for a permanent home. Ellen's mother was there, for her older sister (Ellen's Aunt Elizabeth) had married a Brennan of New London. The town was conveniently close to New York. James enjoyed fishing and swimming, and wanted some land of his own to putter about with.

They chose a strip of land along the Thames River, just where it widens into the Sound. The design for the house was simple but elegant. (It would be immortalized in two of Eugene O'Neill's plays, *Ah, Wilderness!* and *Long Day's Journey Into Night*.) A narrow porch ran across the front and one side of the house. The parlor had floor-to-ceiling windows looking over the long green lawn and the wide blue expanse of the river. The back part of the parlor could be closed off into a windowless room by means of folding doors. This "back parlor" was simply used as a passageway from the living room to the dining room, kitchen, and pantries. The pine-paneled living room took up one whole side of the house. It had windows on three sides and doorways to the porch and both the front and back parlors. Upstairs were rooms for a growing family and several guests.

James had the house built of the finest materials. (Years later, when a back wing of the house was torn down, the contractor offered to do the job for nothing if he could keep the beautiful wood.) The doorways, woodwork, and staircases were all of fine walnut, the floors parquet, and the fireplaces of imported tile. The report in the Boston *Times* that the house had cost $40,000—a fortune in 1883—could not have been far off.

With a new house started, and James starring brilliantly in *Monte Cristo,* the future looked very bright to Ellen in the summer of 1883, and that winter, when her second son was born in St. Louis, her happiness seemed complete. James named the baby Edmund Dantes O'Neill,* hoping that, like Monte Cristo, he might grow up to cry, "The world is mine!"

But now the road schedule of a traveling star proved too difficult for Ellen with a new baby in addition to Jamie. She had been able

* The name of Dumas's character is Edmond but James O'Neill always spelled it Edmund.

to bring Jamie up in one place for his first three years, and now she needed stability for Edmund. So in the fall of 1884, she set up a home for the two children in New York. The first few months weren't bad. From November 17 to the middle of December, James was playing in and around New York, and he and Ellen could be together. But when he went out on the road—Louisville, New Orleans, Atlanta, Savannah—he became bitterly lonely for Ellen and she for him. When he reached Milwaukee in February, James begged her to join him for a while. Ellen's mother could look after the children for a few weeks. So Ellen gave last-minute instructions to her mother and took the train.

Ellen and James had just arrived at the Windsor Hotel in Denver on the morning of March 4, 1885, when they received a telegram: Edmund was seriously ill with the measles. Later Ellen would piece together what had happened. Jamie had caught the measles. After the first few days, his grandmother couldn't keep him in bed or away from the baby, for Jamie was restless and willful. The measles, Ellen knew, could kill a baby. She and James were both in tears when he put her on the train for New York. With the Tabor Opera House sold out for days in advance, James couldn't go with her. So she had to face the long trip to New York alone—filled with fear and guilt. James received a second telegram just before the evening performance of *Monte Cristo*. The baby was dead.

Then he went on stage. As always when he was under great emotion, his voice became hoarse. He could barely force out his lines. But only those who knew of his son's death could see that he was "suffering severely" (as the Denver *Times* noted). Back in New York, Ellen collapsed when she found her little boy dead. She was still ill in April when James at last was able to come to her in New York. Together they brought the body of their baby from the vault in Calvary Cemetery, New York, to New London for final burial. And this was their first act acknowledging New London, Connecticut, as their home.

That summer, Ellen moved into her new home. She would always associate the house with this nightmare time, when she suffered constantly from the thought that her baby might still be alive if she had not left him. Little Edmund Dantes hadn't taken any of the luck of Monte Cristo, but James went ahead and named the house Monte Cristo Cottage. It became only a container for Ellen's misery.

Throughout the next season, touring with her husband, and all through the summer of 1886, when again they were in New London and the house was full of guests, Ellen still suffered bitterly from the death of Edmund, although she kept Jamie close to her all the time. Then, in the spring of 1887, she was struck by a second blow. She had not felt well since the death of Edmund. Now the doctors said that she had cancer of the breast.

A few years before, the word *cancer* had meant death. But in London and Paris, her doctors told James, a drastic operation had been tried out that might save her—removal of the breast and all the surrounding tissues. Ellen might have a chance if she were operated upon immediately. In June, the news went out that James O'Neill and his wife had gone to Europe. Only the immediate family knew the purpose of this trip. There, just before her thirtieth birthday, Ellen underwent surgery that would leave her deformed for the rest of her life.

She had just come up far enough out of the pain to realize that she was alive when a third blow struck. Ellen's mother became ill in New London just as her daughter was recovering from the shock of her operation. On July 28, 1887, Bridget Quinlan died—"chronic Peri Ostitis," the medical report read—and she was buried on the first of August from the home of Ellen's Aunt Elizabeth on Ocean Avenue. Eleven days later, James and Ellen sailed from England for home.

Misfortune often breeds further misfortune. The succession of shocks that Ellen had suffered brought on a final disaster. To relieve her constant mental and physical suffering, the doctors gave her morphine again and again, and only when the damage had been done did they realize that they had made her an addict. It would take twenty-five years for doctors to realize that they were responsible for creating most drug addicts. Ellen's case was not uncommon, but it was no less terrible for that. At intervals for the rest of her life, when emotional strain became too great, Ellen would have to struggle against the desire for morphine.

Life had cruelly hurt her, but both Ellen and James hoped her wounds might be healed if she had another child. The baby was born on October 16, 1888, in the Barrett House in New York, and they called the boy Eugene Gladstone O'Neill, after "the grand old man," James said. Ellen cherished her baby with a fiercely protective love. Never for an instant would she let this last baby out of her sight. She was always a beautiful, gentle presence watching over him. This was the woman Eugene O'Neill grew up calling "Mama."

CHAPTER TWO

"Mama's Baby, Papa's Pet"

I<small>T</small> was a strange, kaleidoscopic world that Eugene O'Neill grew up in, for he traveled with his father's company. Ellen had learned that she and James could not bear separation. She had also learned what might happen to an infant left in the care of others. So Eugene grew up in a bewildering world that was always sliding past the windows of trains, a world where even the four walls of the room in which he went to sleep and awakened were always changing color and pattern. Only in the summer, the world would suddenly compose itself into a house, a long green lawn, stretches of pinkish-beige sand, and the sparkling blue of water: New London.

But with the first cold weather, the nomadic life would begin again, the adult hotel world, train world, theater world. In this perpetually moving world, Eugene found only three presences he could depend on—Mama, Papa, and Sarah, the English governess—

and to these three he attached himself perhaps a little more tena-
ciously than would a child who could count on the other elements
of his world.

Always he was enveloped by the protective love of Mama. The
least sign of sickness in him frightened her. And he gave her much
cause for fear. He was an extremely sensitive baby. George C. Tyler,
James O'Neill's charming young advance man, had vivid memories
of walking the floor with the "howling" Eugene "at four in the
morning." The child was easily disturbed. He caught cold easily,
too.

Particularly frightening for Ellen were the times when Eugene
got sick and James was not with her. Often James would send her
ahead to the next big city to spare her the hardships of a series of
one-night stands; then she had to rely on George C. Tyler.

Later, Tyler often recalled a time in Chicago in December, 1891.
"I was routed out of bed by a hurry-call from Mrs. O'Neill—Gene
was dying, it seemed, and something had to be done about it at
once. So I got into some clothes and went in and had a look at him
—he was sort of black in the face and gasping and raising Cain—he
looked to me like a pretty sick baby all right. I went hotfoot for
the house-doctor. And of course he was out. There was nothing for
it but to dive out into one of those fine, cold, windy nights they
have in Chicago—I was wearing nothing much but a pair of pants
and an overcoat—and dig up a doctor. When I found one, he hud-
dled on a similar costume and we came galloping back to the hotel
like the last act of an old melodrama—then it turned out that the
baby only had a routine case of colic."

The worst time for Ellen came when Eugene got sick in the spring
of 1893. He was so sick that even the *Dramatic Mirror*, which rarely
found out anything about James O'Neill's personal life, reported in
April, "Mr. O'Neill's little son, by the way, who has been quite
seriously ill is convalescing." Perhaps this was the attack of typhoid
Eugene reported later. Whatever it was, Eugene's illness gave Ellen
a horror of going to New London. She associated New London with
death, and for a while she had terrified visions of taking Eugene
back there in a coffin as she and James had taken Edmund. James
loved the New London place, but he decided for Ellen's sake that

they should spend the summer at a farm he owned near Bound Brook, New Jersey. There Eugene recovered gradually, tenderly watched over by Mama and Papa.

No wonder they doted on him; Eugene was a beautiful child. For the first few years of his life his hair was very light, contrasting sharply with his huge dark eyes. Then, he was a delightfully quiet, obedient little boy. He became a favorite with his father's sister Margaret, Aunt Maggie Platz, whom they visited whenever James O'Neill played in Cincinnati. Although she had four children of her own, she always made a fuss over Eugene.

Eugene played with his cousins in Cincinnati, but he rarely had playmates for long. Usually he had to amuse himself. In February, 1893, when James O'Neill was playing through Texas, Ellen rented a house in El Paso, so that she could be near her old school friend from Saint Mary's, Loretta Ritchie, who was now Mrs. Emerson and had two little girls of her own. One of the girls, Helen Emerson, remembered seeing Eugene "playing in the front yard, rolling down the little incline and banging into an iron fence" one day when she brought a note from her mother to Mrs. O'Neill. She noticed "how the grass leaves were sticking" to his clothes.

When Mama and Papa took Eugene to dinner at the Emersons', he was dressed exquisitely in a velvet suit with a large embroidered collar. Twice that February, Mama and Eugene took Mrs. Emerson and her daughters to Meyer's Opera House, where they sat in a box and saw James O'Neill in *Fontenelle* and *Monte Cristo*. Eugene was used to joining his mother when she went visiting or entertained friends at his father's matinees.

When Mama couldn't take him along, Eugene was entrusted to Sarah, the governess, who took him to the park or the zoo or the circus or the aquarium. Once, to his delicious horror, she took him to the Eden Musée in New York where there were lifelike wax figures of criminals committing appalling murders. Sarah was the first to thrill and terrify him with stories of the evil in the world. Eugene was very fond of her.

But summer was the happiest time for Eugene. Much later, when he took to writing poetry, he would write of "Gold summer days": "The sand that shudders in the sun's hot rays," "The bright green lawns that lean down to the bay," "The pungent smell of oily pitch and tow"—all New London images, the images of his happy boyhood summers.

Mama and Papa spared nothing to keep him happy. When he became fascinated by the trains they traveled on and began to admire the engineers, Papa bought him his own railroad, not a tiny one, but one big enough to carry Eugene, with tracks running all around the house at New London. Eugene was both the engineer and fireman of his train. According to his cousin Alma Platz, he burned up half a ton of coal a day chugging about in his engine.

Another of the great joys of his boyhood was raising chickens. Mama and Papa were both proud and amused at the earnestness with which Eugene took up chicken farming. He read about it, cared for the chickens expertly, and kept "a business eye on the market price of chickens and eggs," which, his cousin Alma Platz recalled, he sold to his father "considerably above the market price." The toughness of Eugene's chickens became a family joke, but Papa continued to buy them.

Papa was also proud of Eugene's reading. James O'Neill himself had always been a great reader, and the house was full of books—complete sets of Hugo, Dumas, Shakespeare, and the Irish novelist Lever—all comfortably worn with constant rereading. Eugene would always remember his father's pleasure when he took to reading Irish history on his own, and learned all about Shane the Proud and the glorious O'Neills who were kings of Ireland.

Eugene enjoyed every moment of those New London summers. He loved splashing about in the blue waters of the Sound; he loved to sit on the porch with a book and dream; he loved playing on the lawn with the sound of his mother's piano floating out to him from the parlor; he loved drawing pictures of the boats that sailed by on the Thames River; but most of all he loved the sure presence of his family—of his practically grown-up brother, Jamie, who was always away at school in the winter, of Sarah, of Papa, and more than anyone, of Mama.

Mama was the great presence of those happy summer days. She seemed to Eugene the most beautiful woman in the world. ("The loveliest looking woman I ever saw," Eugene's cousin Bessie Sheridan said of her.) She was always dressed elegantly in simple but expensive clothes—people who knew nothing else about her remembered her beautiful clothes—and she inculcated in both Jamie and Eugene a taste for immaculate grooming and fine dress. Eugene was very proud of his mother.

The happiness he experienced in his mother's love is shown by the way he depicted the mother in all of his mature plays. By the time he wrote them, of course, he had been influenced by Jung's *Psychology of the Unconscious* and the vision it gives of a world of men struggling, unconsciously, to return to the peace and security of the mother. But Jung merely supplied intellectual formulas for Eugene's own strong feelings.

Again and again in his plays he depicted the profound love of a man for his mother, and always he made the mother a symbol of lost happiness. In *The Great God Brown,* Dion Anthony cries to be buried with his mother, "because her hands alone had caressed without clawing," and in *Desire Under the Elms,* Eben can express his intense love for his dead mother only in the broken phrases, "She was kind. She was good." In *Strange Interlude* and *Dynamo,* the love for the mother is actually sublimated into a cosmogony.

Eugene used his mother's beautiful copper-gold hair as the dominant characteristic of the mother image that all the men in *Mourning Becomes Electra* seek to recover. Significantly, at the time he wrote this play, he himself had found a woman strikingly like his mother, with her beautiful dark eyes, and even more important, a woman who could envelop him in the protective love he had felt about him when he was a little boy in his mother's arms: this was his third wife, Carlotta Monterey.

But the metaphysics of "God the Mother" was well in the future for the little boy who spent such happy summers in New London as "Mama's baby, Papa's pet." Still in the future, too, was September, 1895, a date that was to fall across Eugene O'Neill's life like an ax, shattering its organization, altering it drastically and irrevocably.

CHAPTER THREE

The Betrayal

O<small>N</small> one thing James O'Neill was determined: his sons were to have the education he had been cheated of. He had been hauled out of school at the age of ten and put to work. His wide reading— of Congreve, Farquhar, Shakespeare, Greek drama—had never made up, he felt, for his lack of formal schooling.

Eugene would be seven in October, 1895, and it was high time for him to start school. James O'Neill decided to send him to Mount Saint Vincent on the Hudson, a place he found particularly appealing because the rolling land had once belonged to Edwin Forrest. There, Forrest had built an exact replica of a medieval castle, and Forrest himself had lived in the stone foreman's cottage where Eugene would sleep.

James O'Neill had admired Forrest ever since 1869, when, as a beginner, he had supported Forrest in *King Lear* and *Jack Cade*.

Later, James always defended Forrest, who had a reputation for savage bursts of temper. "Mark me, he was intolerant of presumptuous stupidity," said O'Neill, "but where he saw you were eager to learn, and showed a capacity to understand his teaching, no more gentle being ever lived, and no grander soul ever hid itself beneath a certain ruggedness of manner."

James O'Neill liked to tell about the night he had played with Forrest in *Jack Cade* and had just come off stage. He could hear Forrest stamping and growling in his dressing room, and a moment later Forrest's dresser came out, smiling broadly.

"What's the matter?" asked James.

"I was laughing at what the old man just said about you."

"Tell me."

"It may hurt your feelings."

"No, tell me."

"Well, he said, 'That fellow O'Neill will make a capital actor if he ever gets rid of that damned brogue!'"

"I'll take care of the brogue," said James O'Neill, and he did. So Edwin Forrest was dear to the memory of his own climb up in life, and it pleased him to think of his son Eugene living on Edwin Forrest's own estate.

The school had several advantages. It was close to New York, the theatrical center, so that James and Ellen could visit Eugene often. Ellen liked the school, for it was like Saint Mary's. The nuns ran it primarily as a girls' school, but a small school for boys under twelve had just been added. It was mainly for the younger brothers of the girls, but the nuns took a few outsiders like Eugene. The grounds were beautiful, looking out over the wide Hudson to the Palisades.

Eugene was told in the summer that he was to go to Mount Saint Vincent in September. Exactly what this meant he couldn't be sure; a child lives in the present. At the end of August, shortly before he was to go, something happened that diverted his parents' attention from him completely. That Thursday in New London started like any other. James O'Neill was busy all day, conferring with his manager, William F. Connor, trying out new actors, and rehearsing his company. At dinner Eugene learned that Jamie, Papa, and Will Connor were going into town to see the Corbett Combination at the

Lyceum. The play, Papa said, was simply an excuse to let "Gentleman Jim" show off his sparring technique, but Jamie and Papa were eager to see Corbett in action. Eugene had already been put to bed when Papa, Jamie, and Will Connor set out along the short cut to town over the railroad tracks.

Eugene woke up the next morning to find the house in turmoil, Mama upset, and Papa lying in bed all bruised and bandaged. Just as Papa and Jamie and Mr. Connor had reached the trestle over the Howard Street Bridge, a freight train had come along. They had all stepped aside to let the train pass, but Papa had missed his footing in the dark and fallen through the trestle sixteen feet to the stone paving of the street below.

"God is certainly good to the Irish," was Connor's comment when they reached Papa and found him miraculously alive, and, though shocked and badly bruised, with no bones broken. The priest who came to visit Papa the next afternoon said, as he was leaving, "Ah my son, the Lord was with you then, or you would have been killed without a doubt." "But don't you think, Your Reverence," Papa replied with twinkling eyes, "that it would have been better if He had been with me before I fell?"

Mama had been seriously frightened when Will Connor and Jamie helped Papa into the house, and from then on she was busy caring for him. He had to cancel his engagement to play *Virginius* at the Lyceum on August 24, and not until September 7 was he able to join his company in Maine. Meanwhile, although he began to hobble about on crutches the Sunday after his fall, Mama had her hands full caring for him, and Eugene for once was on the outskirts of things.

In the midst of all this, the time came for him to go to Mount Saint Vincent. He was taken there and left—a shy, bewildered boy who felt lost and frightened among the strange children and the alien, black-robed women, so terribly unlike his beautiful mother. And he was left, not for a few hours, but for days and weeks and months, which were filled with the anguish of loneliness and with yearning for Mama, for Papa, for the familiar presences that made up his universe. The hurt went deep. He felt that he had been betrayed, cheated; that those he trusted most had senselessly, cruelly rejected him.

The feeling of rejection was hideously substantiated when Christmas came and all the other children went home. Only he, Eugene, remained alone. He knew that an actor must play on Christmas day. He knew that his parents were far away in Memphis, Tennessee. But he could not be reconciled to being left alone. The lavish presents his parents sent didn't help a bit. All he knew was that when every other boy went home, he alone was left.

The anguish of those vacations spent at school rankled in him always. His Sheridan cousins in New London wondered at his constant complaints at being deprived of Christmas—they knew of his presents, but not of his loneliness. Almost thirty years afterward, when Eugene, close to the breaking point, turned to a woman who seemed a reincarnation of his mother, his first frenzied confession to her was of his agony during those vacations when he alone was left at school.

Later, too, he talked of his pain each fall, when, after a summer of secure love, the whole terrible betrayal was repeated, and again he was sent away in spite of all his tears. Whatever he suffered from the other frustrations of childhood, this was the experience of which he always talked with the greatest bitterness—never forgetting the shock to his love for his parents and his trust in them when they banished him to school.

Indeed, the fear of love, the distrust of love, became one of the central problems of Eugene O'Neill's life and one of the central themes in his plays. In *Days Without End*, for instance, he shows that John Loving "had always been afraid of love" after losing the love of his parents (by death), and that his fear of love became "a dread of life—as if he constantly sensed a malignant Spirit hiding behind life, waiting to catch men at its mercy, in their hour of secure happiness. . . . " In *Welded*, too, O'Neill shows the fear of love resulting in the desire to "murder it—and be free." In *Dynamo*, Reuben Light loses his faith in life with his faith in his mother, who, he feels, has betrayed him to his father: "She cheated me! . . . when I trusted her! . . . when I loved her better than anyone in the world!"

After he had been banished to Mount Saint Vincent, Eugene had terrible doubts about his mother's love and a feeling that she had betrayed him. But he knew that he had been sent away to school at his father's wish, and his father, Eugene felt, was the cause of his suffering. From this time on, although he still showed Papa the old love and admiration, inside he was nursing a sense of rejection into the hatred that would erupt in his adolescence and never fully leave him afterward. Only the violence of his later rebellion against his father, his readiness to see rejection in almost anything his father did, showed the depth of his boyhood love for him. Later, when he had embarked on a whole program of life directed at flouting his father, he would forget how deeply he had been molded by him. And if, at his father's death, Eugene thought of him as a "stranger," an "alien," it was only because he had warred within himself and imprisoned the part of himself that was deeply identified with James O'Neill. No one in the course of his life would influence him as profoundly as this familiar stranger toward whom he felt a great love embittered into a great hatred.

PART TWO

PAPA: THE OLD MAN

CHAPTER FOUR

James O'Neill

Actually, Eugene O'Neill knew very little about his father's life. James O'Neill himself never knew much about his origins. He told A. M. Palmer, who wanted some biographical information for his "History of the Union Square Theatre," that he hoped to pick up "some points" of his early life on his first trip to Ireland, "the land o' me birth." What he picked up was either very little or unfit for publication, because he later talked poetically of being born "one opal-tinted day" (October 14, 1846) in "the shadow of Strongbow's castle" in Kilkenny, Ireland, but he said nothing about his family.

The only certainty is that they were miserably poor people. If James O'Neill's death report in New London is correct, his father was Edward, his mother Mary. They probably came to Buffalo about 1855, for in the city directory of that year is listed an Edward O'Neill, "mechanic," and that was the trade to which he apprenticed his sons. "It was a favorite saying of my father that if he had ten sons every one of them would be brought up to a trade," James O'Neill would say. "Little faith put he in professions; a good honest trade was his idea of the best equipment he could bestow upon his children." So at the age of ten James O'Neill was sent into a machine shop to work twelve hours a day in a freezing shed for a miserable fifty cents a week.

With all of his sons started as machinists, Edward O'Neill deserted his family and fled back to Ireland. He must have died there, for the Buffalo directory of 1857 lists his wife Mary Ann as "widow of Edward." William O'Neill, a "machinist," and John O'Neill, an "iron-finisher," apparently remained in Buffalo when Mary O'Neill, her daughters, and James moved on to Cincinnati, where they subsisted perilously till James's older sister married and he, at fourteen, went to Norfolk, Virginia, to work in his brother-in-law's clothing store. "The Civil War was on and my brother-in-law sold military uniforms and did a thriving business," James recalled. After the war, James O'Neill went back to Cincinnati, and he was working there as a file cutter when he decided to become an actor, and went on to become one.

Eugene always thought his father had become an actor by sheer chance, for he knew the story of how his father had been playing billiards next door to the Cincinnati National Theater one night when the stage manager came rushing in looking for supers to go on stage. But it was no accident that James O'Neill spent his evenings around the theater, or had his "glass" and billiards in the National Saloon where stage people hung out. Even in Norfolk, he had spent his evenings "poring over a Shakespeare given me by an elder sister, or losing myself in the land of romance at the theatre where I was an established gallery god." And even then he had begun to wish. "What's an Irish lad without his dream?" he would say.

The billiard story became the grand legend of James O'Neill's life, which he told often, and always (despite his usual accuracy) differently. Sometimes he went on stage to carry a spear in support of Edwin Forrest; sometimes, wearing "velvet breeches, satin embroidered coat, ruffles at wrist and throat with a perfect golconda of diamond knee buckles and shoe latches," he went on in *The Colleen Bawn;* sometimes he was given a line to speak, which he managed to utter, "but there was a ringing in my ears and a sensation of drowning in deep waters swept across my heart."

In one version, he had no lines to speak, but was carried away by the play. "The dialogue between the leading woman and the heavy man was somewhat spirited, and finally it led up to a situation where she confesses her love for him, which he refuses." So James O'Neill told the story. "I had my own ideas of chivalry, and possibly my high regard and respect for the weaker sex caused me to jump into the breach. Having forgotten for a moment where I was, I said to her: 'I'll take you! He's no good, anyway!'" Whereupon the audience howled and the heavy man ordered him from the stage. "I made my exit somehow or other," James O'Neill continued, "and was greeted with jeers of derision by the actors and a lot of my friends and acquaintances, who had consented to act as supers to help out the stage manager. It was then that I announced my determination to go on the stage. I said to them: 'You're all laughing at me now because you think I made an ass of myself. I'm going to be an actor; I'm going to be a star; and you'll be coming to me some day asking for a position under me, and then the laugh will be on the other side of your face.'"

This fable portrays vividly the real force that made James O'Neill an actor: his steel-hard determination to drive on in the face of failure and ridicule. Again and again in his life he wrested final victory out of defeat through sheer refusal to give up. And the lowly file cutter with the impossible brogue who started out at the Cincinnati National did end by having everyone there—from Kate Fletcher, the leading lady, on down—come to him for jobs; and they got them, too.

James O'Neill's rise in the theater was shared by Alfred Hamilton Seaman—"Pop," he was familiarly called—who started as James O'Neill's benefactor, very quickly became his parasite, and ended, James O'Neill thought, by becoming his betrayer. That is why James O'Neill never mentioned Pop later, only once referring to him as "an old actor" who had given him lessons in acting when he first started going on stage as a super for twenty-five cents a performance.

With Pop, James O'Neill had joined a shoestring traveling company that went bankrupt by the time it reached Quincy, Illinois. There James experienced "the hunger and horror of being stranded without funds." Nevertheless, he struggled on to St. Louis, where he got a low-paying part in the St. Louis Varieties and shared a miserable room with Pop for a few cents a week, which, when the Varieties closed, he couldn't pay. "I remember that one morning we found a few of our clothes tied in bundles on the floor," James O'Neill said later. "Our trunks had been replevined for our room rent." Mrs. O'Neill, the landlady, "tartly informed me," said James, "that even if she and I bore the same name and came from the same part of Ireland that would not pay room rent." James O'Neill saved himself and Pop that time by getting the role of Baron Puck with the Gommersal English Opera Company even though he couldn't "sing a note." "I got two weeks' salary out of the job," he said later, "and my partner and I were able to pay our way on a freight steamer from here to Cincinnati."

Pop remained the "partner" of O'Neill's next few years, from the day he started out as "walking gentleman" at the Cincinnati National on August 31, 1868. He rose to juvenile lead before the year was out. The next year he was playing leading roles in support of Neil Warner, and the year after that, in Cleveland, he had vaulted to leading man at Ellsler's Academy of Music. James O'Neill and Pop roomed together in Cleveland at 19 Johnson Street, and Pop acted as "Jimmy's" dresser. Pop followed Jimmy to Chicago, too, and there, without a doubt, James O'Neill laid out the money to establish Pop as "Alfred H. Seaman, Theatrical Costumes."

It was Nettie Walsh who caused the rift between Alfred Hamilton Seaman and James O'Neill, for Nettie turned to Pop when O'Neill left her. So intimate did they become that Nettie named her child Alfred Hamilton O'Neill after Pop, and at the time of the scandal she and Alfie were living with Pop in a flat on West Harrison Street. It was Pop that James O'Neill meant when he pointed out, in his answer to Nettie's charges, that she had received attentions from "divers men" and that "she is now living with one of said men, who is not her husband, but provides her with the means of support and enjoys the marital relations of a husband." Indeed, from the beginning, James O'Neill had suspected that Pop was behind the whole scheme to blackmail him by means of a divorce suit. He had gone to Pop at once and said, "The whole case rests with you," but Pop had refused to budge. That was why, in his counter charges, James O'Neill spoke darkly of Nettie's being "under the influence of sundry designing persons who seek to ruin his professional prospects."

But Pop didn't want to ruin him. "If he'd behaved right at first nothing would have been said about the case," Pop told a reporter from the *Inter-Ocean*. "I wouldn't see him harmed; but I won't see him wrong anyone." Indeed, Pop bragged to everyone, "I brought him out." To a *Tribune* reporter who asked Pop if he had found James O'Neill as a bootblack, Pop replied, "Never said anything of the kind. Of course I brought him out, but he was no bootblack. He was only a file-cutter when I knew him first, and I put him on the boards in Cincinnati. Yes, sir, Jimmie, although I say it myself, is one of the finest—here Jake! Oh Jake! You remember Jimmie in—" and Pop, if he hadn't been interrupted, would have gone on, with Jake Murray to corroborate him, to brag of James O'Neill's acting.

The divorce suit ended for good James O'Neill's association with Pop Seaman. It ended, too, his troubles with Nettie Walsh. But the scandal itself had raised the ghost of another woman with whom James O'Neill's name had been linked before his marriage. This was the beautiful, dark-eyed Louise Hawthorne, whose terrible death at twenty-nine coincided with James O'Neill's first success in the Union Square Theatre Company. He was the last person to see her alive and one of the first to see her dead.

Talk about James O'Neill and Louise Hawthorne had started immediately after James O'Neill became leading man in Uncle Dick Hooley's "Parlor Home of Comedy" in the fall of 1874, and began to play the part of passionate lover to Louise Hawthorne in a series of adaptations from the French. With all the intense love between them on stage, people began to assume that they must be lovers off stage, too. But the public didn't know that George Morton, also of Hooley's stock company, was Louise Hawthorne's husband.

True, George Morton was not with Hooley's company when it went to San Francisco in May, 1875, or during the following year when James O'Neill and Louise Hawthorne played together in San Francisco, along the Pacific slope, and in bonanza mining towns like Virginia City, Nevada. When they returned to Chicago, Louise Hawthorne delayed her departure for New York, where George Morton awaited her, so that she could see her friend James O'Neill open in *The Two Orphans* with the Union Square Theatre Company on June 27, 1876.

Louise Hawthorne stayed through two acts. Then suddenly she felt so sick that she returned to the Tremont House. As soon as she entered the lobby, she learned that her friend Kate Girard had had a hemorrhage and rushed to Kate's room in the hotel. She was still at Kate's bedside when James O'Neill returned from his performance, which had been a great success, and knocked at Louise's door to give her the sleeping car ticket he had secured for her that afternoon. Finding she wasn't in, he left the ticket on her table and returned to his own room further down the hall on the sixth floor. A little later, Louise came to his room. He told her where to find her ticket; they talked for a few moments and then they parted.

James O'Neill was still up two hours later when a terrified bellboy came to tell him that something was wrong with Miss Hawthorne. At two-thirty in the morning Miss Hawthorne's bell had rung violently, and Shafer, the night clerk, had sent the bellboy up with a pitcher of ice water. The boy had knocked, waited, knocked again. Getting no answer, he had hurried down the hall to the speaking tube and asked Shafer what he should do. Shafer told him to go back and knock louder. This time he rapped very sharply, listened, and then froze with fear when he heard a low moaning from inside the room. He fled down the elevator to tell Shafer.

Shafer, unperturbed, told the bellboy to show another guest to his room on the third floor and then rouse Eldridge, the house clerk, and Miss Hawthorne's friends, including James O'Neill. James hurried down the hall. The door of Louise Hawthorne's room was open. He saw the bed with the covers thrown back, the packed trunks, a handful of clothes on the bureau. The long windows were open and the wind was blowing a mist of rain onto the floor. Eldridge was just coming out of the empty bathroom. James O'Neill stepped to a window, pushed aside the curtains and draperies, looked down the seven-story drop to the court below, and said, "She must have fallen out the window."

Then he, Eldridge, and Will Chapman rushed for the elevator, groped their way through the basement with a lantern, hastily unlocked the door to the inner court, and found Louise lying on the wet pavement, her long hair streaming down her back. Later, Will Chapman said that all he could think as he stood there stunned was that Miss Hawthorne was lying out in the rain and must be gotten in at once. They rushed forward to lift her up. When they raised her head, a great red mass slipped out and fell heavily to the pavement. Her skull had been smashed.

Later, they figured out what must have happened. Louise had been taking a medicine which, she had often complained, made her dizzy. She had apparently run for help, groped toward the window for air, and, losing consciousness, had pitched over the low sill. The *Dramatic News* spiced its account of the story with lurid hints of suicide—which brought an indignant letter from George Morton protesting this "stain" on his wife's memory and pointing out that "there was not the slightest motive for such an act—her prospects had never been brighter." Nevertheless, a rumor spread through Chicago that she had killed herself because of her unrequited love for James O'Neill, and people went on repeating the rumor long after the coroner's unequivocal report of "accidental death."

Despite the shock, James O'Neill immediately took charge of everything. He was a man to count on in time of disaster. He sent telegrams to George Morton and Louise's father, sent for Jordan, the undertaker, had Louise's trunks sealed and sent to New York, arranged for the funeral at the Tremont House, which hundreds of her friends and admirers attended, and finally helped to carry her coffin down to the hearse.

Only a few months later, James helped to arrange another funeral —for the actors burned to death on December 5, 1876, in the Brooklyn Theatre fire, in which four hundred people had been trapped. He was one of the pallbearers for Harry Murdoch, and it is easy to imagine his thoughts. Murdoch had gone to the Brooklyn Theatre to take over James's role in *The Two Orphans* so that James could open in Manhattan with Clara Morris in *Miss Multon.* "According to the ratio of chances," James O'Neill said, "if I had gone there, I should have been the victim, and not poor Murdoch."

Despite such experiences, James O'Neill never lost his zest for living or his joy in work. He enjoyed every moment of the struggle that changed him from a stage-struck file cutter with a heavy brogue at twenty into one of the foremost actors in America at thirty.

He had had to work hard to iron "the Kilkenny twist," as he called it, out of his tongue. "Oh, that brogue!" he would exclaim, chuckling, whenever he recalled how a critic had praised him in 1869 for his playing of King James of Scotland and then added the crushing remark, "But Mr. O'Neill must be reminded that King James was not an Irishman." He never did conquer the brogue altogether. As late as 1891, a critic from the New York *Spirit of the Times* attacked him for pronouncing *past* as "parsed" and *austere* as "oystare." But the faint remnant of the brogue only served to measure his victory over it; critics were always praising him for his diction.

His rich baritone voice, too, which became so famous, was his own creation. "It was a tenor at the beginning," he recalled. "I was my own instructor. I worked it out in my room; never had a lesson in vocal culture in my life."

He listened avidly to the great stars at rehearsals and begged them for more advice afterward. When Joseph Jefferson suggested he read drama, he dove into an orgy of reading—Congreve, Farquhar ("Kilkenny bred, both," he noted proudly), Goldsmith, Sheridan, Boucicault. "I devoured them all," he said, "together with every French and German comedy I could find."

In December, 1869, Joseph Jefferson sent for him after a performance of *Rip Van Winkle*, in which James had played Hendrick—"a part to which I brought a rich Irish brogue." James was terrified, but Jefferson said pleasantly, "My boy, you got six rounds of applause to-night, and that is good. Very good, but there are eight rounds in the part and we must get them."

" 'We,' mind you!" James O'Neill exclaimed when he wrote up this memory for *Theatre Magazine* in 1917. "Then as if time were nothing to him, the kindest and finest of men and actors showed me the points at which I might succeed in winning the coveted 'round' and pointed out the reasons for my failure to do so. A lesson in acting money could not have bought! The following night, alas, nervousness and an over desire to do my best caused me to blunder in my delivery so that instead of eight, I achieved only seven signals of approval from the audience. 'Better, my boy, better' was the star's comment with never a hint of rebuke for my failure to capture the other round. But at every subsequent performance the eight bursts of applause were mine."

James O'Neill learned eagerly from all the visiting stars who came to McVicker's in Chicago during his two years there. He never forgot the kindness of Charlotte Cushman, who taught him the business "Macready used to do," and gently tapped him on the shoulder when she was pleased. "I learned from her," said James, "the art of so emphasizing one word that the meaning of a sentence was clear." Charlotte Cushman was so pleased with her young disciple that she told a reporter this was "the pleasantest engagement of her life," and she borrowed James O'Neill from McVicker to play Macbeth to her Lady Macbeth at a special engagement in Buffalo.

Edwin Booth was James O'Neill's greatest idol. "There was none like Booth!" James often exclaimed, and at the mere mention of Booth's name, he would cry, "Ah! now you talk of the best-natured and sweetest-tempered, as well as the greatest of them all." He worked far into the night during Booth's engagement at McVicker's, for he had several roles a week to learn. But he always said, "Those days were about the happiest I ever have had in my theatrical career." So eager was he to learn from Booth that he almost became Booth. "He dressed like him, walked like him, posed like him, and finally came to speak like him," one critic wrote.

James O'Neill had great triumphs in those days. One night, when he played Macduff to Booth's Macbeth—one of O'Neill's admirers recalled—a great roar went up from the audience. Booth went out to take a bow, but immediately returned, realizing it wasn't he they wanted. A moment later the audience began to shout "O'Neill! O'Neill! O'Neill!" Then James O'Neill went out, "blushing like a boy," to find the audience on its feet, applauding and waving handkerchiefs at him in a frenzy of appreciation.

"After the study of a single year he is the equal of some stars, and the superior of many more." So John McLandburg wrote of him in June, 1873, at the end of his first year at McVicker's. Then, as a postscript to paragraphs of praise, McLandburg added, "He must work, *work*, WORK!" James O'Neill never forgot the advice. Years later (often ascribing the words to Charlotte Cushman) he would repeat again and again that "work, *work*, WORK!" The words embodied his own indestructible determination.

The reviews of his first ten years of acting show his rapid progress from a "nervous," "uneven" youngster to a polished artist. By 1877, after his year with the Union Square Theatre Company, which was known for its "repressed" style of acting, he had gained, according to the San Francisco critics, "greater self-control and intensity." From then on he would be known for his quiet, natural style of acting. Later, one critic would doubt that he could do *Monte Cristo* because "his line is not melodramatic acting; he belongs to the modern repressed school."

From the beginning James O'Neill had shown real creativeness. "I couldn't copy any man," he himself said. He could disregard advice if he thought it hampered his originality. He showed this during Booth's engagement in his second year at McVicker's. Tommaso Salvini, the great Italian artist, had been fascinating Chicago with a frenzied, brutal Othello. "The papers almost hinted that Booth would not dare to play it after him," James O'Neill recalled. "That was Booth's cue to put it up." No one in the packed audience on opening night appreciated Booth's intellectual, restrained Othello more than James O'Neill, who was playing Iago. "Rarely," he said later, "have I been so thrilled, as with the acting, fiery and stately by turns, of Mr. Booth." But no sooner had Booth triumphed as Othello, than he decided to complete the victory by playing Iago, a role that Salvini never attempted. Panic-stricken, James O'Neill realized that *he* would have to play Othello after both Salvini and Booth.

"I was in a quandary," James O'Neill said, when he told the story to a Boston critic in 1900. "I knew that everyone who would be in the house that night would know me; that nearly all of them would have seen Salvini and Booth, and that they would expect me to fail.

To imitate either one or the other of the well-known actors too closely would be bad policy; yet how to introduce something original puzzled me. It came like a flash at the last rehearsal. We were going through the third scene of the third act. You know it:

> *Villain, be sure of it—give me the ocular proof,*
> *Or by the worth of man's eternal soul*
> *Thou hadst better have been born a dog*
> *Than answer my naked wrath.*

" 'Of course, this is your scene, O'Neill,' Booth said very kindly. 'I will be at the side here whenever you want me. And, by the way, O'Neill, I wouldn't wear the sword in that scene if I were you. You will find it in your way.'

"Now the sword was one of those dear old curved scimitars with a highly decorated scabbard from which it was seldom drawn. Going off, the thought struck me and I tried to draw it. It came only half-way, as I expected, and then clanged back with a great deal of noise. It suited my purpose perfectly. In the evening when I went on for the scene referred to I wore the sword. As I worked myself up, I sidled across the stage toward Booth:

> *If thou dost slander her and torture me,*
> *Never pray more—abandon all remorse.*
> *On horror's head horrors accumulate.*
> *Do deeds to make the heaven weep, all earth amazed,*
> *For nothing canst thou to damnation add greater than that.*

"I had drawn near to Booth as the words were said, and the sword had been gradually half-drawn.

> *Nay, Nay! Thou shouldst be honest.*

"Bang! Back went the sword at the words and down came the house. But never mind that part of it. What I want to point out is that as I went to my dressing-room after the curtain fell it was Booth who called me back because the audience wanted me. 'The scene is yours,' he said. 'You couldn't have done better,' and he pressed my hand. Yet I had disregarded his advice and had not imitated him in any way."

The rest of that evening was more beautiful than any daydream of success: not just the ovation after the scene with the sword—which the stage manager assured him was "the most prolonged round of applause I have ever heard!"; but also the moment when John Barron, who had played Ludovico, came to him and told him what he at first refused to believe, that Booth had said of him, "That young man plays Othello better than I ever did!" This was in February, 1874, when James O'Neill was twenty-seven.

The great victory, of course, was not the one bit of stage business he had introduced, but, as the critics pointed out, his portrayal of a distinct third Othello, different from both Salvini's and Booth's. Always in the face of almost certain failure, James O'Neill could force a victory through sheer indomitable will. Yet he never took himself too seriously. He was always ready, as Willie Seymour said, to give and take a joke.

Even when he was playing Romeo to Adelaide Neilson's Juliet in April, 1873, he couldn't resist a bit of mischief. Night after night, said James, Adelaide Neilson had bent over him in the death scene of *Romeo and Juliet,* giving the audience "the impression that she kissed me, though her lips met only empty air."

"One night, as the dying hero, I thought to better the situation. . . . I let my chin sink on my chest with a last breath, and she stooped over for the touching but unsatisfactory final salutation. In that moment I suddenly threw back my head so that any mere stage illusion was out of the question; I was too clearly in view of the audience for that; and Romeo had a kiss of the sterling variety!

"Down went the curtain and up sprang Miss Neilson. 'How could you? How could you?' she cried.

" 'How could I what?' I asked in turn, as innocently as my training in simulation would allow.

" 'How, how—' and she hesitated; 'How could Romeo throw his head back after he was dead?'

" 'Miss Neilson,' I answered, 'your Juliet was the cause of it. It would make anyone come back to life!' "

Louis James, a fellow actor, enjoyed telling how James O'Neill avenged the whole of Hooley's company on Barry Sullivan, the domineering English actor who had alienated all the actors at the

Baldwin Academy in March, 1876, by his surly manner and refusal
"to allow anybody to shine but himself."

"So James O'Neill," said Louis James, "decided to give him a dose
of his own medicine. When Othello was put on Jim delivered the
lines of Iago with a melodramatic vehemence that completely an-
nihilated the effect of the most forceful speeches with which Barry
Sullivan, as the Moor, was wont to evoke thunders of applause. In
the course of the performance Mr. Sullivan took Jim aside and said,
'My boy, is this your conception of Iago? You know the lines are full
of subtlety and should not be given with so much fervor.' 'Well,'
answered Jim, 'that's the way I generally play the part, and it's too
late to tone it down this evening.'" The other actors were delighted,
and they all had a good laugh after the show.

James O'Neill was one of those rare men who can also laugh when
the joke is on them. And so he did at the joke that Mike Kennedy,
Ned Buckley, and Billy Crane pulled on him when they were playing in Virginia City, Nevada, in July, 1875. Knowing how eager
James was to get hold of a mine, Ned Buckley introduced him to a
mine owner in the billiard room of the International Hotel. The
mine owner, who was actually an actor from another company, took
O'Neill out to a huge cave about a mile from town in which there
was a well so deep no one had ever plumbed its bottom. There he
and O'Neill were leapt upon by bandits (actually more actors), who
threatened to toss O'Neill down the pit. It was an elaborate melo-
drama, but O'Neill caught on to it very soon and the whole thing
ended in a jolly party, with a demijohn of whiskey going the rounds.
O'Neill enjoyed the "hilarious farce" so thoroughly that he wrote it
up at length for the *Dramatic Mirror* in 1899, dwelling with delight
on how he had been "forced to the brink of the chasm in spite of my
cries and protestations; my hair standing on end, my blood con-
gealed with horror, and a cold perspiration bedewing my body."

For all his gaiety, James O'Neill could be firm when he felt his
interests threatened, and at such times he was a hard man to move.
During his first year with Uncle Dick Hooley, he had overcome a
"newspaper cabal," organized by Fred Williams, the stage manager,
to push Harry Murdoch into the first place in the company. In the
end Williams left the company altogether, and James O'Neill saw to

it that Billy Crane, the comedian, became stage manager in his place. "In this way we started a friendship that is warm to this day," Crane would say.

James O'Neill could act firmly in questions of money, too. In the summer of 1881, when Hamlin, the Chicago theater manager, refused to give him better terms for a new contract, he immediately signed on with Uncle Dick Hooley. To Hamlin's threats of a lawsuit, O'Neill quietly replied, "I contracted with Mr. Hamlin for a three weeks' engagement which I carried out to the letter"; and he added, "Had Mr. Hamlin been more liberal" he would still have the O'Neill company. Once O'Neill had gained his point, he and Hamlin were friends again.

Politely but firmly, James O'Neill could drive a hard bargain. He always got good terms in his contracts, not just in salary, but in his choice of roles. He had a clause in his contract with the Union Square Theatre, for instance, that he was not to play with Charley Thorne unless he had a role of equal strength. He always insisted on the privilege of turning down a role he felt beneath his powers.

Of course, he made mistakes; not just little ones, either. In the spring of 1881, after turning down many excellent offers, he signed a four-year contract with J. M. Hill, who offered to star him in *Hamlet* if he would take the role of Joe Thatcher in *Deacon Crankett* for the first year. James O'Neill "bit" on the promise of *Hamlet,* to find himself, the next fall, playing a poor role in a weak play in little coal-mining towns where the audiences stamped, catcalled, and commented loudly on the action of the play. He suspected, by then, that Hill had never intended to star him in *Hamlet.*

When *Deacon Crankett* opened in New York on November 7, 1881, Hill received a telegram from James O'Neill a few minutes before curtain time, saying he was ill and couldn't go on. A few days later, O'Neill asked to be released from his contract. Harrison Grey Fiske, editor of the *Dramatic Mirror,* decided that O'Neill was only ill under contract. "A very dapper, lively young man fashionably attired, conversing hilariously with his friends one week later on Union Square—this was O'Neill released. Silly fellow! He throws away the best opportunity that ever was or can be placed before him, simply because a foolish pride prevented his playing a part here which, in the blindness of conceit, he considered beneath his powers."

Fiske was wrong on both counts. Dr. Howe, a physician just across the street from O'Neill's rooms on West Twenty-fourth Street, testified that James O'Neill had certainly been ill. "Monday afternoon about five o'clock I found the patient suffering from malaria, and he was in a high fever and unable to leave the house. He told me that he had been really ill for two weeks, but would not give up to the feeling. He said he *must* go to the theatre that evening, but I expressly forbade it, and wrote a note to that effect to Mr. Hill, his manager." James O'Neill had been ill. He had also taken advantage of his illness to break a contract which had turned out to be a mistake. Hill had never really intended to star him in *Hamlet*.

Because of his incurable readiness to like and trust his fellow men, James O'Neill was frequently cheated. From his boyhood days when he sold newspapers and bought a pack cheap that turned out to be yesterday's papers, to the last years of his life, James O'Neill was not only easily taken in, but very slow to realize that he had been taken.

When the Cumberland Mine in Arizona—owned by James O'Neill, John E. Owens, and a few other actors—failed, nothing could convince James O'Neill that he had lost his money. "I don't consider that I have sustained a loss," he told an incredulous reporter from the New York *Dramatic News* on April 8, 1881. "I am certain that both Mr. Owens and myself will get all our money back, and more, too. I haven't lost faith in the Cumberland by any means." Then he added comfortably, "But even if nothing should ever be realized from the Cumberland, I have six other claims out there, which will bring me in all the money I have expended."

"The assertion has been broadcast, too," James O'Neill continued, "that we were swindled out of all our investments, and that Ciprico was at the bottom of it. Now, that is likewise untrue. We know that every dollar we invested was spent in buying machinery. Owens put in something like $25,000, and it was used immediately in that way. As to Ciprico, he is the poorest of the lot; he is one of those men who are always under a cloud, always in debt. There was no swindle at all. You will yet see us get our money back." But they never did.

Right after James O'Neill's death, his good friend George C. Tyler confided to Eugene, "Your dear daddy's queer investments were a continual source of worry to both Will Connor and myself. When we protested, he pooh-poohed. But there was a pathetically humorous side to it all. He was nearly always 'done' by an Irishman! Such a lover of his own people was he that any plausible swindler had simply to possess an Irish name in order to get his ear, and if he happened to have an O' in front of it, all the king's men couldn't hold the dear fellow back. And yet, he was really cautious when Will Connor advised—and Will loved him more than he loved anyone in the world. Strange, wasn't it?"

It was strange. James O'Neill, who was ready to trust almost everyone, could, at times, be unreasonably suspicious. And he invariably distrusted his managers. He later declared that they had swindled him out of thousands of dollars. When he began starring in *The American King* in 1882, he and his manager E. M. Gardiner parted company before the tour was two months out. He suspected his second manager, Ernest Stanley, almost at once. According to James, "Stanley was to devote his entire time and attention to my business, and before he had been with me a week he was bragging of another attraction he had to handle while his contract with me was in force."

In the case of Will Connor (who did love him dearly), James O'Neill revealed clearly the psychological origins of his chronic distrust of managers. "I think Mr. Connor is working for his own interest, not mine," he told Tyler by letter on January 25, 1899, at the time Liebler and Company was forming. "He has averaged about 4000 a year with me and I am sure he does not appreciate what I have done for him." James O'Neill told Tyler that he wished Connor "well" and hoped he would become "a big man," but he didn't want to work "*under him,*" so he hoped Connor would not get the third interest in Liebler and Company. "This is confidential. He is still in my employ and we are friends. I will do anything to help him but I don't want him to become my master. I will help him to master anyone else but I draw the line at / Your friend / James O'Neill."

Connor did buy the third interest, yet he and James O'Neill remained close friends. But James O'Neill never got over the secret distrust of a man in the position of a "master." Perhaps the feeling stemmed from his experiences, first with his father, who had forced him into a trade and then deserted him, and later with Pop Seaman. It remained a curious contradiction in the personality of a man usually trusting and openhearted to the point of naïveté.

All his life O'Neill was known for his spontaneous generosity. Flushed with his first success in *Monte Cristo,* he happened to meet Bonnie Whitton, the old Cincinnati property man who had helped him in his youth, and at once presented him with a fifty-dollar bill for old times' sake. Again, on learning that the man transporting the company's scenery had been injured severely in a runaway, O'Neill started a subscription for him, heading it with fifty dollars. He could always be counted on for from twenty-five to fifty dollars a year by the Actor's Fund, and he handed out larger sums privately to people in difficulties. As Fred Wren, a less fortunate actor, said of him, "He is liberal, giving according to his means, which is ten times more than Rockefeller and Carnegie give. He does not teach a Sunday school class and never lets the world know of his charities." His friend Tom Dorsey summed him up as "a soft-hearted man, always good for a touch." Everyone found him "kind-hearted and generous to a fault."

James O'Neill was a big man in other ways. He never stooped to the little ways men have of exalting their egos. He never stood on dignity; he was as cordial to a stagehand as to the manager of a theater. He was universally admired for his "modesty." Billy Crane would always remember James O'Neill's comment on Mrs. Maeder, a lady who was perpetually recalling her triumphs as Clara Fisher, the child star. "When she fairly got started on the splendors of her past," Crane recalled, "James O'Neill used to say: 'Deliver me from former greatness.' It was almost a prayer with him."

Something in James O'Neill's serene, kindly Irish face caused him to be taken frequently for a Catholic priest. He once told a Chicago *Times* reporter of the days when he was touring the Northwest "with my wonderful one man show." The whole town of Spokane had watched him as—clad in "a frock coat buttoned high" and "a long linen duster"—he assisted two Catholic Sisters of Charity out of the stagecoach and into the house where they were staying. After watching the sun rise over the falls of the Spokane River, James O'Neill returned to the hotel, where he found a small crowd waiting for him. "It was quite common then for me to be visited by a number of people upon my arrival in a place, and I thought nothing of it," he said. "A little Irishman, who was acting as spokesman for the party, began to introduce Mr. Flynn, Mr. Doyle, Mr. Flannigan, Mr. Moriarty, Mr. Maloney and others until I thought I had struck a new Hibernia.

"He said, 'We were not expecting you.'

"I said, 'I thought my coming had been announced. I sent some notices of it.'

" . . . I talked a while with my visitors, and was about to excuse myself when what was my surprise to have my little friend propound: 'Your riverence, will you be kind enough to inform us if you will have any confessions before you say mass?' A light broke upon me at once, and when I explained who I was, great was the amusement at the comical blunder. The boys packed the house to overflowing for me that night, and what a time we did have after the show!"

Far from comical was the occasion, a year after Eugene's birth, when James O'Neill was taken for a Catholic priest in New York. The adventure impressed James so strongly that he wrote it out for the *Dramatic Mirror* in 1896. "I was playing an engagement in the city, and after the Saturday matinee found myself on Eighth Avenue, on my way home. It was about half-past five in the afternoon; the streets were covered with a heavy fall of snow and crowded with the usual throng of busy buyers of Christmas presents. The professional beggar was out in full force, and I could not help contrasting his ragged person with the well-dressed people in the brilliantly lighted stores.

"The comparison made me weary at heart, and for the moment I wished that every poor man once in his life could get a chance to play the part of a rich man. Imagination sometimes is better than reality. Would that every *Edmond Dantes,* the prisoner of cell 17, could be metamorphosed into a *Count of Monte Cristo!*

"But I am digressing. Between Seventh and Eighth Avenue, there are several rows of houses inhabited by poor people. As I was passing one of them, the door between the narrow alley and the side walk was suddenly thrown open and a little girl came tumbling head foremost toward me. She was only about ten years of age, and the force required in opening the door had completely exhausted her.

"I picked her up; she was crying, and in answer to my questions whether she was hurt or not, she did not reply, but merely hid her head in her hands and continued sobbing. Unable to get a word from her, I finally forcibly raised her head, and made her look into my eyes. My long dark coat was buttoned tightly, and the collar turned up. The little girl's beautiful and expressive eyes, dimmed with tears, looked into mine, and by soothing and caressing her, I at last succeeded in calming the frightened little soul.

"She looked up and noticed my appearance—she watched my coat, my hat, and scanned my features closely. Then she whispered 'Father,' and raising her voice, said, 'Yes, yes, you are a father, a priest, are you not? Please come with me to mamma. She is sick and alone and no one with her.' I could not refuse the child's request, neither could I explain the mistake to her, and she, by that time, had me almost pulled through the narrow doorway. She led the way up a rickety staircase and into a small room. May I never see such a sight again!

"A thin, emaciated woman with hardly any covering on a body that was continually racked by a consumptive cough, stretched on a mattress in a cold, fireless room! The little girl knelt down by her mother's side, threw her arms around her bony neck, saying softly, 'He is here, Mamma, the good father is here, and he will cure you all right.' "

James O'Neill rushed away and found a doctor, but the woman died shortly after he came. James and the physician left the child with neighbors overnight, while they arranged for her to be admitted to an institution. Later, the doctor wrote him that she was "getting along splendidly."

The fact that James O'Neill was so often taken for a priest became a family joke. Eugene O'Neill was certainly remembering that joke years later when he fled the United States incognito with a woman very like his mother, for he chose as his pseudonym "Reverend William J. O'Brien."

If James O'Neill resembled a priest, he certainly had nothing other-worldly about him. All his life he was the center of a crowd. Even when a crazy women, a dressmaker named Bridget O'Neill, decided that James O'Neill was her long-lost husband—this was in November, 1889—and haled him into court, his friends crowded the courtroom, although the hour was painfully early. When the dressmaker accused the actor of watching her "wildly" from the stage, everyone laughed heartily, but James O'Neill very kindly said, "I am very sorry for the lady; it is a case of mistaken identity." He testified that he was forty-four, not thirty-five, as the woman said her husband was. "I wish I was," he added, to the amusement of his friends. He said he had never worked as a farm hand "except upon my own farm. I have a place in New London where I bury stones in the summer," and again everyone laughed.

His life was one long fellowship. His happiest memories were always crowded with other people—his memories of San Francisco, for instance, with its exacting critics. "Yet how hospitable, how jolly and unconventional we all were at the time!" he wrote in 1899. "What true Bohemians we were, and what flashes of wit used to illumine the Arion Symposium when all the bright fellows gathered there to discuss Harry Grimm's Budweiser and edibles, Shakespeare's plays, acting, music, mining, politics and kindred topics. There could be seen Harry Edwards and 'Bob' Eberle hobnobbing with Barton Hill; George Barnes, the dramatic Solon of the *Morning Call*, teaching Peter Robertson of the *Chronicle* the hidden mysteries of theatrical censorship; and George Jessup and Alfred Balch, molders of theatrical opinion on purely commercial lines, watching with feverish expectancy Joseph Murphy of 'Kerry Gow' fame, as he ordered champagne and more substantial delicacies for the host of well-wishers by whom he was generally surrounded; and above the din of voices, the clink of glasses, the shouts of waiters and the clatter of knives and forks could be heard the honey-dew dialect of my friend, James Connor Roach, and the more persuasive and Doric tones of 'Sconchin' Maloney, as they argued over the merits of the poets and politicians of their native land, occasionally substituting the Gaelic tongue for the less familiar and more difficult speech of the Sassenach. Ah! These were halcyon days, and as for the nights, they have no parallel now, for Bohemianism is a thing of the past, and the money changer sits upon the throne of the artist."

Although he never became as familiar with some of the "gun fighters" and "desperadoes" that Mike Kennedy and Billy Crane hobnobbed with in those days, he had, he said, "a large circle of acquaintances . . . among them being keen mining sharps, men of varied accomplishments, some of them Harvard bred, others from Oxford and Heidelberg, and still a few from dear old Trinity College, Dublin. Many a social glass did we have together, and when not compelled to go to my hotel after the performance to study some new part, it was my custom to meet them and talk over the scientific, literary and psychological subjects men of their calibre had made their special study."

He loved good conversation, stimulated by a social glass. His friends were legion: actors, producers, managers—all knew him and loved him. Everywhere he went he had friends, and in New London he knew everyone in town. His house was constantly full of visitors, not just members of his company, but hosts of other friends. He was "hospitality personified," according to Fred Wren; and Eugene's friend Art McGinley would recall enthusiastically that the house at 325 Pequot Avenue was a place "where you always found a very cordial welcome" and that James O'Neill was "the most fascinating man I've ever known."

This was the man Eugene O'Neill grew up calling "Papa."

CHAPTER FIVE

Monte Cristo

AMONG the first words Eugene O'Neill ever heard were surely "Monte Cristo"; he grew up hearing of the play, seeing it, watching rehearsals of it. *Monte Cristo* had been running five years when Eugene was born, and it went on running—despite James O'Neill's efforts to shake it—right up to 1912. Eugene never understood why his father had let *Monte Cristo* happen to him—why he went on playing the role long after he had come to "hate the very thought of it."

Monte Cristo had begun happening to James O'Neill as early as April, 1881, when he turned down an offer to do leading business in the stock company at the Chestnut Street Theatre in Philadelphia, saying he preferred to star. The rise of the American small town and the extension of the railroads had made it possible, economically, for every popular actor to organize and become star of his own "traveling combination." The age of the actor-managers had come, and it quickly replaced the stock theater system in America. James O'Neill was one of the first of the actor-managers.

The traveling star found it a great advantage to be identified with one role, for everyone then wanted to see him in it. By the time he had covered the United States in a play, he could begin again, for in two years a town would have a whole new population of play-goers waiting to see him. So an entire generation of actors either chose or were forced to restrict themselves to a single role. James O'Neill in *Monte Cristo* was simply the most popular of them, for his play embodied the myth of the nation: the lowly man who rises to the pinnacle of wealth and power.

James O'Neill felt the pressure to limit himself to one role as soon as he formed his own company to produce *The American King* in 1882. Asked whether he would stick to that play, he replied, "There are financial reasons why I should like to, and there are artistic reasons why I should not. I would like the money; but I do not want to become known as a one-part actor."

Actually his tour with *The American King*, he soon admitted, was far from being "a pecuniary success." He received good reviews, but played to pitifully small audiences. When he reached Cleveland and some friends complimented him on not having changed a bit, he replied grimly, "I have got to that point in life when every year counts."

Such was his position in January, 1883, when he received a telegram from John Stetson, who was planning to put on a series of romantic revivals in New York—first *The Corsican Brothers,* and then *Monte Cristo* and *The Three Musketeers.* Stetson asked, "Will you play the 'Corsican Brothers,' at Booth's theater, and when can you begin, and what salary, for balance of season? Thorne ill, and compelled to resign his position. If you will entertain it telegraph me quick."

Without hesitation, James O'Neill wired back, "No." But that was not the end of it. John Stetson looked up O'Neill's advance schedule, found he would be in Albany from January 18–20, and took the next train. There he argued one whole afternoon until James O'Neill agreed to take the lead in *Monte Cristo* in February at a salary of

$600 a week. Chance had brought Charles Thorne a fatal illness when *The Corsican Brothers* opened in New York on January 8, 1883. The same chance brought James O'Neill the fatal role of Monte Cristo.

James O'Neill's career in *Monte Cristo* began with a failure. Blizzards trapped him in Chicago long after rehearsals had started in New York. Only three days before the opening on February 12, 1883, did he get to New York. He rehearsed feverishly from ten in the morning until seven at night and then, exhausted, studied the long, intricate role of Edmond Dantes. At his best, James O'Neill was not a "quick study"; he never had been. He begged Stetson to postpone the opening, but Stetson said, "I know all the newspaper boys and will tell them that you had only three rehearsals." But in the last-minute rush, he forgot. The result was a debacle. All the newspapers "roasted" O'Neill, the *Spirit of the Times* declaring that he "was only tolerable when he tried to imitate Fechter, who was inimitable." (Fechter had originated the role.)

"The critics were right that time," said James O'Neill. "I was bad. I knew it. But I got at the play with hammer and tongs. I rehearsed all day in my rooms. By the end of the week the play was going well." The *Mirror* said that he had "improved remarkably," but, as James O'Neill declared later, "The public saved the life of the play." So began *Monte Cristo*. The rest was applause, crowded theaters, enthusiastic audiences—a popularity that came out victorious over streetcar strikes, riots, below-zero weather, rainstorms, and all competition.

With Stetson—famous for his ferocity and profanity—James O'Neill kept on pleasant terms. "I've met smoother-mannered men," he agreed, when a critic mentioned Stetson's reputation, "and he sometimes thoughtlessly uses to his people the words that Senator Nye argued was a term of endearment in Nevada. But, for all that, he's not a bad sort of fellow in the main." Stetson agreed, pleasantly enough, to give O'Neill a larger share in the profits of *Monte Cristo* his second year, but at the end of that year came trouble.

James O'Neill wanted to continue *Monte Cristo*. Stetson flatly declared it was "a lemon that has been squeezed dry." He wanted O'Neill to support Mary Anderson in *Romeo and Juliet* at a salary of $20,000 for the season. James O'Neill took a day to think it over.

He loved Shakespeare, but he would not be the star and Stetson would be his master. So he quietly declined and, instead, offered Stetson $1000 for the rights to the Fechter version of *Monte Cristo*. Stetson exploded. In the end, James O'Neill doubled his offer, saying, "Besides, you boasted last night to some of your friends that I was one of the actors with whom you had never quarreled, and you're not going to begin quarreling with me now, are you?" James O'Neill came out owning *Monte Cristo*—and *Monte Cristo*, in a way, came out owning him.

"We have a pile of letters the size of a small haystack, all asking for *Monte Cristo* dates." So Ed Zimmerman, O'Neill's manager, announced jubilantly the next fall, and O'Neill exclaimed, "Will I play *Monte Cristo* next season? Well, I rather think I will," pointing out the splendid business he had done so far. "Altogether, the route, which was fixed up by Mr. Zimmerman and myself, is an excellent one, with all doubtful cities left out. In fact, it's the first time I've had a chance to say where I'd play and where I wouldn't, and haven't been handicapped by some queer advance agent." Asked one year later how long he would confine himself to *Monte Cristo*, James O'Neill answered with prophetic honesty, "Altogether too long, I'm afraid."

He cleared $35,000 the first year he owned *Monte Cristo*. The standing-room-only sign was always up in the theaters he played, and sometimes there wasn't even standing room and several hundred people had to be turned away. The next year, incredibly, was even better. So great was the demand for *Monte Cristo* that he organized a second company, with Horace Lewis as Dantes, to play the small towns he couldn't reach. But that was a bad idea, for Lewis began to think of himself as a rival to James O'Neill, and all the entrepreneurs were now alerted to the gold in *Monte Cristo*. Within a few years, three rival *Monte Cristo* companies were playing the small towns, keeping out of the way of James O'Neill. A burlesque of the play called *Monte Cristo, Jr.* had quite a vogue, as did a sequel *The Son of Monte Cristo*. James O'Neill made so much money he was able to invest $20,000 in a cattle ranch in Montana—a pet enterprise of his friend Nate Salsbury—and thousands more in real estate in Chattanooga, New London, New York City, and New

Jersey. Soon he was said to own an orange grove in California and a mine in Colorado, too.

But in the midst of it all, he did not forget that he was an artist. The three roles that he played in *Monte Cristo*—the young Dantès, the gentle Abbé Busoni, and the stark avenger—gave full scope to his talents. And *Monte Cristo* would give him the money, he thought, to realize his great dream of devoting his life to Shakespeare—or to the Passion play, in which he had acted in San Francisco in 1879.

"Never before or since have I felt as I did when I made my first appearance as the Christ," James O'Neill said. O'Neill had been "simply dumbfounded" when Tom Maguire decided to put on Salmi Morse's Passion play in San Francisco that year and gave him the role of Christus. He had been ready to refuse the role until he learned that the Catholic archbishop, Joseph Alemany, approved the play. But then the uproar began. Protestant ministers arose against "this blasphemous work of sacrilege and dishonour"; the San Francisco Board of Aldermen rushed through an ordinance against it, and mobs, threatening lynching, gathered at the theater on the opening night, March 3.

Ellen was "thoroughly frightened." Indeed, James O'Neill himself later confided to his friend Nate Salsbury, "I was uncertain up to ten minutes before I went to the theatre, whether I should not give up the whole thing. My wife threw herself upon her knees at my feet, and pleaded with me to send word that I would not go on. She said the people would kill me."

Once at the theater, however, he thought only of the role. "As a Christian I approached the rendition of that glorious character with a sense of awe and veneration simply indescribable," he said. As he came out of his dressing room, Willie Seymour came up to him merrily, about to speak. "The joke died on my lips," Seymour confessed later. "I thought I stood in the presence of Our Saviour. . . . "

In silence James O'Neill moved on stage. "Actors spoke only in a whisper, scene-shifters and carpenters tiptoed, and the breathing of the leading characters could be heard as they arranged themselves for the scene," he later told a reporter from the Pittsburgh *Leader*. Of the rest of his performance, he often said, "To me it was not acting; it was devotion." He came off stage in a trance. "The first night of the Passion play," Louis Morrison would recall, "he came into the dressing room after his first scene and sat down. For a few minutes he did not speak. Then mechanically, from sheer force of habit, he reached for his pipe. When his hand touched it, he seemed to awake. He started and looked at me. I said, 'Don't Jim; not now'—and he didn't."

The rest was a furious uproar from people who hadn't seen the performance, and praise from those who had. "If ever an actor was exalted by his work," James A. Herne, the actor and playwright, declared, "Mr. O'Neill was exalted by coming so closely in spiritual touch with Jesus Christ. I have never heard or read anything anywhere which so ennobled and dignified religion as did that play and that actor." James O'Neill and Ellen treasured a rosary from Jerusalem sent him by the poet Charles Warren Stoddard in memory of his "marvelous impersonation." After all her fears, Ellen was filled with admiration for her husband. "My wife likes to associate me with the character," he would later say, smiling.

So she had the courage to support him when Maguire, on April 15, 1879, put on the play to test the new ordinance against it. James O'Neill preferred to go to jail himself rather than allow an amateur to botch the role in his place, and so he was arrested. Later he was released on bail till the case came up for trial. On April 22, 1879, the courts declared the ordinance legal, James O'Neill paid a $50 fine for the "misdemeanor" of impersonating Christ; and there were no more performances of the Passion play in San Francisco.

A little over a year later, James O'Neill was again prepared to brave public fury by playing the role of Christ in a New York production of the Passion play under the management of Henry Abbey. James told a *Tribune* reporter in November, 1880, "If the public will support me, I shall devote the remainder of my life to this great work. I have no desire to go back to the routine work of the stage at all. I believe I can do more good by this presentation than any of the ministers from their pulpits."

Far from supporting him, the public was ready to tear him to pieces. The ministers, the newspapers, the politicians—all broke into violent denunciation of the play, of its author Salmi Morse, and particularly of the man who would play Christ. "Good God," the Rev-

erend Newman exclaimed, "we shudder at the presumption of the
man who would dare to try to do so." "Every time my name was
mentioned," James O'Neill remarked later, "it was coupled with my
assumption of the character as an act of audacity, when, Heaven
knows, I never felt in a more humble frame of mind in my life all
the time I was acting it."

When "Abbey got cold feet," and withdrew *The Passion* from
production on November 27, 1880, James O'Neill was left defenseless. He had counted on overcoming the fury against him by the
beauty of his performance. He never got the chance. Instead, Abbey
put him into *A Celebrated Case,* and he found himself suddenly,
on December 6, playing before a scattered, hostile audience. "Mr.
O'Neill seemed cold, unimpassioned, and ill," one critic noted. James
O'Neill himself confessed later, "I firmly believed myself at the end
of all success as an actor."

Two years later, James O'Neill turned down the role of Christ
in Salmi Morse's third attempt to put on the Passion play, for he
feared "prejudice" would again crush it. He was right. Lawsuits
bled Salmi Morse to bankruptcy so that he had to give up his attempt, and a year later he was found drowned in the Hudson River.
"Poor old Salmi," said James O'Neill, refusing to think, as many
people did, that Morse had committed suicide. "My theory of his
death is, that, brooding over his misfortunes he sought to forget
care and took a glass or two too much; after which, wandering in
the vicinity of the river—a favorite walk of his—he lost his balance,
fell in, and was unable to recover himself." Then he added, "I hope
he is in Heaven!"

Despite all this, James O'Neill never gave up the idea of playing
Christ in the Passion play. In 1889, he planned to produce *The Passion* in Omaha, Nebraska, using the money he had made from
Monte Cristo. But as soon as he applied for a permit, the Episco-
palian Church and the Y.M.C.A. there rose up in arms against it.
In 1891, he again talked of putting on *The Passion,* and in 1896 he
announced that he would play Christ in "an Eastern syndicate's"
production of the Passion play, but both these projects died in embryo. Public opinion was still too hostile.

James O'Neill's other great dream of devoting himself to Shakespeare also proved to be hopeless. With the retirement of Booth and Barrett, the audience for Shakespeare seemed to disappear. Only Tom Keene made money with Shakespeare in the hick towns, where the people liked him, James O'Neill said, "for the same reason that they always buy Rio coffee—because it is coarse and rank."

But James O'Neill didn't give up. He put on *Hamlet* in Mobile, Alabama, on January 16, 1886, and played it again on February 1 in Birmingham. The newspapers were kind. They found his portrayal "enjoyable," decided that "his soliloquies were meditations not recitations," and praised his freedom from rant, but James O'Neill knew perfectly well that if he devoted himself to *Hamlet* he would quickly go bankrupt. Theatrical companies were collapsing all around him in the South that year, but *Monte Cristo* drew crowded houses. Later, from 1893 through 1896, by playing a repertory that featured *Monte Cristo* at most performances, he did manage to keep on performing *Hamlet,* but in those depression years he would have gone under fast had he tried to devote himself to Shakespeare.

James O'Neill could not escape *Monte Cristo* through Shakespeare or the Passion play, nor could he turn from it to contemporary American plays. "I have always been willing to encourage the American drama," he said, "but dramas of native authorship of sufficient strength and merit to suit my purpose are few and far between. I am not referring to comedies or comedy-dramas. Bronson Howard, Henry Guy Carleton, Augustus Thomas, and others are very clever playwrights in that line. But take tragedies like *Francesca da Rimini* and *The Gladiator,* both written by American authors of a former generation. They may write plays of equal strength today, but I must confess they have not been submitted to me."

Nevertheless, James O'Neill did try new American plays, such as *The Envoy* by E. J. Swartz, which he put on at the Star Theatre, New York City, in May, 1891. "New York," he remarked to the editor of the *Dramatic Mirror,* after the play's quick failure, "is the town of towns for fads, skits, and horse-play. The dramatic outlook is black. Perhaps, though, it is not the people, but the financial state of the country that is to blame. It is my experience that when the country is going through bad times—as at present, when business is dull and the money market is stringent—then the people, by way of contrast, want to see light plays that do not tax the brain; and that when the business world is prosperous, so that men have a cheerful day, then the people, for the same reason, are willing at night to see a serious play."

He tried other new plays too—*The New South, Don Carlos de Seville, The O'Neill*—but none of them succeeded. The public seemed interested only in romantic melodrama, and when James O'Neill found a successful one, *Fontenelle,* he decided almost immediately, as Will Connor confided to William Seymour, that the part was "not good enough for him" and that he was "wasting time." If he must be restricted to romantic melodramas, James O'Neill thought, it might as well be the best of them, *Monte Cristo.* But he was becoming desperately tired of the part. "I find it hard to remember the words sometimes," he told a reporter in October, 1891. "I have repeated them so often that now they demand considerable effort."

James O'Neill did not give in to *Monte Cristo* quite as easily as his son Eugene would later assume. Nor was Edmond Dantes the only role he played between 1883 and 1900. Although he never shook *Monte Cristo* for more than a year at a time, the catalogue of the other plays he produced is fairly long: *Hamlet, The Dead Heart, The Envoy, The New South, Fontenelle, Don Carlos de Seville, Richelieu, Virginius, The O'Neill, Courier of Lyons, The Dream of Mathew Wayne, When Greek Meets Greek,* and *The Three Musketeers.*

The shy dark-eyed boy growing up in the house at New London saw many plays in rehearsal besides the perennial *Monte Cristo.* But *Monte Cristo* was always there—and years later, forgetting the other plays and unaware of the forces that had kept James O'Neill from his highest ambition, Eugene would think his father had simply "fallen for the lure of easy popularity and easy money."

CHAPTER SIX

The Inheritance

EUGENE O'NEILL got from his father far more than the quarter of a million dollars he inherited. By the time he was six he had absorbed a set of values, a way of looking at life that would stand intact through all the wars he later fought against them. Whenever he returned to his childhood world of faith and love, he also returned to the ideas of honor and decency he had acquired from his father.

For all his tolerance, James O'Neill had an ironclad code of behavior. Even when the trouble with Nettie Walsh came, he wanted to believe he had acted "squarely and honorably from beginning to end." He believed in acting "squarely and honorably" and passed on the belief to his son. From his father, Eugene also caught the "fighting spirit," the desire to battle through all difficulties to success, the willingness to "work, *work*, WORK." In addition, Eugene learned the ideal of service to others, the idea, as James O'Neill put it, that "life is really worth living, after all," not only on one's own account, but "through the fortunate circumstances which enable one to come to the assistance of a fellow-being." James O'Neill had founded his whole career on the belief that an actor is best pleased "when he knows that by his efforts he has been able to convey some sense of comfort and satisfaction to his audiences." Service to others became for Eugene one of the great ideals of life.

Never would he be able to alter, much less annihilate this set of values. It stood impregnable in the midst of his later philosophizing and emerged again and again in his writing. The whole code appears in an early poem Eugene wrote for the New London *Telegraph* describing "A Regular Sort of a Guy," who "fights where the fighting is thickest," keeps "his honor clean," shuns "the petty and mean," and has "a pat on the back" for "the lowliest bum on the street." A little later, in the early play *Abortion* he also presented the ideal of "playing out the game" like "a regular sort of a guy." Evelyn tells her fiancé, after watching him win a baseball game, "It struck me as symbolical of the way you would always play, in the game of life—fairly, squarely, strengthening those around you, refusing to weaken at critical moments, advancing others by sacrifices, fighting the good fight for the cause, the team, and always, always, whether vanquished or victor, reserving a hearty, honest cheer for the other side."

Nor did Eugene slough off the code in his later, mature plays. Whenever he presented love triumphant, he also presented the values of his happy childhood, before his faith in his parents' love was shaken by the long exile at Mount Saint Vincent. Particularly in *Ah, Wilderness!* and *Days Without End* (both written in 1932), triumphant love and the early code appear hand-in-hand. In *Ah, Wilderness!* both Nat Miller and his son Richard represent a tolerant but firm code of honor. Nat Miller is, as his brother-in-law tells him, "too decent for your own good." He is incapable of "a dirty, spiteful trick" like using his newspaper for personal revenge. His son Richard is also the soul of honor; his father can say with certainty, "Richard won't lie."

The same code inspires one side of John Loving's split personality in *Days Without End;* and John's wife Elsa lives, as Lucy says, "in some lost world where human beings are still decent and honorable." This "lost world" is Eugene O'Neill's childhood world, the world of his father's values. Curiously, Eugene seems to summon up his father as a presence in this play in which he rejects all his intellectual searching to return to a simple faith in love. How else explain the presence of Father Baird, John Loving's "guardian," who embodies John's childhood values and witnesses his return to them, but, as many critics have pointed out, doesn't really function in the play at all? In earlier drafts this figure was simply a "country doctor," but finally he became a Catholic priest, although his priesthood is entirely superfluous to the action of the play. Perhaps, unconsciously, Eugene created the "guardian" as an avatar of James O'Neill, who was always either playing a Catholic priest on stage (the Abbé Busoni in *Monte Cristo*) or being taken for one off stage. Perhaps Eugene O'Neill couldn't resist having his father symbolically present in this play in which he renounced the ideas of his years of revolt and returned to the simple faith in life and love of his father's world.

From James O'Neill, Eugene took not only ethics but attitudes. He absorbed his father's love for the Irish and his immense pride in being Irish. Eugene knew the story, famous at Liebler and Company, of how James O'Neill, usually innocent of "turf knowledge," insisted on placing money on a horse when he learned that the name of the jockey was O'Neill.

"But O'Neill isn't a horse," the boys had insisted. "O'Neill is the jockey. And the horse he is to ride stands no show to get in the money."

"Ah," said James O'Neill. "What is the name of the horse?"

"Irish Lad."

"Irish Lad?" said James O'Neill, pulling out his money. "Irish Lad and O'Neill is too good a combination to miss. You can't beat them." And to all protests he replied, "They can't beat an O'Neill on Irish Lad." The big joke, of course, came when Irish Lad actually did come in first—at odds of twelve to one.

Eugene was aware of the associations of his middle name "Gladstone." He was still more conscious of the associations of the name O'Neill, which had been borne by the kings of Ireland. When Eugene was five, his father put on a play written especially for him by William Greer Harrison, *The O'Neill, or the Prince of Ulster*, telling how Shane O'Neill, "Shane the Proud," Earl of Tyrone and King of Ireland, had escaped British captivity, pleaded the case of his persecuted country before Queen Elizabeth, and triumphantly brought home rule to Ireland. Remembering Shane O'Neill, the Earl of Tyrone, Eugene would call his son "Shane" and later would substitute "Tyrone" for his family's name "O'Neill" when he wrote the autobiographical plays *Moon for the Misbegotten* and *Long Day's Journey Into Night*.

Eugene caught all his father's enthusiasm for Irish culture. "I have always wanted to go to Ireland. My father, of course, knew the old Irish legends and folklore," he said in 1923. "I started to study Gaelic, but it was too difficult, and I had to give it up." Eugene also knew the legends and folklore. He named his daughter Oona and his dog Finn. When a young writer, Patrick O'Neill, whom he had helped, complained of getting rejection slips, Eugene said proudly, "We O'Neills regard them merely as convincing evidence of the terrible amount of stupidity in the world." Eugene was always eager to declare, "I'm all Irish."

Of course, in the years of his revolt, Eugene often roused his father by attacking the Irish, and when he presented that revolt in *Long Day's Journey Into Night*, he depicted his father as a bit of a bigot who had to see everyone he admired, including Shakespeare, as an Irish Catholic. Actually, James O'Neill's love for the Irish was part of a general love for humanity. Asked if the Irish weren't particularly gifted in drama, he replied, "I am not much of a believer in national characteristics, though I must admit that the history of the stage contains many illustrious Irish names, both as dramatists and actors, but I don't wish to be considered provincial, and a man of genius is equally dear to me, no matter what country he comes from, be it Judea or Ireland. We all come from a common source, no matter where we were born, and when God gives man or woman genius He has little regard for the geographical place of their birth."

From James O'Neill, too, Eugene learned to expect financial reward for success. Despite his contempt for "greed" and "material-ism," Eugene often drove a hard bargain on rights to his plays and manuscripts.

But, above all, Eugene learned from his father to value art: "I began with a background of poetry. My father was reciting poetry all the time. Instead of singing in the bathtub, he'd break out into Shakespeare." James O'Neill talked about art, too. He thought all great art came from "soul." "The man who feels, who aspires, who wanders in thought from this world and mingles with the higher in-telligences has a soul that lends itself to artistic effort; in short, he is a genius," James O'Neill told Harrison Grey Fiske in 1899. "He may be a poet, a painter or an actor, and I am proud to say that in my profession there have been many geniuses; though, alas, they are growing smaller in number year by year, for the sensation monger has supplanted the poet, and the sycophantic counter jumper has usurped the place of the real actor."

All through his childhood, Eugene heard his father talk bitterly of the commercialization of the theater, of the subordination of art to money. "I hope no one ever calls me a star again. I wish to be known as an actor, and that is what very few of the advertised 'stars' of this country are today. . . . The once honored title 'star' has come to mean nothing more than the ability to secure a big bank account and unlimited amount of printers' ink and billboard space. One apparently no longer has to act to become a star. It is a matter of money, not art."

"Almost the first words of my father I remember are, 'The theatre is dying,'" said Eugene. "And those words seem to me as true to-day as when he said them." Again and again, he heard his father say, "The stage has never been in such a diabolical condition." Commercialization and mechanization were destroying the theater, according to James O'Neill. "Art in the theater is losing ground," he told a reporter from the Chicago *Tribune*. "The honorable profes-sion of acting is becoming a trade. Wagner, in his revolutionary opera, dimmed the supremacy of the human voice and made it but another instrument in his orchestra. The producer of the present day has robbed the actor of his foremost place on the stage and made him simply an ingredient. He is no longer the first consideration; he is simply one of the parts, sometimes an inferior part, of the mixture of electric lights and garish scenery which is nowadays called the drama.

"A great artist once said that it was not scenery but silence that the actor needed, and of another artist—David Garrick—a critic wrote: 'By his transcendent genius he could make bare walls look like gilded palaces.' But that was, of course, when poetry and imagination had their place in the world, and the blending of poetry and imagination brings inspiration—and inspiration is no longer tolerated in the art of acting.

"Everything must be carefully planned and executed with mechanical precision. . . . Individuality is gone and hopelessly lost, and art without individuality is impossible—the impersonal is always mechanical."

From his father, too, Eugene learned that "the play's the thing." "I have always believed that there is but one way to hold an audience, and, in fact, to obtain one," said James O'Neill, "and that is to give them an interesting play, and present it in a creditable and capable way." For a "creditable" performance, "the actor must lose his own identity and for the time being assume the personality of the character in which he is cast." James O'Neill always spoke out against the actor who allowed "his own personality to override" his role. "In the days of the old school actor this sort of slipshod performance would have been hissed from the stage," he declared.

Very early, Eugene also learned from his father to respect tragedy above all other forms of drama. "Tragedy deals with the passions in their highest and grandest moods," James O'Neill remarked in 1899. "It carries the actor completely out of himself; transports him as it were to scenes beyond the ken of ordinary minds."

Simply, unconsciously, Eugene absorbed his father's ideas on art and began his apprenticeship in drama. James O'Neill had always believed that a playwright should serve some sort of "dramatic apprenticeship," in the theater, or at least receive "a series of lectures on the art of constructing plays," but he would have been astonished had anyone told him that he himself was supplying a dramatic apprenticeship for the boy who would grow up to be hailed as the long-awaited "great American playwright." He had no desire to bend his sons to a stage career. If anything, he hoped they might become lawyers. So he took Eugene along to rehearsals purely by way of camaraderie. Easily, without pressure, Eugene learned the theater inside out.

Later—although he never thought of his debt to his father—Eugene set great store by his knowledge of the theater. Asked in 1946, "How can one learn to be a playwright?" Eugene answered, "Take some wood and canvas and nails and things. Build yourself a theater, a stage, light it, learn about it. When you've done that you will probably know how to write a play—that is to say if you can."

Eugene's knowledge of the theater started early. His cousin Alma Platz recalled the remark Eugene, at five, made about a neighbor who called at the Platz home in Cincinnati. "Suddenly he turned to his father, and in the tone of a veteran showman delivered this judgment, 'Ugly old woman. Wouldn't do for the stage.'" Eugene's theatrical education was already well under way.

From watching rehearsals, Eugene learned the value of "strong situations," as his father called them: father and son about to fight, not knowing their relationship (*Monte Cristo*); brother against brother (*The Two Orphans, When Greek Meets Greek*); the husband whose child has been begotten by a trusted friend (*The Manxman*). He would use such situations in his own plays—more meaningfully, perhaps, but just as surely for their dramatic value.

Had James O'Neill not been one of America's last great actors, Eugene O'Neill might never have been its first great playwright. He never could have revolutionized the theater had he not known it so thoroughly that expressing himself dramatically came as easy to him, after his New London boyhood, as swimming in the Sound. Perhaps his greatest asset was his ability to communicate large ideas directly through strong situations and exciting theater.

Not only did Eugene learn by watching rehearsals, he also heard talk of the theater from morning till night, for the house at New London was always full of actors in the summer. Everyone talked theater. James O'Neill loved to theorize and often did; for instance, he might launch into a discussion of the resemblance between Greek drama and minstrel shows, saying of burnt cork, "It furnishes a kind of mask which does not entirely obliterate the player, but does disguise him sufficiently to give that little flavor of romance and impersonality which is so essential." Eugene listened.

He listened, too, to his father's frequent statements on the need for a repertory theater. Asked, in 1895, why America had such a "dearth of serious plays," James O'Neill answered, "One of them is that the lack of stock companies has deprived us of the very best training schools for actors." In 1925, Eugene echoed his father's ideas, saying, "The immediate future of the theatre is in the actor. Until he gets his real opportunity, we others—I speak as a playwright— . . . but wait for ours." Eugene, like his father, believed the answer for the actor was a repertory theater. "For actors are conceived by and born of the parts they have been permitted to play." He had absorbed these ideas along with the cold boiled lobster at the dinner table in New London.

In addition, from his father's box at the Lyceum, Eugene saw all the shows that came to New London, and many came, for New London was a "try-out" town for Broadway plays. As soon as Eugene was old enough, James O'Neill often took him and his friends to the theater in the evening. One of his boyhood friends, Ed Keefe, recalled those evenings with delight. "He was always a lovely companion with us," he said of James O'Neill, and then added, "A marvelous man! A lovable character!" Eugene enjoyed those evenings too. Theater going became as natural a part of life as eating.

Later, Eugene would think that all he learned of the theater from his father was to despise it. "My early experience with the theatre through my father really made me revolt against it. As a boy I saw so much of the old, ranting, artificial, romantic stage stuff that I always had a sort of contempt for the theatre." But Eugene could never take a fair view of what his father had meant to him. He loved him too much and hated him too much ever to see him straight.

CHAPTER SEVEN

Seeds of Revolt

T HE exile to Mount Saint Vincent seemed endless to Eugene, for he was also deprived for two years of summers at New London, and he sensed uneasily that something was wrong with his mother. When the spring of 1896 came, Ellen couldn't face the thought of New London with its associations of loss and suffering. So the family spent the summer at Twilight Park in the Catskills, and although Eugene was with his parents again, he missed the green lawns and blue waters of New London.

They didn't go back the next summer either. "I like my place at New London," James O'Neill explained in May, 1897, "but the sea air does not agree with Mrs. O'Neill." But it wasn't the sea air, for they took a cottage, finally, near the beach on Staten Island. Eugene couldn't know of the shock his mother had received the winter before—just as he could not know of her deeper trouble—but he could sense the tension in her. Jamie knew, for the story got into all the newspapers, including the New London *Day*. And that, perhaps, was why Ellen O'Neill couldn't bear to spend the summer in New London.

This time the source of the scandal was Nettie Walsh's son, Alfred Hamilton O'Neill. He had grown up in poverty and the thought of his wealthy father must have filled him with bitterness. He finally acted. On March 9, 1897, the news broke that a young man claiming to be James O'Neill's son was suing the actor for $20,000. Alfred O'Neill declared that his mother, being "a mere child" and "inexperienced in the ways of the world" had been frightened out of her legal rights as the wife of James O'Neill.

Shortly after he filed suit, Alfred Hamilton O'Neill obviously came into money, for he was no longer a hand in the E. M. Davis Soap Company, but a "soap manufacturer." He must have settled with Maloney and Scofield, James O'Neill's attorneys. In any event, he did not file a reply to James O'Neill's reply, his complaint was dismissed "for want of equity," and he never troubled his father again. With his patrimony, he struggled on. First he called himself a "promoter," then, in 1904 he listed himself as "A. Hamilton O'Neill, manufacturer's agent." By 1910, when Jamie and Eugene, the acknowledged sons, seemed hopeless failures, he would seem, ironically, to be the only son of James O'Neill who had made something of himself.

All that the scandal meant to Eugene was the loss of the New London summer. But the year after, when Papa came up to Mount Saint Vincent to get him, Eugene found out that he was going back to the home he loved, to the blue waters of the Thames River, to happy hours rocking on the porch with a book, where he could hear his mother's piano playing and look up to see his father at work on the lawn.

Even after three years in the stone cottage at Mount Saint Vincent, Eugene still felt the same shattering loneliness when the time came for him to return to school. He didn't like that world of little boys. He had grown up in an adult world and rarely enjoyed playing with other children. When the rest of the boys joined eagerly in the haying at the invitation of the farm men, Eugene preferred to stay at the cottage with "his nose in a book," to the great astonishment of Sister Mary Florentine. His schoolmate Ewing Philbin said that "he kept pretty much to himself."

The nuns spoke of Eugene later as a very "good" boy, "a gentlemanly little fellow, neat about his appearance, and very obedient and cooperative." Obedience was required. Ewing Philbin thought "the Sisters were more strict than they should have been." Eugene, apparently, thought so too. Later he spoke of Sister Martha, "who used to knuckle us on the bean," and, writing to George Jean Nathan about the days when they were "little convent boys," he asked, "Remember how Sister Mary used to paddle your behind to the chime of the Angelus and never miss a beat?"

Perhaps Eugene felt Mount Saint Vincent too deeply as the place of exile from his parents' love to care much for the beauty of its long, tree-shaded drives, which were heaped with chestnuts and leaves when he returned each fall. But he did like to walk over the rustic bridge to a grotto on an island in the middle of a little lake, where a statue of Our Lady of Lourdes stood in the light of a stained-glass window. Long afterward, when Eugene depicted his mother in *Long Day's Journey Into Night* as a virgin soul misled into marriage, and invented for her a girlhood "true vision" of the call to be a nun, he set it in the shrine of Our Lady of Lourdes at Mount Saint Vincent, where he himself had knelt as a boy.

Eugene was happiest at Mount Saint Vincent in the spring of 1899, for then his parents were near him. James O'Neill had come to New York for a big production by Liebler and Company of *The Three Musketeers* at the Broadway Theatre. There had been a kind of race to get the play out before E. H. Sothern put on another version called *The King's Musketeers*. Tyler had sent the whole company out to Louisville, Kentucky, so that James O'Neill could rehearse *The Musketeers* with the stars who would support him—Blanche Bates, Margaret Anglin, Wilton Lackaye, and S. Miller Kent—while carrying out his own company's engagements in *When Greek Meets Greek*, *Monte Cristo*, and *Virginius*. The strain of doing both was too much for James O'Neill. By the time he dismissed his own company to open in *The Musketeers* in Montreal on March 7, he had a cold that got steadily worse during the week he played there. When the company reached New York, he was really sick, but insisted on going on. He did brilliantly at the beginning of the play, although his wonderful voice was hoarse. But then his voice began to fail. He broke down, jumbled his lines, and all the fire went out of his performance. He struggled through one more night and then collapsed. He could not return to the theater for several days.

Once he was well, of course, his D'Artagnan was praised by everyone. "Mark the effectiveness of O'Neill's sword play," said the *Dramatic Mirror*, "the fire of his love-making, his buoyant and agile grace of movement, his mobile facial expression, the ease with which he doffs his plumed hat, and the swagger with which he wears his ever-ready rapier. This is D'Artagnan himself, and I advise every young actor who gets the chance to study the impersonation in every detail."

Eugene spent happy hours at the theater with his mother. She took him about backstage, introducing him to the actors and actresses in their dressing rooms. "His mother brought him to see me," Margaret Anglin would recall, "a little dark-eyed boy in a sailor suit. He was diffident until I said, 'Don't be afraid, I'm not going to kiss you. I have little brothers of my own and know they don't like it.' Then we became friendly."

Mama even invited Eugene's classmates to the theater. Stephen Philbin remembered that all spring, after the theater party, "Eugene, I and others vigorously fenced with foils made from the mulberry and cherry trees." He and the others thought Eugene belonged to a "finer world than our less distinguished families." For once Eugene was not left alone and desolate during the Easter holidays. He was with a loving mother and a father the other boys admired and imitated.

That summer in New London Eugene and his friend Eddie Keefe watched his father rehearsing Maude Odell, Nora O'Brien, Edmund Breese, Gertrude Bennett, Edgar Forrest, and Mark Ellsworth for the fall tour in *The Musketeers*. On his father's bookshelves, Eugene found the rest of Dumas's novels, read them all, and then started in on the novels of Victor Hugo.

Eugene went back to New London the next summer, too. He had celebrated his first Holy Communion on May 24, 1900, and in June left Mount Saint Vincent for good, as the school didn't take boys over twelve. Eugene, at twelve, was shy and awkward; his legs were beginning to be too long and somehow in the way. When he wasn't reading or swimming, he liked to hang around the stable and watch his father's coachman rub down the new horses. They were a gorgeous pair, but a family joke. James O'Neill had picked them up in an out-of-the-way stable in New York at the bargain price of a little over a thousand dollars (they were easily worth double the price) and had had them shipped to New London. When he burst into the offices of Liebler and Company in the Knickerbocker Building "to acquaint the boys of his luck," Connor and Tyler exchanged glances, and instead of congratulating him, told him that sharpers all over New York were selling smart teams at absurdly low figures, spot cash, and then never delivering them. James O'Neill became so worried that he didn't wait for the elevator, but "tore down four flights of stairs," and ran to the stable, where the hostler told him the proprietor had just driven away with the team. It looked bad. When James O'Neill got back to Liebler and Company, George Tyler offered to bet his next month's income against a fresh roasted peanut that O'Neill would never see the horses or his money again.

James O'Neill telegraphed, worried all night, and telegraphed again in the morning. Still no horses. At a neighboring livery stable, he learned that the one where he had bought the horses had been occupied only a few days by strangers. He had just returned to Tyler's offices, entirely discouraged, when he found a telegram from New London, and read it in a husky voice: "Team just received in good order." "Say, Tyler—I wish I'd risked that peanut," he remarked.

Eugene, watching the coachman, learned all about horses and about racing too, for the coachman owned a few race horses of his own. From him and from Jamie, Eugene learned to read the racing-form sheets and studied them so avidly that he knew them by heart. One glorious day the coachman took him out to the Sheepshead Bay track to see the races and introduced him to a famous trainer, Al Weston. "They started to talk horses, of course," Eugene said later, "and the minute they'd mention a name I'd break in and say, 'Oh, yes: Laddie Z, by Buzzfuzz out of Guinevere; ran second

at Morris Park, June 16th; fourth at Sheepshead, July 10th.' I knew
them all; I couldn't help it. After an hour of this, Weston gave me
a hard look and said, 'Kid, either you'll be a jockey or you'll get
yourself killed.' "

He had a grand time that whole summer. For once he was free of
the fear of being deserted in the fall. This year, when he entered De
La Salle Institute in New York, he would just be a day student, for
the whole family was to live in New York because Liebler and Company was putting on *Monte Cristo* in New York and Boston. It was
to be a spectacular production, with ornamental candelabra nine
feet high in the ballroom scene, trees covered with crystal snow
and ice glittering in the rays from concealed electric lights, a full-
rigged ship to appear on stage in the opening scene, and so on. No
wonder Papa was disgusted at the mixture of "electric lights and
garish scenery" which was taking the place of the old drama. But
it was what the public wanted. Meanwhile, Annie Ward Tiffany,
Frederick de Belleville, S. Miller Kent, and Augustus Cook all came
to New London for rehearsals.

Mama found the apartment at 8 West Sixty-eighth Street—Papa
was too busy with rehearsals to join the search—but it was Papa who
went to take possession of the place. He asked the car conductor
to let him off at Sixty-eighth Street. At number 8, he politely announced to the lady he found there, "I have come to take possession
of the apartment."

"I don't understand you, sir," the lady replied, astounded. "This is
my apartment and I have no intention of giving it up."

"This is number 8, first floor, is it not?" Papa asked. "I have a
lease for this apartment—here it is."

The lady glanced at it and smiled. "This paper reads number 8
West Sixty-eighth Street," she said, "and you are four blocks away
—this is Sixty-fourth Street."

Papa had a few sharp comments to make on car conductors, but
the family laughed heartily at his mistake.

The O'Neills moved into the apartment on Sixty-eighth Street,
and every morning Eugene set out for De La Salle Institute on
Fifty-ninth Street at Central Park South. In the afternoon he came
home to find Mama waiting for him, and, after November, Papa

too, on the days when there was no matinee. And he wasn't deserted at Christmas. His presents were put in his hands by Mama and Papa—not sent to him in his loneliness, a kind of payment for being abandoned.

But he had not lost the old bitterness, and his father unwittingly increased it. In the turmoil of adolescence, Eugene's shyness became more intense. He became uncomfortably aware of his body, shrank into himself so that his sudden height would seem less exposed, and, sensitive to rebuff, mumbled his words. Then would come a powerful slap on the back and his father's rich voice saying, "Get that hump off your back; straighten up there; open your mouth and let the words come out." He would find it even harder to speak up the next time. And there were other humiliations as he tried to find himself in a world where love and admiration were invariably captured by his father.

Rebellion was rising in him, too. He could not read the works of Victor Hugo without learning that some people regarded the Catholic Church, not as a simple projection of Christ's teachings as Papa and Mama did, but rather as a tool of oppression that kept the masses servile by means of a mixture of superstitious fear and idolatry. He couldn't forget either that it was to a Catholic school, to the care of nuns and priests, that his parents had exiled him. And the anguish he had suffered at Mount Saint Vincent made him question the Church's teachings about Divine Providence and a kind God. At De La Salle, he found himself observing the religious ceremonies from the critical viewpoint he had absorbed from the revolutionary romantic writers.

He had been a very "good," a very "obedient" little boy. Now, all the individuality that had been repressed to make him very "good," very "obedient" suddenly came out. He was ready to revolt against everything he had bowed down to as a child. All he needed was opportunity and someone to show him the way. Under any circumstances he would have rebelled, but his rebellion might never have carried him so far beyond everything he had loved and believed if he had not found a leader in his brother, Jamie—Jamie, who was gay, charming, reckless, and already hopelessly blighted.

PART THREE

JAMIE: THE MASK OF MEPHISTOPHELES

CHAPTER EIGHT

James O'Neill, Jr.

J AMES O'NEILL, JR., started out in life with everything—beauty, brilliance, wealth, a father ready to back him in any profession he might choose, a mother who adored him—and with all these gifts, his life frittered itself out in mediocrity, drunken stupor, bitterness, whores, and death. Why? Perhaps he was poisoned by too many gifts, by too much love. No one who saw him as a boy or later as a man with his mother ever took long to realize that Jamie had been spoiled.

Very quickly Jamie learned that his mother could deny him nothing, that to her whatever he did was charming, that in her love there were no demands, only adoring acceptance. Nowhere again in the world would he find such a love, and so he would love no woman as he did his mother. He would never marry, and he would let go all hold of life when he lost his mother. For his first ten years, he had to share his mother only for the little over a year that his brother Edmund lived. Otherwise he was the center of her universe —except, that is, for his father, who always came first with her.

From his father, too, he had received great affection. In the morning, as soon as Papa awoke, he would call for Jamie, and the two of them would romp about the bed together, Jamie shrieking with pleasure. But from the beginning, Jamie felt the difference between his father's love and his mother's. All his life James O'Neill had driven himself with the "work, *work,* WORK" formula. Now he demanded as much of Jamie as he had of himself. Always in his father's love, Jamie felt the pressure.

From his father he learned the bitterness of not having reached an expected mark, and fearing that humiliation unconsciously, he protected himself by relinquishing the desire to succeed. If he didn't strive for a goal, he couldn't fail. Between the demanding universe of his father and the accepting universe of his mother, Jamie very quickly made a choice. The guiding principle of his life would be a calculated irresponsibility; he would be deliberately irresponsible, refusing to live on any other terms than as his mother's gay, charming boy who could be denied nothing.

And he was a charming boy—clever, with an irresistible sense of humor that would become more and more bitter as the trap he made of his own life began to close in on him and he found himself, with the years, reduced to a dwarf following in the gigantic footsteps of his father's career, just as he had always followed him in love for his mother. But the trap had not begun to close when his little brother Eugene looked up to him as the dazzling sophisticate who could take on and best Papa in an argument. Only the beginnings of Jamie's end could be seen when, for all his brilliance, he managed to get himself expelled from Notre Dame University for serious infraction of the rules—drinking.

Very regretfully the priests let him go without his degree. He was popular and promising—and besides, they all admired his father— but they had to let him go. They had all been guests of James O'Neill whenever he played South Bend. He always had several boxes full of guests from Notre Dame and Saint Mary's, with Mrs. O'Neill and Jamie doing the honors. Even after Jamie was expelled, when he had first started acting in his father's company, he and his father were invited to the St. Patrick's Day performance of *Twelfth Night* by the university players at Notre Dame on March 17, 1902. "Young O'Neill, his father and the company were guests of honor," the *Mirror* noted.

The same calculated irresponsibility that kept Jamie from a university degree kept him from choosing a career for himself in which he might have walked independent of his father. Acting was easiest; he had picked up a knack for it watching his father's company rehearse; he had acted with the university players at Notre Dame. He could drift into it easily, without struggling, without trying to achieve anything. He could just go on being Mama's gay, witty, charming boy, getting his way.

Later, James O'Neill had his press agent write up Jamie's debut this way: "James O'Neill, Jr. was suspiciously silent upon the theme of his future field of usefulness. His father's suggestions about the law rebounded from a wall of discouraging silence. At dinner one night the young man timidly approached the subject.

" 'Father, I—I've decided what profession I should—like to adopt. You and mamma won't like it very well—at first—but—'

" 'You want to go upon the stage?'

"The boy nodded. The father sighed. 'Well, I'll give you a chance to begin,' said the actor. 'It will be a very small chance,' he resolved.

"James O'Neill, Jr. was assigned to the smallest roles in the James O'Neill company. 'I gave him $20 a week, and almost nothing to do,' said the actor. 'But by a slip in my plans he was made understudy for the man who plays my son in Monte Cristo. The young man did not make good, and there was nothing to be done but let the understudy play it. My son played the son in Monte Cristo. He did so well that we had to let him go on playing it. His salary went from $20 to $50. That spoiled my plans and settled his future.' "

Characteristically, James O'Neill wished to picture his son as successful in spite of rather than because of him. And the story was essentially true, only exaggerating Jamie's success. Of course, that first year (1901–1902) when Jamie played Albert de Morcerf to his father's Monte Cristo, he didn't do badly, and the press was usually kind, when he was noticed at all—speaking of his "excellent work" or the "splendid impression" he made, although critics were already noting, "Mr. O'Neill is apparently years younger than the handsome young man who is his son, both in real life and in the play."

Certainly, James O'Neill had high hopes for Jamie. Just as he had always made a comrade of his boy, now he shared a dressing room with him, and took him along to parties after the theater. It was always "James O'Neill and his son" now, entertained by the Knights of Columbus in St. Paul, Minnesota, at "a wrestling match and boxing bout," for instance, or by the Elks. And Jamie really had talent; his acting was capable for a beginner. Only later would James O'Neill realize that Jamie's beginning was his high point. What he could do effortlessly, out of a spontaneous interest in the novelty of acting, was his best. Later, he would become increasingly slipshod.

But at the beginning, with his gaiety and charm, it seemed as if Jamie might go anywhere. As a matter of fact, Will Connor remarked to James O'Neill and Jamie in August, 1902, as they sat smoking in the offices of Liebler and Company, that Jamie would soon be as big a man as his father.

"Oh, I don't know," Jamie replied, taking a deep breath and inflating his chest, "on chest measurement, I think I've got the pater pushed way upstage."

James O'Neill agreed "figuratively," for Jamie, he said, was the "chestiest" youngster he ever had met; but if it was a case of material inches—well! James O'Neill stood erect, inhaled, and winked at Will Connor. Just then, Herman Friedmann, the clerk, came in with a wire tape measure.

"Ah," exclaimed Jamie, "just the thing! If Mr. Friedmann will let us take his tape a moment we shall see."

"We shall see!" cried James O'Neill, stripping off his coat and waistcoat. Jamie followed suit. Friedmann carefully measured Jamie's chest, and announced, "Forty inches."

James O'Neill threw back his shoulders and smiled. "For the entire office force, Jamie," he said, "at the buffet across the street."

"Father," said Jamie, "you're on."

Friedmann stretched the tape around James O'Neill's chest. Then he let out a link. Then he let out another, and announced, "Forty-four and one-quarter inches!"

"I especially stipulated the chest," said Jamie, "not the waist measurement."

"But this is the chest," protested Mr. Friedmann.

The Thirty-eighth Street elevator had to make two trips to transport all of Jamie's guests to the Normandie buffet. All told, the check came to $6.90.

"Present this bill with my compliments," said Jamie, "to the elderly, gray-haired gentleman at the other end of the line. He has a wallet filled with bank notes sewed to the inside of his shirt that increases his chest measurement exactly five inches." Then he turned to his father and added, "Pater, I hate to give you away. But $6.90 for a single highball—this is too much for a poor young actor!"

This was Jamie: gay, witty, always the victor in verbal battle, always, in the end, getting his way, always, under the veil of humor, his father's rival, with a keen eye for his father's weakness, but always in reality bested by his father, no matter how delusively he turned his defeat into seeming victory. Later, when the defeats became more frequent and obvious, Jamie's gay banter would take on an increasingly cruel edge, and finally, he would go for long stretches without speaking at all in his father's presence.

It would take just ten years for Jamie to reach that point. Meanwhile, he rode high, dazzling the New London youngsters with Broadway sophistication, keeping a crowd in stitches at a bar, getting his way irresistibly with the women. His life ran over those ten years quickly, leaving a trail of vignettes: James O'Neill, Jr., Lionel and John Barrymore gaily organizing the "Sons of Actors" club; James O'Neill, Jr., emerging from the Actor's Club with an eye blacked in a brawl; James O'Neill, Jr., rumored "almost engaged" to Elfie Fay, vaudeville darling, "Belle of Avenue A"; James O'Neill, Jr., flush with poker winnings, drunkenly sleeping in a hotel lobby while his pocket is being picked; and so on.

Meanwhile, the drinking became more and more important to him. James O'Neill had always been a heavy drinker, but by choice, with the ability to stop. He never *had* to drink, and he never allowed drink to get in the way of his responsibilities, or even of his self-possession. "I've seen him pretty well loaded," his friend's son, Tom Dorsey, Jr., would remark, "but never that he couldn't handle himself." But liquor would be much more dangerous for his sons. Once started, they would *have* to drink; they would *need* another glass. Jamie was never merely a "social" drinker, but always a desperate drinker. He drank himself out of Notre Dame and, finally, out of his theatrical career—missing performances, going on stage "all corned up," as one of his contemporaries put it.

He used women as he used drink, for release of tension, and always he *used* them. His love belonged to one woman, his mother; with the others he took perpetual revenge on her for being his father's wife. He went the round of easy chorus girls and prostitutes, preferring what his brother Eugene would call "bedlock" to wedlock. He knew all the ways of access to compliant women, and he would leave the New London boys gaping with tales of hotels in New York where widows were on the lookout for young men. Jamie knew all the ways and delighted in a "hard-boiled" display of what he knew.

He was, perhaps, a doubtful guide for a struggling young adolescent seeking to find himself and the meaning of life. But he was a singularly alluring guide and very ready to take charge of his little brother Eugene. To Eugene he seemed, then, and for a long time afterward, a bit of a hero: so sure of himself, so ready for gay battle with his father. In Jamie, Eugene found a general to marshal his scattered rebellion, and so, blindly, trustingly, he enlisted himself under Jamie in a war against his parents, against the whole universe of his childhood.

CHAPTER NINE

The Devil of Hate

To Eugene, Jamie's face always had a "Mephistophelian cast," partly because of his aquiline nose and cynical expression, but mostly because he had been the devil who came to Eugene in his innocence and taught him disobedience and the knowledge of sin. Even when he was still a very "good" little boy, Eugene was always ready to follow Jamie in daring sorties against the authority of his father.

"I remember once, when we were all together in New London," Eugene told Hamilton Basso in 1948, "he was telling my brother James and me about how hard he had to work as an actor. 'You call that work?' my brother said. My brother bet him ten dollars that he could learn the whole of Goldsmith's 'The Deserted Village' in one week and I bet him the same amount that I could learn the part of Macbeth. My brother and I studied together. We were very close, my brother and I. We were a very close family—perhaps *too* close. Anyway, after our week was over, James and I stood before my father. My brother ran through 'The Deserted Village,' collected his money, and then my father started to cue me my lines as Macbeth. I gave them back to him without a hitch. My father closed the book and looked at me. 'You certainly have a good memory,' he said, 'and I see you've worked hard, but never go on the stage.' " Eugene laughed when he recalled this.

The story was typical, he and Jamie in conspiracy against the Old Man, but Papa somehow getting in the last needle. As Jamie and Eugene grew older they took more pleasure in their alliance, egged each other on to more flippant hostility in talk of the Old Man, until finally the humor went out of it, and they could call him "a lousy tightwad bastard," or worse. What they had managed to do was suppress all the affection, admiration, and comradeship they had felt for their father as children under an exhilarating contempt, a clean enmity.

Years later, critics would always think Eugene O'Neill had been misled by a superficial knowledge of Freud, when he depicted sons —in *Strange Interlude, Desire Under the Elms,* and *Mourning Becomes Electra*—who feel love for the mother and open hatred for the father. They would think Eugene O'Neill hadn't understood Freud's Oedipus complex—in which the son feels both love and hate for the father, but represses the hatred. They would believe Eugene O'Neill simple-minded for portraying sons in open, uncomplicated hatred of the father, and would pity him for designing plays according to intellectual theories he couldn't grasp, rather than according to life.

But in no case would Eugene O'Neill be following personal experience more closely than in depicting father-son relationships. What he and Jamie felt, and consciously acknowledged between them, was open hostility for their father. They had repressed not the hate, but the love. Only indirectly, in the intensity of the hatred, would they show the love.

In *Mourning Becomes Electra,* Eugene shows how—underneath a surface hatred for the parent of the same sex—a child identifies with him, admires him, so much so that he finds himself taking over his parent's personality after his death. In his autobiographical play *Long Day's Journey Into Night,* too, Eugene carefully delineates the suppressed bond of love beneath his own and Jamie's surface hostility for their father.

But during Eugene's adolescence, when he and Jamie became allies in rebellion, only the conscious hatred existed. It was Jamie who taught Eugene how to reject his father's values by turning to a forbidden world of drink and whores. It was Jamie who put his brother wise to life by brutally placing him, a very young boy, in the hands of hardened prostitutes who taught him quickly—without any glossing of romance or beauty or affection—the crude mechanics of sex.

What was the impact of these experiences on a sensitive boy whose ideas of love had been shaped by his father's code of honor, his own adoration of his mother, and the exalted sentiments of romantic novels? Shattering, of course. Eugene O'Neill would never altogether succeed in separating his ideas of sex from his initial experience of it as a deliberate revolt against love, as a kind of nasty rape.

Later, when he got to Harvard, Eugene O'Neill would tell his friends all the lurid details of his varied experiences with "sexually aggressive nymphomaniacs" and prostitutes. "But what was significant about those exciting experiences of Gene's was his own passive role in them," Corwin Willson, his classmate, later observed. "It is my belief that Gene's abundance of early experience with women in ways that psychically were without beauty and were actually degrading colored his entire outlook. His attitude toward women much resembled the indignant cry of the man who complained, 'She gave me the clap.' He never discussed homosexuality with me but he sure was hipped on what over-amorous women can do to a rather passive man. Always Gene's stories ended by the woman hungrily pouncing on him. I must admit I was all ears. I had never known women like that. In my experience, a man worked hard for what he got, but the end-result was satisfying and the association of the experience with beauty constant and lasting."

For Eugene, sex (particularly as represented by a prostitute) became a symbol of the revolt from love—the pure love he had felt for his mother—and of a spiritual violation, a rape. Again and again in his plays these dual associations are apparent. In *Ah, Wilderness!* Richard, in revolt from the pure love he believes has betrayed him, turns to the prostitute, who makes the grossest advances to him, "squirming around on his lap," clearly leeching for his five dollars, not his person, and leaving him with the feeling that "she was everything dirty."

Similarly, in *Welded* and *Days Without End*, both plays that deal directly with the revolt from love, Eugene O'Neill presents that revolt as an ugly sexual experience. Michael Cape in *Welded*, when he flies from love, flies directly to a prostitute, telling her, "You have the power—and the right—to murder love! You can satisfy hate." In *Days Without End* John Loving submits to the repellent sexual advances of his friend's wife in order "to kill" love, and emerges sick with loathing.

The association of sex with the violation of love makes for a curious representation of sexual love in O'Neill's plays. He associates love with the mother—with the *pure* love for the mother—so his women often have to undergo a kind of spiritual identification with the mother before his heroes can accept their love. In *Desire Under the Elms,* for instance, before Eben can give himself in love to Abbie, she has to promise, "I'll kiss ye pure, Eben—same 's if I was a Maw t' ye—an' ye kin kiss me back 's if yew was my son—my boy—sayin' good-night t' me!" Only when Eben is sure that his mother's spirit approves, that, as Abbie tells him, "She's tellin' ye t' love me," can he give himself in love. Only when the woman has the seal of the mother upon her, can the sexual union be one of love.

The same idea appears in *Moon for the Misbegotten,* Eugene O'Neill's requiem for his brother, Jamie, where, as was certainly true of Jamie, only the mother means love, so that sexual union becomes a violation of love. James Tyrone has fornicated with "a blonde pig" every night on the train bearing his mother's body back to New York, as a "revenge" for being "left alone." He can give love to Josie only when she takes on the role of his mother and allows him to cry his "heart's repentance against her breast," only when the mother's "blessing lies" on her. But there is no reconciliation of sex with love. The moment Josie makes sexual advances to him, James Tyrone treats her with hatred as a prostitute.

This dichotomy between love and sex occurs in many of O'Neill's plays. In *The Great God Brown* it appears in one person: Cybel, the earth mother. Approached sexually, she claps on her mask, "the rouged and eye-blackened countenance of the hardened prostitute," but once Dion agrees that they will never be "anything less" than friends, that is, that their love will be nonsexual, she removes her mask and becomes entirely the peace and beauty of the mother, and "Mother!" is what Dion, without his mask, can call her.

The same dichotomy appears in *Dynamo,* where the "Great Mother of Eternal Life," a sublimation of Reuben's love for his mother, "wants," Reuben thinks, "some one man to love her purely." His sexual union with Ada bars him, he thinks, from the love of the Mother God, so first he rejects Ada, then attempts to unify her with the Mother by having her pray to Dynamo "with your arms like her arms, stretching out for me!" In the end, having given way to his passion for Ada, he thinks, "Mother! . . . I've betrayed you . . . " so he kills Ada (sexual passion) in order to gain the pure love of the mother.

Many of the plays reflect the sense of violation and guilt that his early sexual experiences brought to Eugene O'Neill. Yet for all his remorse, he continued to follow Jamie. The part of Eugene that was still boy—the romantically idealistic, code-bound Eugene—suffered horribly from the feeling that he had degraded himself and his mother. But a new Eugene, molded in the Mephistophelean image of his brother James, took pride in the most sordid exploits, seeing in them a grand freedom and revenge—freedom from the anxiety that had corroded his love for his parents after his exile to Mount Saint Vincent—revenge for all the suffering his love had caused him.

Eugene found other advantages in this new personality. It was a great protection; it armored him in cynicism. It covered his hypersensitivity with a dashing pose, broke down humiliations in advance with a scornful sneer. Eugene felt that, having tasted sin, he could look a long way down on the naïve herd.

But within him, the little boy Eugene remained intact, often sick with disgust at the activities of the Mephistophelean Eugene. What had happened was really a split in his personality. For the rest of his life, Eugene would feel himself torn by this inner split. Talking of himself, he told Nina Moise when he was thirty years old, was like having "Jekyll" describe "Hyde" or Hyde Jekyll. "One part of me fiddles betimes while Rome burneth and while the other part perishes in the flames—a martyr giving birth to the soul of an idea."

If the plays are any clue, one part of his personality seems to have been organized around a core of love, the other around a core of hate. One part was the little boy Eugene: sweet, sensitive, trusting in and needing desperately the love of his Mama, his Papa, easily hurt, full of high ideals of honor and decency, accepting wholly the values—not only moral, but also economic and political —of the world of his parents. The other part was the Mephistophelean Eugene: the rebel against love that left him vulnerable to pain, against faith that made him subject to betrayal, against all the values of his childhood.

To the Mephistophelean half of Eugene belonged the intellect, the thinking man who would run through all the *avant-garde* theories—philosophical, political, and ethical—and take to himself all the revolutionary playwrights and novelists. To the other part, the little boy, belonged the emotions, the unquestioning acceptance of beauty, the faith in and love for his fellow men. Each part was incomplete. The far-ranging, questioning intellect lacked love and faith, so that O'Neill's social criticism was limited to the destructive, the negative. The loving part clung to a child's simple scheme of values.

The split is often presented in his plays. In *Welded* and *Days Without End,* he pits the little boy against the Mephistopheles, and gives the victory to the little boy, so that faith in love triumphs. The split is graphically represented in *Days Without End.* Two actors represent the one character John Loving, each depicting one side of his split personality. One part of him, John, is the boy, the "romantic idealist" with a simple faith in love. The other part, Loving, is the rebel, the "mocking rational something in him that laughs with scorn," the "devil of hate." A similar split occurs in Michael Cape of *Welded* and also in his wife. Again, thinking, the "rational," is on the side of the devil of hate. "Thinking explains. It eliminates the unexplainable—by which we live," Michael tells his wife, and she adds, "By which we love."

The same split appears in other plays, in *The Great God Brown*, for instance. With the first knowledge of evil, Dion Anthony "became silent for life and designed a mask of the Bad Boy Pan in which to live and rebel," a mask that grows perpetually "more defiant and mocking, its sneer more forced and bitter, its Pan quality becoming more Mephistophelean." Without his mask, he is the little boy, laying his head—lovingly and trustingly—in the lap of Cybel, the mother. In *All God's Chillun Got Wings*, a similar split occurs in Ella Downey. She can be either a murderous devil, filled with hate, or a loving child. In order to relax into love, she must relinquish her adult personality and become pure child.

Not only was Eugene aware of the split, but those he lived with and loved in later years always had to be ready for his sudden transformation into a savagely cruel "devil of hate." His second wife, Agnes Boulton, described this part of him as "a strange being who was not the real Gene at all." His third wife, Carlotta Monterey, has said that he was a "peculiar mixture"; gentle, with a childlike smile, but able to turn around in an instant and become "vicious, like a rattlesnake."

In the years of his rebellion, few people got close enough to him to see the split. From the outside, he simply looked like an extraordinarily serious adolescent, with a face so grave it appeared to be scowling. His father's friend Tom Dorsey was amused by the boy Eugene. "Always the gloomy one," he said later, "always the tragedian, always thinkin'."

What he was thinking of came out among his friends—Hutch Collins, Eddie Keefe, and Art McGinley—when he would suddenly burst into poetry, the "Ballad of Reading Gaol," for instance, intoning with all the intensity of personal experience, "Yet each man kills the thing he loves," or Byron's *Childe Harold*, "I have not loved the world, nor the world me." From his brother Jamie, Eugene picked up a taste for modern poetry, particularly for the works of Wilde, Dowson, Kipling, Swinburne, Rossetti, and Edward Fitzgerald. He had great parts of the *Rubáiyát* by heart, and often quoted from it. "Drink! for you know not whence you come nor why."

This was the "philosophical" justification for drinking and whoring that Jamie presented to Eugene, the rationale of the *fin de siècle* poets flying from the crudities of middle-class society into the world of the senses, of wine, women, song. From Jamie and the *fin de siècle* poets, Eugene learned to look at prostitutes, as he would say in *Long Day's Journey Into Night,* as "fascinating vampires instead of poor, stupid, diseased slobs they really are." He learned to see beauty and nobility in deliberate self-destruction: in drinking past the point where he knew what he was doing, in submitting to the sexual advances of women repellent to him in every way. He learned to echo his brother's cynical talk, and to break out, on his own, in revolt against the Old Man. This was his heritage from his brother, Jamie.

CHAPTER TEN

Betts Academy

O F course, James O'Neill saw the change of his good little boy into a rebellious adolescent, difficult at home and a real problem at school. Eugene wasn't doing well at De La Salle Institute. James O'Neill began to wonder whether the priests weren't too strict for his boys, whether Eugene wouldn't be better off at another school. He didn't want Eugene to go the way of Jamie. So he inquired into preparatory schools and came up with Betts Academy in Stamford, Connecticut.

It looked like just the place for Eugene. A special aim of Betts Academy, according to the catalogue, was "To make the *individual*, not the class, the basis of work." Betts, as a matter of fact, made a specialty of problem children. A number of millionaires' sons—all with problems in schoolwork—attended Betts Academy, although the fees there ($600 a year for board and tuition) were moderate in comparison to the other Connecticut schools that prepared boys for Yale University. Wealthy Latin Americans sent their boys to Betts Academy, too, assured that individual treatment would overcome the language problem.

The school was nonsectarian, but supervised church attendance on Sundays was compulsory. James O'Neill looked over the extensive school grounds high on Strawberry Hill, talked with William Betts, the headmaster, and decided to enter Eugene there in the fall.

All that summer the house on Pequot Avenue was swarming with visitors. Harriet Ford came down to discuss her new version of *The Danicheffs*, called *The Honor of the Humble*, with James O'Neill, for he would star in it that fall. With her were Will Connor and George Tyler, full of talk about Eleonora Duse, whom they had just signed on for a hundred performances in America. A little later the cast for *Honor of the Humble* came down to start rehearsals—among them the gorgeous May Buckley, who, Jamie told Eugene, had figured in a lurid scandal the year before when a handsome deaf mute, mad with jealousy (and drink and dope, the newspaper boys had suggested) had tried to kill her in Papst's Hotel. Jamie kept May dazzled with his swift patter, and Eugene looked on, awed by his brother's skill. Finally, Edmund Breese came down to arrange for taking over James O'Neill's role in *Monte Cristo,* and the whole family went over to Willimantic, Connecticut, to watch him open on September 3.

Jamie was going to be on his own that year, out from under the Old Man's wing. Tyler had got him a part in *Audrey* supporting Eleanor Robson, Selene Johnson, and Forrest Robinson. So Jamie would be in New York that fall, and he promised Eugene he'd show him the town on weekends. Cheered by Jamie's promise, Eugene went off to Betts Academy late in September, 1902.

Mr. Betts, Billy, as the boys called him behind his back, was a dynamic little man in knickerbockers, who would electrify a class by shouting "That isn't so!" and leaping over a chair when he received a wrong answer, or by spitting on his hand and violently rubbing out an error on the blackboard. When he wanted a boy's attention, he would call out, "See here, please," hissing the *see* so that it came out "S'ere please." The boys could tell when he was coming down the hall well in advance by a noise he made in his throat, a sort of grunt.

Eugene soon got to know Billy Betts, his grunt, and his "S'ere please," for it was Betts who disciplined the boys, and Betts who issued permission to go to New York on a weekend. Very frequently in the next four years Eugene would find himself en route to Betts's study to answer for one misdeed or another. (At Betts he was always called Eugene *James* O'Neill in honor of his father.) The misdeeds started at once, too, for if Eugene had any clear program for life at the time, it was to rebel against all authority, against anything his father was *for*.

His father wanted him to do well at school, but Eugene felt a vast contempt for the whole academic program at Betts. In class he allowed his mind to wander. "As a student, Gene was somewhat of a dreamer," his classmate William Trausneck observed, "and I have heard Boyd [the Latin teacher] yell, 'O'Neill, wake up!' in the classroom on many occasions, but Gene always knew the answers." As his roommate that first year, Wesley D. Sawyer, would remark with a certain awe, he had "a uncanny way of getting his lesson without too much studying which he didn't like." William Jenkins had the impression that Eugene "didn't have to study" because it was all "too easy for him." Much of it actually was. Eugene O'Neill came to preparatory school with a wider knowledge of literature than most men have when they graduate from college. No wonder he could astonish the other boys by his brilliance, without studying.

It was only in mathematics that he couldn't coast along. Arthur G. Walter, his mathematics teacher, whom the boys called Algie, recalled, during an interview in 1936 with a Stamford *Advocate* reporter, how Eugene had hated mathematics. "He was constantly complaining about the uselessness of the study. 'What is the good of studying that stuff?' and 'What good will that be for me?' He would never become actively angry but withdraw into himself and sulk."

Betts Academy stressed athletics. All the boys were required to participate, and the Betts teams usually came out on top. Billy Betts always had a few boys working their way through school tending furnaces who invariably turned out, "by coincidence," as Harold

Green observed later, to be star pitchers or batters or football play-ers. So Betts always had excellent teams, and the student parlor was crowded with trophies. All the boys were out, after classes, prac-ticing football or baseball or hockey—all, that is, except Eugene. He made it very clear to his classmate William Jenkins that he thought "athletics were a waste of time," indeed, that "school was a waste of time," but that he was supremely bored with sports.

Actually, in his heart of hearts, Eugene was not quite as far above the herd as he wished to appear. He made "sub" on the second team in baseball, and his classmate Trausneck thought he had "a good arm." He was not above playing catch with his cousin Phil Sheridan in the summer at New London, and at school he would sit by the hour sunning himself on a big rock and watching the boys practice football or baseball. He would even ask a question now and then.

But he had adopted the pose of the confirmed rebel and he would have died rather than admit an interest in anything the other boys found absorbing. Of course, he had always kept out of group games. "During the evening recreation hour when the other boys would be urging me to start games and play them with all their heart," Algie Walter recalled, "O'Neill would listlessly enter if he was coaxed but would show no interest or enthusiasm to be the winner. If he was at the foot it was all right with him."

He was, of course, under his mask of cynical indifference, very shy and sensitive. "He was a dreamer, no mixer at all," Algie Walter remembered, "—liked to go off for walks by himself, you know, or spend hours reading in his room." With the other boys he kept his distance. "If we had a rough-house party in a room," T. G. Tread-way recalled, "he generally sat in a corner with his mind 90 miles away. He was a very quiet chap. I never knew him to be chummy with anybody." He rebuffed advances from other boys, too. "He was sort of hard to draw out," said John Pero. "He would answer a question, but wouldn't go beyond it."

Most of the boys at Betts had no conception of the intellectual upheaval and emotional explosions that were going on behind the silent façade of Eugene O'Neill. Nor did they have any idea of the sophisticated Broadway world to which his brother Jamie was in-troducing him. "While other boys were shivering themselves into a fit of embarrassment at the mere thought of a show girl," Eugene himself would later say, "I really was a wise guy." During his last two years at Betts, however, the other boys did become aware that Eugene O'Neill was years ahead of them and that when he took off for a weekend in New York (as he did more and more frequently), he would be moving in a world of show girls and drink quite beyond their own wildest dreams.

Only in Hans Schleip, "Heinie" as the boys called him, did Eugene find a fellow sophisticate who was interested in the theater and in women, and knew his way around. Heinie Schleip's father ran Papst's Café, next door to the Majestic Theatre at Columbus Circle in New York, and Heinie had had an early education in what Eugene would later humorously call "the pace that kills." When Eugene couldn't get tickets to a show from Tyler, Heinie's father could usually get them seats in a box at the Majestic. During his last two years at Betts, Eugene was always taking off for New York with Heinie Schleip in quest of wine, women, and song, Eugene looking very suave and sophisticated—"Quite a dapper dressed boy, Gene was," Harold Green observed—to the envy of their schoolmates.

When Eugene did go with other Betts boys to a dance at one of the girls' schools in Stamford, he let everyone know that he found it contemptibly tame. "He wouldn't dance," William Jenkins observed. "He just sat around and made remarks about it." He gave Jenkins the impression that "this was all country-bumpkin stuff" for him. As, indeed, it was.

Meanwhile, despite his contempt for the classroom, Eugene went right on avidly educating himself as he had been doing ever since early childhood. The latest thing in theater was "Ibsenism." In it he sensed a fulcrum for revolt. So he began to read Ibsen, learning how a moralistic middle-class society can turn any expression of joy in living into evil dissipation—how the mask of Pan is gradually compressed into the mask of Mephistopheles, as he would later express it in his own play *The Great God Brown*. Already he was voyaging beyond his brother Jamie, beyond the viewpoint of the *fin de siècle* poets.

His greatest excitement came when he discovered Shaw's *Quintessence of Ibsenism*. He read and reread it during his last year at

Betts, underlining in red ink each passage that thrilled him, until finally hardly a sentence remained that wasn't underscored in red. The book came as a revelation to him. He now understood exactly what was wrong with the romantic plays he had grown up on. Vistas of social and intellectual revolt opened before him. He saw how a corrupt drama stemmed from a corrupt society; he saw how false standards and hypocrisy create a false, artificial art.

With apt quotations from Shaw, he found he could dumfound his schoolmates in argument. He began reading Shaw's plays, too, absorbing them so completely that years later, when he created the character of Captain Brant in *Mourning Becomes Electra,* he would make him almost an exact duplicate of Shaw's Captain Brassbound without even being conscious of the plagiarism.

Shaw set him on the path of political inquiry that would lead him eventually to Marx, Engels, and Kropotkin. At the same time, Shaw gave him a glimpse of a mystical faith in a life force beyond individual life which he found strangely appealing. At last he had the intellectual ammunition to fight the whole army of his childhood beliefs. Into the framework of his schoolboy rebellion he began to put the most advanced ideas of his time.

But he was still a schoolboy rebelling against all rules without troubling to find out whether they were good rules or bad. After his first year at Betts, the headmaster knew what to expect of him and assigned him a room directly opposite that of Algie Walter, who had charge of the dormitory, so the teacher could keep an eye on him. Often, late at night, Walter would find Eugene reading and smoking in his room. Smoking was strictly against the rules; almost everyone smoked, nevertheless, but the other boys did most of their smoking in the lunchwagon in town, and when they did smoke in their rooms, they did so leaning out of the window with the drapes closed behind them. But Eugene scorned such subterfuges. He smoked openly. "All this," Algie Walter remarked ruefully later, "was part of his rebellion against discipline. He was constantly rebellious against the regulations of the school and critical of authority. He had a very determined mind of his own."

James O'Neill was frequently in conference with William Betts over his problem child. He was very anxious to have Eugene straightened out once and for all. If Betts thought punishment would do it, he was ready to back him to the hilt. He "was always eager to cooperate" with Betts, Walter would recall, "in any measures to advance his son's studies." All of which simply reinforced Eugene's determination to rebel.

Eugene was far too preoccupied with his own upheaval during the years at Betts to have any insight into the undercurrent of frustration in his father's life. His father looked solid enough to him. He was always the center of an admiring group, beloved of everybody, even Eugene's friends, who were always captivated by him.

One after another of the new plays Liebler and Company found for James O'Neill ended in financial disaster. A few months on the road with *The Honor of the Humble* lost them so much money that they considered it a blessing when the scenery burned in Canada in December, 1902. *The Manxman* did little better. The next year, with A. Conan Doyle's *The Adventures of Gerard* and the curtain raiser *Sacrament of Judas,* Liebler and Company were lucky to break even. Everyone acknowledged James O'Neill as one of the finest actors on the American stage, but his popularity, except in *Monte Cristo,* seemed to have melted away. An ever deepening strain of bitterness flavored all his talk of the American theater.

Absorbed in his own awakening intellectual power, Eugene looked at his father from a great psychological distance. Home for Easter recess in March, 1904, he watched the rehearsals for the all-star revival of *The Two Orphans,* unimpressed, from long habit, by the famous actors—Clara Morris, Kyrle Bellew, Charles Warner, Grace George, Margaret Illington—who were acting with his father. He began to recognize the artificiality of this play where the good were so good, and the evil so very evil.

That summer, too, he learned something that demolished any simple ideas of good and bad he still had. But it hurt him cruelly. The lesson came from Jamie, as the other shattering lessons had, only this time Eugene tried not to believe it, for it defiled the shining image he had kept intact in the midst of his most savage rebellion: the image of his beautiful mother.

Not that it was Jamie's fault. He and Papa had decided that they couldn't keep the truth from Eugene any longer—especially after one nightmare time when Mama had run out of the house in her nightdress and tried to throw herself off the dock. From Jamie Eugene learned that his mother was addicted to dope—that, when she was suddenly cut off from it, she would go almost crazy for need of it, that many of the times Mama had been "ill," this had been her illness. "God, it made everything in life seem rotten!" he would write of it later in *Long Day's Journey Into Night*.

Whatever positive feelings toward life Eugene had were centered in his mother. If she proved corrupt, nothing decent remained in the world. Eugene suffered horribly in the first days after Jamie told him. Only gradually did he come to terms with the knowledge by fitting it into a myth he had evolved to preserve his mother from the hatred he felt for his father. When he thought of his mother, he liked to see her as a kind of enchanted princess—pure and sweet and undefiled—but captive in the castle of a wicked giant. "And my mother?" he would have Dion Anthony say in *The Great God Brown*. "I remember a sweet strange girl, with affectionate, bewildered eyes as if God had locked her in a dark closet without any explanation. I was the sole doll our ogre, her husband, allowed her and she played mother and child with me for many years. . . . "

When he portrayed his mother directly in *Long Day's Journey Into Night*, he created a similar myth, showing her as a simple convent girl, misled into marriage, but still a child and pure: a virgin mother. Dion Anthony says of his dead mother, "The last time I looked, her purity had forgotten me, she was stainless and imperishable, and I knew my sobs were ugly and meaningless to her virginity." Later, Eugene would be fascinated by the psychological origins of religions, seeing them as "the best case histories" of man's inner life. Very deeply, he understood the need to believe in a virgin mother.

By picturing his mother as a captive princess, he could attribute all the uncertainty he had felt in her love to the "ogre," his father, and he was finally able to accept even his mother's addiction to drugs by making his father the culprit. By imagining that his father, out of sheer miserliness, had called in cheap doctors who accustomed her to morphine, he was able to exonerate his mother and soothe himself. He still held this belief years later, and offered it as the cause of the mother's addiction in his autobiographical play, *Long Day's Journey Into Night.*

In his third year at Betts, Eugene knew that his mother was not with his father and Jamie, who were touring in the all-star revival of *The Two Orphans.* She was in a sanatorium. When she rejoined her husband, she was apparently her old self. Sarah Truax, a young actress in the company, recalled, "Mrs. O'Neill traveled with us sometimes, and they were both very good to me. They took me to the Old Absinthe House in New Orleans, and I tasted absinthe for the first time." She never remotely suspected that her charming hostess had just fought off drug addiction.

Eugene suffered alone over his mother's trouble. He couldn't sympathize with his father, embittered by his wife's addiction and by Jamie, who was back on his father's hands after *Audrey,* so that James O'Neill had to get him parts in *The Adventures of Gerard* and *The Two Orphans,* and finally in the one act of *Virginius* which James put on for a brief but lucrative fling at vaudeville in the spring of 1905. James O'Neill was ashamed that his son could not get a job on his own and still couldn't handle anything but minor parts. Eugene's sympathies lay with Jamie, not his father.

Nor did he perceive the bitterness behind his father's announcement in June, 1905, that he was going back to *Monte Cristo* because the "managers and public" wanted him in it. "The more I see of other pieces, the better I like Monte Cristo," he said, "and when I produce it this time, if I meet with the success I anticipate, I'll keep on playing it until I retire for good from the stage. Jefferson played Rip Van Winkle for forty years and while he sandwiched in The Rivals and one or two other little pieces, it was Rip made big money, and things have got so now that all there is in acting is money. If animated by a love of art, a man wants to produce a legitimate play, it takes a small fortune to do it . . . and after all this risk and trouble, you are likely to make a failure." Eugene simply thought derisively, "*Monte Cristo,* again!"

But he listened when Will Connor came down to New London and talked of how he'd left Liebler and Company to join Lee Shubert in managing an American tour for Madame Sarah Bernhardt, and of how they expected to run into trouble with Klaw and Erlanger's syndicate. Eugene had been too young to understand what was going on back in 1895, when his father, with Minnie Maddern Fiske and Francis Wilson, had tried to organize opposition to the syndicate and failed. But he had heard his father attacking the Klaw and Erlanger monopoly on bookings, and he absorbed some of the excitement of battle as Connor and Papa discussed the strategy of the Bernhardt tour. Connor was not going to knuckle under to the syndicate. If they wouldn't let him play their theaters, he would find other ways; Bernhardt could perform in a tent the way Barnum and Bailey did, if necessary. Eugene listened, fascinated, and thought of getting tickets from Connor to see Bernhardt when she opened in New York that fall.

That was about as far as his plans for himself went. Papa was beginning to bother him about what he wanted to do when he graduated from Betts in the spring, but he couldn't say. The same listless indifference he had felt for the competitive games at Betts he now felt for the game of getting on. He had no idea of what he wanted in the way of a career. He knew that he wanted to go on reading, thinking, discovering what life was all about, but he couldn't tell his father that. All he could say for sure was that he didn't want to go to Yale. Betts boys automatically went to Yale; they believed it the school for "he-men." His father didn't insist on Yale. He could go to Princeton. But what did he want to study? How about the law? The law, James O'Neill declared, was "the foundation of all success." He often regretted that in his barnstorming days he had turned down an offer by a prominent politician to adopt him and send him through law school. With a knowledge of the law a man might do anything, he told Eugene. What about the law? Eugene thought that might be all right. He could offer nothing in its place. So James O'Neill sent his son Eugene to Princeton University, fully expecting him to emerge a few years later standing firmly on the law, "the foundation of all success."

CHAPTER ELEVEN

Jamie's Footsteps

EUGENE thought he might, too. Established in his rooms, 30 University Hall, that September of 1906, he felt himself very much a college man. Confidently, he wrote "Eugene O'Neill" inside his French book, *Contes de Daudet,* and then, in bold numerals, his class, "1910." He expected to emerge with a B. Litt. from Princeton in 1910, just as surely as he had come out of Betts Academy with a prep-school diploma. The process, he felt, would take care of itself with no exertion on his part.

Yet for all his lackadaisical approach, Princeton held no more avid student than Eugene O'Neill. His mind was seething with questions; he was eager for ideas, for answers. But in the classroom he found no answers, only a concentrated dose of academic sawdust. The stale abstractions of mathematics that he had hated so furiously at Betts were now shoved down his throat all week long, and no one at Princeton, any more than at Betts, seemed to know why the meaningless mess should be gone into to begin with. Algebra, Spherical Trigonometry, Physics—these were the required courses. Eugene dozed, for they came early in the morning, or daydreamed through the endless chalk-filled hours.

Next in order of idiocy Eugene put compulsory chapel, twice during the week plus every other Sunday, and he couldn't cut it either, or else he would have to make it up, getting as many as eight chapels in two weeks, a lethal dose. Usually, Eugene managed not to listen to the sermons, but sometimes he found himself unable to shut them out, particularly those of Professor Henry Van Dyke which he found "so irritatingly stupid," as he would later recall, "that they prevented me from sleeping."

The courses in French, English, and Latin were easy, as they had been at Betts, but Daudet and Livy, as taught at Princeton, seemed far removed from what Eugene wanted to know, and the study of Shakespeare in class, he would confess years later, "made me afraid of him." "I am perhaps excusing myself for the way I loafed and fooled and got as much fun and as little work as I could out of my one year at Princeton, but I think that I felt there instinctively, that we were not in touch with life or on the trail of the real things." But then, remembering the confused turmoil of his youth, Eugene would add with characteristic honesty, "Or perhaps I was merely lazy. Who knows just what is going on inside of him?"

Lazy he was not, as he roamed hungrily through the bookstore of Benjamin Tucker, "the old philosophical anarchist," during his weekends in New York, searching for books on sociology and philosophy that would put him "on the trail of the real things." Only outside of class, Eugene would later say, "my awakenings came."

One tremendous awakening came to him that year with his reading of Oscar Wilde's *The Picture of Dorian Gray*. He had picked it up casually, interested because Papa had talked of seeing Wilde's *Salome* in Europe the preceding summer and the newspapers had talked of its "elegant pollution." Besides, Eugene had once heard enough bowdlerized scandal about the trial of Oscar Wilde to conclude that he was guilty of "bigamy." So he was interested in Wilde's novel, but he was by no means prepared for the "indelible impression" that the book made upon him.

He wouldn't analyze the fascinated recognition he felt as he followed the progressive corruption of Dorian Gray; he would never explain that "indelible impression," but what the book meant to him is clear enough. Here, for the first time, he saw set down in writing the mysterious split, the oppressive duality he had felt in himself ever since Jamie had showed him the path to rebellion in debauchery. "Suddenly," as Oscar Wilde put it, "we find that we are no longer the actors, but the spectators of the play. Or rather we are both. We watch ourselves, and the mere wonder of the spectacle enthralls us." So Eugene found it. Like Dorian Gray, he had already experienced debauchery, and like Dorian Gray, "The more he knew, the more he desired to know. He had mad hungers that grew more ravenous as he fed them."

Reading the book alone in his rooms, Eugene saw his whole youthful torment rendered meaningful. The hunger for experience, the debauchery, the sick guilt and longing for lost purity, and yet, triumphant over all, the further riotous search for sensation, were somehow resolved in the comforting precept of Lord Henry, "The aim of life is self-development. To realize one's nature perfectly— that is what each of us is here for."

While Eugene was still awhirl with the emotional storm aroused by *Dorian Gray,* he found a book at Benjamin Tucker's that came as another dazzling revelation, and one that led him far beyond his own personal torment. In Nietzsche's *Thus Spake Zarathustra* he found not only vitriolic words to express his hatred of the conforming herd, but also a rhapsodic vision of human grandeur, a meaningful universe to replace the shattered rubble of his Catholicism. No single experience of his life would mean as much to him as this book, for he would read and reread it year after year, and at each reading make it more intimately a part of his thought, of his way of looking at life. He was eighteen when he found *Thus Spake Zarathustra,* and he was still rereading it and carefully copying out excerpts from it thirty years later. At a few points he disagreed with its doctrine, but he never tired of it as a poetic revelation of what is wrong with the world and what is right with the world.

Of course, that first ecstatic reading of *Zarathustra* at Princeton gave him only the surface of it; his understanding would grow through all the rereadings of the following years. What he took first was the ammunition to fight the conventional world he had been rebelling against since his puberty. "Too long have they been admitted to be right, these petty folk," said Nietzsche. "Thus at last they have also been given power. Now they teach: 'Good is only what the petty folk approve.'" For the first time, Eugene found a meaning for his rebellion against conventional virtue. "Beware of the good and just! They would fain crucify those who invent their own standard of virtue—they hate the lonely one," Nietzsche told him. "O lonely one, thou goest the way of the creator; Thou wilt create for thyself a God out of thy seven devils." This, then, was the meaning of all his torment; he, Eugene, was the lonely one, the creator of new values.

In Nietzsche, too, he found the words to express his contempt for the irritating stupidity of the sermons of a Henry Van Dyke. "In order that I might learn to believe in their Saviour they ought to sing better songs," Zarathustra told him, "and his disciples ought to look saved-like." For his instinctive mockery of the adulation accorded Andrew Carnegie when he presented Princeton with a lake that year, Eugene found such words as these: "Many a one I have found who strained himself and puffed himself up. And the folk cried, 'Behold a great man.' But of what good are any bellows? At last the wind escapeth from them." And for the superficial patriotism in the air at Princeton functions, Eugene found his definition, "The state—the idol of the superfluous."

As for his occasional twinges of guilt at the bought love in which Jamie had initiated him, Nietzsche soothed him with "Verily it is still better to act wickedly than to think pettily." For his restless, wandering spirit, his inability to see in any practical goals a direction for his life, Eugene found at least a philosophical justification: "And whatever may become my fate and experience—a wandering and a mountain-climbing will be part of it. In the end one experienceth nothing but one's self." He was armored, too, against the hostility of the unthinking boys around him, and when they taunted him for his absorption in his own philosophical upheaval by calling him "Ego," he could think to himself, in the words of Zarathustra, "Thy neighbors will always be poisonous flies."

At the same time, he enjoyed drinking with the boys—that grand reinforcement the adolescent finds in noisy gaiety, uproarious freedom. But side by side with his "general hell-raising," as he would later call it, Eugene pursued his own intellectual development. He was reading Jack London and Conrad, too, finding further justification for his lonely fight. Indeed, the only thing he wasn't doing much of was studying.

Of course, French, Latin and English were a cinch for him. Even without much studying, he came through at midyear with a "3" in each. Princeton had seven numbers for grading, "1" being best and "7" worst. A "3" at Princeton was considered a "gentleman's grade," above average, but not too conspicuously so. It was mathematics that was Eugene's downfall. Spherical Trigonometry he managed to squeak through with a low passing grade, but Algebra and Physics he realized were hopeless. He was failing both courses so emphatically that he saw no sense in presenting himself for the farce of an examination. So he took his failures without that indignity.

That was how he came through at midyear, not well, but by no means disastrously either. He registered for the second semester of English, Latin, and French, for another dose of Algebra and Physics, plus a new horror, Conics. If anything, Eugene pursued his formal education with even less enthusiasm now that a semester of college had revealed to him the full sterility of the classroom. "Why can't our education," he would later ask fiercely, "respond logically to our needs? If it did we'd grab for these things and hold on to them."

But if Princeton wasn't educating Eugene O'Neill, he was educating himself. In the bookstore of Benjamin Tucker and in the Broadway theaters, he found what he was looking for. At the Easter recess in March, he went to see Alla Nazimova in *Hedda Gabler*. "I do remember well the impact upon me when I saw an Ibsen play for the first time, a production of 'Hedda Gabler' at the old Bijou Theatre in New York—and then went again and again for ten successive nights," he recalled years later. "That experience discovered an entire new world of the drama for me. It gave me my first conception of a modern theatre where truth might live."

He would speak similarly of his discovery of Strindberg and the Abbey Theatre plays. If only he had known then that he was educating himself to become a playwright. But at the time, his rapturous return to the Bijou Theatre each night seemed just another of his crazy larks, aimed at nothing better than the ability to think of himself as Eilert Lovborg "with vine leaves in his hair" when he went on a spree with his classmates.

And more and more, he was indulging in such sprees, "curing the soul by means of the senses," as Oscar Wilde put it. He fancied himself as Eugene O'Neill, class of 1910, raising hell. Even years later, he would be ready to recall cheerfully, "My allegiance is always with Princeton. I like Princeton. I had a good time there, even though I only stayed a year." The pursuit of a good time took him weekends to New York and evenings to Trenton, where some grandly low-down taverns could be found. One night he and his friends stayed so late in Trenton that they missed their connections and had to walk back after midnight along the trolley tracks, a good ten-mile hike. One of the boys took a shot with a stone at a glass insulator overhead, and in their mood of reckless joy this seemed a glorious idea, so they all gathered stones and, as they walked along, flung them, laughing triumphantly at each new shattering of glass.

A few days later, Eugene was standing before Dean Fine, author of the *College Algebra* he avoided studying, and chairman of the disciplinary committee at Princeton. Dean Fine solemnly informed him that breaking the glass insulators of trolleys was an irresponsible act that endangered the lives of other people, and that to impress on Eugene and his fellow culprits the seriousness of their crime, the college was suspending them from all classes for at least two weeks.

Of what was Eugene thinking as he heard this lecture? Of all the classes he'd cut, of all the examinations he would flunk? Of the senseless stupidity of studying Conic Sections? Or was he thinking, deep down, of the shock to Papa when Jamie had got himself expelled from Notre Dame, of Papa's great pride in having him at

Princeton, and the blow it would be to the Old Man to have him
follow in Jamie's footsteps? Whatever he was thinking, he told Dean
Fine that he wanted to resign altogether. Then, through a long talk
by the Dean on the reasons why he should return to college, Eugene
stood firm. This would be the end of his college career.

In April, just as the Brooklyn *Eagle* was welcoming James O'Neill
back to New York with an encomium on his family life—"Mrs.
O'Neill is his constant companion on the road. Their elder son James
O'Neill, jr., is a member of the 'Monte Cristo' company, and the
younger son is at college studying law"—just, indeed, as Papa,
Mama, and Jamie returned after a whole year away from New York,
Eugene arrived at the Hotel Lucerne and presented his father with
the destruction of his one great dream for his sons—that they would
have the formal education he'd never had. The shock was complete
—the destruction final. Eugene had followed in Jamie's footsteps—
almost as if he had to do what he knew would hurt his father most.

CHAPTER TWELVE

Debris

So James O'Neill found himself in the midst of the debris of his fondest hopes for both his boys. He couldn't understand what was wrong with Eugene—or Jamie either. He remembered his own bitter childhood, working in a machine shop when he was longing with all his heart to go to school. His own two boys had been given the best of everything—and had thrown it away. When he tried to say this to Eugene, the lad was simply derisive or bored. (Eugene himself would call this his "wise guy" period.) James O'Neill couldn't make the boy out.

Perhaps, James thought, he was at fault for leaving the boy alone so much. He and Ella had been exhausted in the spring of last year, for the "farewell tour," as he called it, of *Monte Cristo* had taken them through many one-night stands. So they had gone off to

Europe, sailing on the *Caronia* in May, 1906, before Eugene had graduated from Betts.

James O'Neill had enjoyed the theater in England, particularly the Ellen Terry benefit, and he'd grown pleasantly sentimental over his return to Kilkenny. "I have been down to the old home and found every familiar place the same," he had written back, "but strange faces greet me on every side. I sat for hours on the old porch last night thinking of the dear ones departed." When he and Ella had returned refreshed at the beginning of August, he'd kept everyone in stitches with accounts of his Irish trip.

"An Irish railway porter simply can't help being funny," he had told Tyler and Connor. "On one of my trips through the Emerald Isle I got into a third-class car by mistake with a first-class ticket; a zealous porter wrathfully pulled me out of the car and told me 'I was chating the Kumpany.' After I was comfortably seated in the first-class compartment, he put his head in and asked: 'Is there anyone there for here?' But even this genius was eclipsed by the conductor of the train who, before the train departed, fiercely rang a bell and bellowed the gloomy warning: 'This train shtops nowhere at all!' " Everyone had enjoyed hearing him tell of Ireland—particularly Eugene's friends Ed Keefe and Art McGinley. But he hadn't had much time with Eugene, what with getting his company ready to open in Chicago in August.

Of course, the boy had seemed to be settled. His rooms were waiting for him at Princeton, and James O'Neill was sure he would make a fine lawyer. William J. Betts has assured him that Eugene was very bright, for all his rebelliousness, and was bound to do well at Princeton. The lad's future had seemed perfectly secure.

James O'Neill's tour had taken him out through the Middle West, through California, and back by way of the Southwest, so the whole year had gone by before he could get back to New York and see how Eugene was getting along. Then he had had other troubles. He had been acting in his new play about John the Baptist, *The Voice of the Mighty,* less than a month when he realized that he'd have to go back to *Monte Cristo* if he wanted to act before full houses rather than empty plush seats. Besides, critics were still being "surprised and delighted with some new turn to the emotional scenes" he'd put into *Monte Cristo,* as the Augusta *Herald* declared. So *Monte Cristo* had him again.

He had also had trouble with Jamie, who was with him. The critics had started out by being kind. They called Jamie "a manly looking chap"; he wasn't as good as his father ("The voice is not as smooth and even, and there is not the same magnetic presence"), but they predicted that "the training he is receiving will be invaluable, and something should be heard of him later." But now they were flatly declaring that Jamie was "decidedly weak," and that "his experience has not worked to improve him." The Florida *Times Union* bluntly announced, "When the heart of the father ceases to cloud the judgment of the actor and artist, James O'Neill, Sr., will drop James O'Neill, Jr., from his company; and the plays will be the better therefore." James O'Neill had turned on Jamie, trying to drive him to work harder. But Jamie retorted flippantly, and they quarreled. To his father's bitter declaration that he'd never be an actor the way he was going, Jamie sneered, "What of it?" and flung out to spend the night drinking and chasing women.

And now Eugene, his father's last bright hope, came home with the news that he was out of Princeton and dumped himself on his father's hands. The boy had no idea where he would go from here, was even indifferent to the subject. He left it to his father to decide what he should do next. No wonder James O'Neill chafed at the ingratitude of his children. No wonder he began to talk of putting on *King Lear.* "Lear offers such tremendous possibilities to the actor, for it contains so much that is human and moving and sympathetic," he told a reporter. "The part cannot, I believe, be played with any degree of convincing satisfaction by a young man. To get at the heart and soul of the great, towering old man, one must be backed in his efforts by seasoned powers and vast experience." James O'Neill had certainly experienced ingratitude. "God deliver me from my children!" he often said.

But he had too much native optimism to despair. Even Eugene was impressed by how much the Old Man could take and "keep on smiling." Before long, James O'Neill was rushing about to hire a New York theater for a seven-week engagement. He was going to return to the classics wholesale, get himself a first-class repertory company, and train younger actors in the classic style. He would start with a revival of *Virginius*, that glorious old play that had gone off the boards when John McCullough had succumbed to paresis, and follow it with Shakespeare's *Julius Caesar* so that he could use the Roman settings for both. Jamie would have a part in each play, and maybe the example of a first-rate company would inspire him to improve.

Meanwhile, he had found something for Eugene. College wasn't necessarily everything. Ella's father had made a splendid success of business without any college training, and her brother William had done all right in the wholesale grocery business with only the training he'd got as a bookkeeper. If Eugene didn't want a profession, maybe he was cut out for business. James O'Neill had invested some of Ella's money in Henry Brittain's New York-Chicago Supply Company. Brittain agreed to take Eugene under his wing as a secretary, so he could learn the ropes. Eugene was willing. He didn't know what else to do with himself, and he wanted to stay in New York. James O'Neill, putting aside his pride in his boy "studying law," developed a reborn optimism about Eugene, and his new press representative, James Findlater Byth, announced grandiosely to the newspapers that James O'Neill's younger son, Eugene Gladstone O'Neill, had just "made his successful debut in the manufacturing business."

PART FOUR

JIMMY TOMORROW

CHAPTER THIRTEEN

James Findlater Byth

I NEFFECTUAL, lovable Jimmy Byth! Eugene was drawn to him at once, to his gentleness, to his wistful "lost dog" appeal for affection —and his fear of a kick; and above all, to Jimmy's subtly self-destructive quality, embodied in his insatiable need for "a wee drappie," a "gentle stimulant," a "bite."

Jimmy would stand as a symbol for the next five years of Eugene O'Neill's life, for his drifting, his sense of futility, his self-destructive search—for what? Oblivion? Jimmy's accelerating descent to the bottom would parallel Eugene's own descent, till finally the two of them would reach the bottom together to share drunkenness and despair. Indeed, Jimmy would almost lure Eugene into the final oblivion—death. But that was later.

Eugene did not believe everything Jimmy Byth told him of his past. He suspected that the Scottish manor house in which Jimmy fondly recollected growing up was of the same order as a castle in Spain. But Jimmy's gentlemanly bearing, his Scottish accent, his Edinburgh degree were all verified realities. Although Eugene found Jimmy's enthusiasm for Dickens and Thackeray laughable compared with his own excitement over Ibsen, Shaw, Wilde, and Nietzsche, he always admired the well-educated gentleman in Jimmy.

Very early in his career, Jimmy had come to America and gone into theatrical publicity; in the *Dramatic Mirror* of August 10, 1895, appeared the following notice: "James F. Byth, who for the past three seasons was in advance of *The Devil's Auction* company, is at liberty and may be addressed at this office." After that, he had become the booking representative of the Hopkins Theatre Circuit in Chicago. In June, 1898, he had opened a theatrical agency and exchange in partnership with David Carpos. That couldn't have done well, for when the Boer War started in 1899, Jimmy went to South Africa as a war correspondent for Reuter's.

According to Jimmy, his life was destroyed the day he returned to Cape Town to find his wife "in the hay with a staff officer." That betrayal, he liked to believe, had turned him to alcohol. Actually, Eugene was sure that Jimmy had been drinking long before that moment in Cape Town, that the drinking had broken up the marriage, and that his wife's infidelity was a poetic excuse for the self-destruction that had already become the pattern of his life.

By the time he became James O'Neill's press representative, Jimmy had lost many jobs, but had always got new ones on the strength of his Edinburgh degree, his culture, and his professional skill. But by 1907, the balance was beginning to shift—the drinking, the deterioration, the irresponsibility were beginning to outweigh the charm, the culture, the skill.

Thirty years later Eugene would recall Jimmy's "gentle bloodhound's" face, his friendly, bloodshot brown eyes, thin hair, buck teeth, and small bulbous nose, as well as his curious quality of being partly "prim, Victorian old maid" and partly "affectionate boy who has never grown up." Jimmy's was a strangely appealing personality. When Richard H. Little came down to McVicker's in Chicago to get a story on James O'Neill for the Chicago *Record Herald*, he became so fascinated with Jimmy that he devoted much of his article to him.

"J. Findlater Byth is down on the programme as official press representative for Mr. O'Neill," Little wrote in February, 1908. "His duties consist in seeing that all things concerning Mr. James O'Neill be not kept out of the newspapers. When I said that I wanted to know why Mr. O'Neill played the Count of Monte Cristo and intimated that I would like a complete answer, Mr. J. Findlater Byth in spite of his proud Scotch lineage looked as if he wanted to embrace me. Instead of that he suggested that we go somewhere and have a bite. I speak the language of J. Findlater Byth and I understood that by a bite he meant in his mother tongue 'a wee drappie.'

"Then I pressed my inquiry again upon J. Findlater Byth. J. Findlater did not wish to answer without consulting counsel. Whereupon he disappeared, returning soon with copious re-enforcements in the persons of Edgar Forrest, general manager for Mr. O'Neill, and John G. Magle, the general representative for the same.

"Everybody in authority connected with the James O'Neill company seemed to be present except the carpenter and the mistress of the wardrobes. It looked as if the riddle was about to be answered. J. Findlater Byth suggested that before proceeding to the discussion of the main question that all hands be piped forward to splice the main brace. The main brace was duly spliced. Mr. Magle then asked J. Findlater Byth if they had anything half as good as that down in South Africa. J. Findlater Byth hooted-mon after the fashion of the Scotch and said: 'Oh, no, not at all, old chap.' The general manager explained that the general press representative had joined the Boer army when it wasn't looking, down in South Africa during the late unpleasantness as a war correspondent and had tarried to the bitter end.

" 'And you are a loyal subject of the King,' said the general manager chidingly.

" 'But I was not fighting, old chap,' said the general press representative in defense. 'I was a war correspondent for Reuter's. I was not a beastly pro-Boer merely because duty put me among them, don't you understand?'

" 'But weren't the English soldiers going to tie a rope around your neck and fasten you to a tree until the coroner arrived?' asked the manager.

" 'Oh, yes,' answered J. Findlater Byth carelessly. 'They did have a bit of a rope and there was a bit of a tree somewhere about, and the beggars made no end of a row when they captured me. But they thought I had been fighting, which I jolly well hadn't.'

" 'And so?' asked the manager.

"J. Findlater Byth yawned. 'That's all the story. There is nothing more.'

" 'But you didn't say whether they hung you or not,' said the manager.

" 'But they didn't,' said J. Findlater Byth. 'Didn't you read the dispatches about it? Oh, no, I was not hung at all.'

" 'I'm glad of that,' said the manager. 'I was always worried about that. You never told me before in just so many words that you were not hung in South Africa. Congratulations.'

" 'Silly oss,' said J. Findlater Byth.

" 'He must love it,' I ventured after a time.

" 'He does,' said the manager, looking reprovingly at J. Findlater Byth. 'They've had to put an extra bartender on duty here since he arrived in town.'

" 'No,' I said; 'I mean O'Neill. I was referring to the number of times he has played Monte Cristo. Why?'

" 'I've a good idea,' said J. Findlater Byth.

"The general manager and the general representative exchanged glances.

" 'All together,' said the manager. 'Hip, hip, hurrah! Hip, hip, hurrah! Hip, hip, hurrah! Tiger!'

" 'I was going to say,' said the general press representative, 'that while we all can answer that question after a fashion, why not go back and ask the governor?'

" 'That's Mr. O'Neill,' said the manager. 'Everybody connected with the company always calls him the governor. It's not a bad suggestion.'

"Under the personal direction of J. Findlater Byth we moved back to the theater and made our way to the stage. The second act of 'Virginius' was on. Roman citizens stood about in the wings and a beautiful Roman slave girl who was soon to go and claim the daughter of Virginius as her own che-ild was perched on a throne chewing gum.

"'Hello, Jimmie,' said the girl with a great deal of familiarity considering her lowly position. 'Did you ever get me those postal cards?'

"'That's Edna Porter,' explained J. Findlater Byth. 'She has a small bit in this piece, but she's the page in "Caesar." Clever, deucedly clever, that girl. Pretty, too, hey? What? And there's a girl over there—most extraordinary girl. She's a socialist. Believes in dividing up wealth and sharing property, and raising up the workingman and—er—er—all that sort of rot,' concluded J. Findlater Byth lamely."

In the dressing room, Richard Little asked James O'Neill, "Why have you played Monte Cristo 5,678 times?"

"Mr. O'Neill's face took on a look of deep dejection.

"'Why?' he said; 'well, because I cannot get rid of the cursed thing.'

"This was frankness, anyhow. But J. Findlater Byth interposed. 'Oh, you love your art, governor, and the artistic possibilities of Monte Cristo are so great that you feel it would be an imposition on the public to put aside a play that so appeals to the emotions and has such a great influence on so many.'

"'Do I, Jimmy?' said the governor. 'Thanks. But I would like to bury Edmond Dantes so deep that he would never come to life again. Edmond Dantes is the old man of the sea around my neck. I have carried him twenty-five years, but he won't let go. I can't break his hold. I want to play "Virginius" and "Julius Caesar." . . . But I can't shake this Nemesis, this nightmare, this spectral shape of Monte Cristo. It haunts me and I can't escape it.'

"'You're sick, governor,' said J. Findlater Byth.

"'No,' said Virginius, drawing his toga closer about him, for a draft came in the door. 'I'm not sick. I was never sick in my life. But "Virginius" is one of the greatest plays ever written. It is one of the noblest classics we have. It is my ambition to become associated in the public mind with this character. But "Monte Cristo" will not down. Every year I start out with the fixed determination that I am done with Edmond Dantes forever, and before I know it he has me by the throat and I am climbing the rock once more and shouting: "Mine the treasures of Monte Cristo; the world is mine." ' "

When O'Neill had returned for the next act of *Virginius*, "Mr. J. Findlater Byth called attention to the fact that it was thirteen minutes past ten. Mr. J. Findlater Byth said it was his invariable custom at thirteen minutes past ten to take a gentle stimulant, and we were invited to accompany him." And Little shared a few more of Jimmy Byth's gentle stimulants before the conclusion of the interview.

Often, in the next five years, Eugene would share a gentle stimulant with Jimmy Byth. Often, Jimmy's wistful eyes would fix affectionately on "Gene," so that long after, Eugene would be haunted by those eyes that had almost led him into annihilation. Twice, after he had been reborn as a playwright, Eugene would try to write out his feelings for Jimmy—once in the short story "Tomorrow" in 1916, when his pity for that lovable "lost dog" came out in a burst of naked self-revelation, and again, almost twenty-five years later, in *The Iceman Cometh,* when his profound regret for Jimmy's wasted life had been absorbed in a larger tragic vision.

But in the summer and fall of 1907, when the eighteen-year-old Eugene O'Neill first began joining Jimmy in his gentle stimulants, he saw no tragic ending to this jolly companionship with his father's press representative.

CHAPTER FOURTEEN

The "Wise Guy"

Fʀᴏᴍ the moment the O'Neills closed their New London home and came down to New York in September, 1907, Eugene had a glorious time. His "successful debut in the manufacturing business," as Jimmy would label it, was still a month off. He was free to hang around rehearsals of *Virginius*, joking with Jamie and Jimmy Byth, and then go off with Jamie for wild alcoholic evenings in the company of chorus girls and music-hall beauties. Jamie knew them all— and for Eugene, not quite nineteen, these girls glittered with all the excitement of the world. For the rest of his life he would never tire of recalling those he knew and those he had seen on stage: Bonnie Maginn, Violet Pearl, Anna Held, Lotta Faust, Lulu Glaser, Elfie Fay (really a conquest of Jamie's). Eugene always thought they were the essence of "good fun" in the unmatchable good old days. "I can't imagine anything worse," he would say years later, "than having a date with one of the hard-working ballerinas they have nowa-days instead of chorus girls."

Eugene was proud and astonished by his own success with the ladies. He had none of Jamie's gay patter; he said little until he was very drunk, when he would find himself quoting poetry, but the girls liked him. He could rarely resist watching his darkly handsome young face in the mirror. He was amazed at this successful exterior self that bore so little resemblance to the whirl of uncertainty, guilt, and anxiety he experienced within. Ever more deliberately he culti-vated his pose of the "Bad Boy Pan."

As a very "wise guy," Eugene looked on at Papa's rehearsals of *Virginius* and *Julius Caesar*, critically observing (as some of the critics did on opening night) that several members of the "Roman" populace were chewing gum. "Have you ever seen a production of 'Julius Caesar'"? he would ask later. "Did the Roman mob ever sug-gest to you anything more Roman than a gum-chewing Coney Island Mardi Gras or, in the case of a special all-star revival, a gath-ering of familiar-faced modern actors masquerading uncomfortably in togas?"

The revival of *Virginius* got a big spread in the papers. Before the play even opened, the reporters trooped down to Lyric Hall. Papa could be heard sounding off about how he was going to put on a whole series of Shakespeare revivals—*King Lear, Coriolanus, Henry V, Othello*. "The difficulty in securing good Shakespearian actors is the reason these productions are announced for next season, and not for this," Papa explained. "The present company while on tour will be given the training, in special rehearsals, which the old stock sys-tem used to supply."

When *Virginius* finally opened on September 16, 1907, most of the critics found the play outdated, the scenery garish, the supporting cast weak, but the star magnificent. "I never knew how much of majesty might inhere in a human being until I saw James O'Neill play Virginius," one critic wrote. "His walk is stately as the move-ment of a newly launched ocean liner making its proud way out to sea. His voice is like a deep-toned bell. His eyes, big and luminous like Novelli's, bespeak a boundless vitality."

At the end of the third act, James O'Neill came out and, silencing the applause, made a little speech. "I thank you," he said, "for your generous appreciation. Though for the last thirty years I have occupied a somewhat conspicuous position on the stage, I have seldom visited New York. I am sure I don't know why. I am no worse than other actors. To-night's greeting encourages me to say that I intend to be back among you every year of the few years that are still left to me, playing something of this sort, and when I depart for that bourne from which no traveller returns, I trust you may be able to say of me: 'Ah, well, he could do something else than act dear old Monte Cristo.'" To which one critic responded, "Worse than other actors? Mr. O'Neill has forgotten more about acting than some of our Broadway favorites will ever know."

Papa was covered with praise for his rendition of Virginius. Jamie did not fare so well. One critic did praise him for a "fiery" rendition of Icilius—only he wasn't playing Icilius; Norman Hackett was. Most critics, if they noticed his Lucius at all, decided he was "not suited" to the role. One critic declared caustically, "James O'Neill, Jr. played Lucius, and ran all the way from Rome to the battlefield without turning a hair in his smoothly plastered locks, parted in the middle —which may and may not have been the style in 450 B.C." That was Jamie all over. He wasn't going to disturb his slick grooming for any stage realism.

On the whole, Papa's revival of *Virginius* was not exactly a raving success, but you couldn't destroy the Old Man's optimism. He thought the "bad business" came from having to open too early in New York in order to get a theater. After a two-week run of *Virginius,* he put on *Monte Cristo.* He told a reporter, "though I have an affectionate regard for the romantic gentleman who always bobs up in the nick of time, I must say I have grown dizzy impersonating him," and added, "My revival of 'Julius Caesar' week after next is made with the idea of establishing a repertory, as I really fear I would become hysterical with nothing but 'Monte Cristo' to occupy my attention."

Eugene enjoyed himself during the whole of his father's run at the Lyric; he hated to see Jamie and dear old Jimmy Byth take off for New Haven, Providence, and Boston, the next stops on their tour. But his own time was curtailed now, too, for his "successful debut" at the New York-Chicago Supply Company could not be put off. Papa thought he was going to learn all about business and make his fortune. Eugene knew better.

Every morning he went down to 194 Broadway, off Fulton Street, and entered Room 33, the office of the New York-Chicago Supply Company. He was supposed to be secretary to the president, Henry L. Brittain, and handle the correspondence, of which there was a great deal, for it was a mail-order firm, getting youngsters all over the country to sell ten-cent jewelry for the reward of a phonograph and record. Eugene didn't know much about what was going on, but the stenographer seemed to know exactly what was to be done. No one seemed to expect much more of him than his physical presence. One whole afternoon he spent at his desk carefully copying out Ernest Dowson's "Impenitentia Ultima" on the back of some of H. L. Brittain's stationery advertising his Kodagraph Home Motion Picture Machines and Films.

The office work, he felt, was merely a "bridgehead" to his evenings. His salary of twenty-five dollars a week, supplemented by all the free theater tickets he wanted, went far. He was free—no parents, no schoolmasters to restrain him. A delirious world of drink opened before him, in which he could perpetually retest his surprising power with women.

He was developing into a very dangerous young man. The "swift babies" who had initiated him into the mysteries of sex had not taught him restraint. Now he was swept along by the whole force of adolescent rebellion. Vaguely, in the back of his mind, was the cynical idea that the Old Man was rich and could buy him out of any scrape he got himself into. Indeed, perhaps a part of the satisfaction lay in exactly that—in making the Old Man pay.

Meanwhile, James O'Neill had sorrows enough without Eugene's adding to them. He hadn't been long on the road when the inevitable happened: he had to run *Monte Cristo* more frequently to pay for *Julius Caesar* and *Virginius*. "I am as much a prisoner of the Château d'If as Edmond Dantes ever was," he remarked wryly. The twenty-five years he had played *Monte Cristo* made him feel, he said, older than a California redwood.

"In that time I have seen great actors spring from obscurity to fame, flourish and die. I have seen careers built up and torn down. Children have been born and grown into men and women. Little towns where I once played one-night stands, or passed by entirely, have become flourishing cities. Inventions never thought of when I began playing Edmond Dantes have revolutionized everything.

"And all this time I have been climbing up on a rock, waving a knife and announcing that the world was mine. Do you wonder I want to escape from it all? I want them to remember me as Virginius, but they won't. I suppose that I will be Edmond Dantes throughout the play and down to the final curtain."

He hadn't been long on the road, either, before his plans for establishing a Shakespeare repertory company, of turning his company into "a training school for actors" began to crumble. He alternated the roles of Marc Antony and Brutus for the sheer joy of acting, but his enthusiasm was not caught by the rest of his company. "I don't know where the good young actors are coming from," he complained. "Too many of the younger players are too lazy to study. They want the salary without working for it."

Of course, he had Jamie particularly in mind. Occasionally, Jamie put on a decent performance, or some old friend of James O'Neill would say that Jamie showed "flashes of the talent of his sire," but usually he was roasted mercilessly. The more James O'Neill tried to get him to show some interest in his work, the more indifferent Jamie became. A great gulf of bitterness was opening between the two.

That May, when they returned to New London for the summer, Jamie moved into The Rural View Cottage on Ocean Beach with a fellow "ham," Danny Dennison, rather than live with his parents. That way, he could see a lot of Mama without having the Old Man reproaching him all the time. He liked seeing "the kid," meaning Eugene, there and in New York. The two of them shared an unformulated but almost tangible desire to strike back at the Old Man.

They saw nothing to pity in him. He looked to them, as to the rest of the world, as impregnably sure of himself as ever. His smile was surely as dazzling as ever. "It is a smile that illumines his face as a torch lights a place of darkness," wrote Ada Patterson, who interviewed him in his hotel room when he returned to New York in April.

"After the smile one notices the eyes of the actor," she continued. "They are brown and bright. They have a habit of smiling pleasantly when the lips are motionless. And once or twice when our chat drifted for a moment into deeper channels there was a transitory mist upon them which he quickly wiped away. They are larger and fuller eyes than we see often in the face of a man, and they are boyish eyes, the eyes of everlasting youth.

"All this one notices while the dignified, florid-faced man, of compact figure and broad, well-carried shoulders comes forward in greeting. When his deep-toned voice rumbles richly forth that greeting there is recognizable the fine distant flavor of a brogue. Twas the recognition of this remote brogue that set us speculating as to what national temperament is most distinctly dramatic. 'The Irish temperament is dramatic—yes,' said Mr. O'Neill. He settled comfortably into a corner of the divan in the hotel drawing room. He does everything deliberately, giving the impression of measured force and of a vast fund of unused vitality. 'It is always in the depths or on the heights, tremendously happy or hopelessly miserable. These extremes, of course, make for dramatic comprehension and intensity. But the ideal dramatic temperament is the Irish with a mingling of French. I personally am a great admirer of the French school of acting.' "

No wonder James O'Neill seemed invulnerable to his sons in the summer of 1908, as he strode busily about New London with his pal Tom Dorsey, looking after his real estate, attending to the opening of the "Monte Cristo" garage he had built down on Washington Street for $10,000, or rehearsing his company, including Jamie, in a new play *Abbé Bonaparte,* which he was going to open in Asbury Park on September 1 and then try out in St. Louis, Kansas City, and Omaha.

Abbé Bonaparte failed in a few weeks. James O'Neill could only go back to *Monte Cristo* or close his tour. He closed. For the first time in his long career as an actor, he faced a season with nothing to do. Besides, he had Jamie on his hands. Restlessly he strode about his rooms in the Hotel Lucerne.

At this moment, in walked Eugene with just about everything wrong with his life that a young man of twenty years could manage. First of all, the New York-Chicago Supply Company had gone bankrupt. That was the fault of the depression, not of Eugene. But the boy was entirely without the slightest wish to go into anything else. He simply presented himself to his parents to be taken care of, and he met all his father's advice about getting himself settled in life with sullen withdrawal or spiteful flippancy. The boy was developing almost as sharp a tongue as Jamie—mocking everything his father held sacred: the Church, Ireland, Shakespeare, anything that could get a rise out of the Old Man.

On top of this, Eugene had got into real trouble from playing "loose and fast with all the girls," as his friend Ed Keefe would describe it. Now this was serious. James O'Neill was a fairly tolerant man, but there was a limit to what he would stand for. Sternly, he accused Eugene. Whereupon Eugene went out and got himself the most flamboyant redheaded whore the streets offered, one who, as he would later phrase it, "looked more like a whore than twenty-five whores," and appeared with her that night in his father's box at the Broadway theater. That, for Eugene, was the perfect revenge—to flaunt a prostitute in the face of his family and let the Old Man (and Mama!) take it as best they could.

After that, there was no question of his staying with the family at the Hotel Lucerne. He moved in with Eddie Keefe, his good New London friend, and George Bellows. For a long time he was sunk in the guilt that had overwhelmed him almost at the moment of his triumph. Only gradually did he pull out of it a little, coming to a superficial reconciliation with his father and receiving the hurt forgiveness of his mother.

The Old Man wasn't going to let him starve, at any rate. He gave him an allowance of a dollar a day—a demonstration, Eugene felt, of the Old Man's real lack of feeling for him. As time went on, Eugene began to lift himself out of the blues. Ed Keefe was grand company, even though he, like everyone else, loved James O'Neill and found it hard to sympathize with Gene's rebellion.

Keefe was an artist, as was his roommate George Bellows, and they shared a studio at 1947 Broadway in the Lincoln Arcade across from the Sharkey Athletic Club. Eugene, Keefe, and Bellows went to the club to see the fights, enjoying hugely this otherwise forbidden form of entertainment. Then Eugene would watch Bellows at his easel, recreating in oil the strained muscles of the fighters as they closed on one another in the dim, smoky light at Sharkey's.

Eugene liked the fights. He also liked going to Mouquin's French Restaurant with Ed Keefe (Bellows was no drinker and rarely accompanied them). Mouquin's was a hangout for the whole "Ash Can" school of painters, Henri in particular. Ed and Gene became so attached to the place that they would go there, as they put it, to "watch the rats come in." That meant, simply, that they would outlast all the guests, when, literally, the rats *would* come in.

Eugene talked eagerly with Keefe and Bellows and with a friend from his Princeton days, Ted Ireland, whom Bellows and Keefe "let" stay at the studio, partly because he was an artist, but mostly because he was working and could pay the rent for all of them. In October, Alla Nazimova had put on a repertory of Ibsen—*The Doll's House, Hedda Gabler, The Master Builder;* Eugene had gone to see them all and he talked Ibsen all that year. "The populace think of Ibsen as very dreadful and deep," he would say. "He's deep, all right, and dreadful, like life itself, but he's also intensely human and understandable. I needed no professor to tell me that Ibsen as dramatist knew whereof he spoke. I found him for myself outside college grounds and hours. If I had met him inside I might still be a stranger to Ibsen."

He had discovered for himself, also, the philosopher Schopenhauer and was reading him with almost as much enthusiasm as he had felt when he first explored Nietzsche. He responded profoundly to the cosmic pessimism that explained his own insane follies, which had often seemed to originate in a mysterious force beyond his own individual will. He felt deeply the truth of Schopenhauer's vision of a great life-force working itself out pitilessly through the lives of individual men, tossing them about in a fever of living for no end other than life itself, so that life becomes a perpetual suffering endured for a hope that always proves abortive. He responded deeply to the vision of man as a creature kept in a perpetual state of senseless striving by the power of the will to live. Always Eugene would

agree with Schopenhauer's view of individual human life as the expression of a vast mysterious force beyond self, and Schopenhauer
would sometimes color his thinking and his writing, particularly in
plays like *Strange Interlude.*

Eugene talked enthusiastically of Schopenhauer to his roommates,
to Jimmy Byth, who was no longer with "the Governor," and to
Jamie, who was "at liberty" for a while. The Old Man had managed
to get Jamie a small part in the second company of *The Traveling
Salesman,* starting in January, 1909. This company was set up for
one-night stands in the real "hick burgs": Scranton, Hazelton, Dan-
ville, Bloomsburg, Williamsport, Oswego, Elmira, Corning, Hornell,
and so on. Jamie expected to develop an encyclopedic knowledge of
the bars in small-town America. Meanwhile, with the assistance of
Eugene, he enriched his already impressive knowledge of those in
New York.

But Eugene was beginning to find his association with creative
artists contagious. Bellows worked at his easel untiringly, and even
Ed Keefe—for all his roguish look with his dark hair flopping over
his forehead—worked hard. Eugene started writing poems—little
echoes of Wilde and Dowson and Kipling, but expressions of something in himself as well.

He was on easier terms now with the Old Man, who spent his
days at the Lambs Club and the Green Room Club, talked of writing
his autobiography, or found odd new investments for his money—
real estate, manufacturing firms in New York, even mining claims in
Central America. And when Eugene told his father that Keefe and
Bellows were longing to get out of town to paint some winter land-
scapes, James O'Neill suggested that they go out to the farm in New
Jersey, in Zion near Bound Brook. The place was pretty dilapidated,
of course; no one had lived there for years, but the keys were theirs
if they wanted them.

On January 18, 1909, Eugene, Bellows, and Keefe stood freezing
in the midst of their new home. There was only one bed to stay
warm in, so they matched for it. Keefe and Gene got the bed; Bellows lost. For him they found an old spring and put it on some
boxes. Gene sawed wood for the fire while Ed Keefe and George
Bellows went out into the biting cold to paint snowscapes, their

hands encumbered with mittens so they wouldn't stiffen from the cold. Sometimes Eugene would accompany them for a while, then strike off on long lonely walks over the hills; or he would saw more wood or curl up close to the fire and write poetry or read.

Evenings the three of them would sit around the fire until far into the night, arguing and talking about books and pictures and people. "The talk," George Bellows would later tell his wife, "was either very high or very low."

By the middle of February George Bellows had painted ten pictures and Keefe had two fine oils, but the three of them were beginning to suffer too much from the bitter cold, so they closed up the Zion farmhouse and returned to New York.

Here Eugene drifted unthinkingly into what was to explode into a major debacle, when, for the first time, his reckless search for experience would result not only in hurt to himself and his parents, but in irreparable injury to another person.

It all started with a double date. A friend named Frank Best asked Gene to make a foursome with his girl and a friend of hers, Kathleen Jenkins. After that, the four of them were constantly together. Frank Best was seriously courting his girl, and somehow everyone took it for granted that Eugene had the same feelings for Kathleen—everyone, that is, but Eugene, who was simply following his instincts as he had for the last three years. To Kathleen, he was a romantic figure—this handsome rebellious son of a famous man. She, too, was impatient with the conventional world of her parents. She admired his mockery. She trusted him, sensing—as most women would—the affectionate boy underneath his sardonic exterior. That was, perhaps, the most dangerous quality in him, for it was the most disarming.

Not that Eugene was consciously insincere. He had no idea of getting himself married, but he had no wicked designs either. He was simply doing what seemed most pleasant at the moment. And it was certainly pleasant to be with Kathleen Jenkins, to see her, to touch her.

All that summer he drifted, happily absorbed in the moment. The New London cottage was closed, for the Old Man spent the spring touring with the Lambs Club All Star Gambol as Brutus in a scene from *Julius Caesar*. Then Papa and Mama went out to St. Louis to put on *Virginius* and *Monte Cristo* at the Delmar Garden Summer Theatre in June and July. Finally, they ended the summer at Asbury Park, New Jersey, where the Green Room Club was holding its midsummer dress rehearsal. Papa was now prompter of the Green Room Club. He enjoyed chatting with George M. Cohan, Raymond Hitchcock, and the others, and presided genially, with Mama beside him, over the club's annual clambake at Avon. So Eugene saw little of his parents, stayed in New York with his roommates in the studio at 1947 Broadway, and drifted deeper and deeper into his affair with Kathleen Jenkins.

He didn't wake up to what he was doing until the damage was done, and he found himself trapped with no way to turn. The climax came in September. Everyone descended on him at once. His friends turned against him—Frank Best in particular—and told him he must marry Kathleen; it was unforgivable to treat an innocent young girl this way; besides, marriage would do him good, get him settled in life.

Then Kathleen's parents got wind of the whole thing and marched up to face Mama and Papa in their hotel rooms and demand that something be done. In a way, this brought Papa around almost to Eugene's side, for he got the idea that Kathleen Jenkins and her parents were simply out to hook a rich man's son, and much as he thought Eugene to blame, he thought maybe the girl was more than a bit to blame too, was simply a woman like Nettie Walsh, out for money. Then, too, Eugene was in such a state, his father couldn't be too harsh with him.

At the first realization of his disaster, Eugene's "mask of the Bad Boy Pan" crumbled and left him defenseless. He thought miserably of Kathleen Jenkins's trust in him—Mama and Papa were wrong about her—but he was suicidally terrified at the thought of marrying her. He realized that he didn't love her. The honorable, code-bound Eugene rose in him and scorched him for betraying innocence, but he shrank from the thought of a life bound hopelessly to a woman he didn't love.

Papa wanted to buy the girl off, but Eugene knew Kathleen didn't want that. He felt he had to go through with the marriage, and he did, on October 2, 1909, at Trinity Protestant Episcopal Church, Hoboken, with only Marc and Helen Lackley as witnesses. But that was as far as honor led him. He shrank from further contact with this girl, who was suddenly a stranger to him.

He turned to his parents for help, and, of course, Papa came through. Earl Stevens was out in San Francisco preparing for an expedition to Honduras to care for James O'Neill's mining properties there, and he would need an assistant. Eugene could leave immediately to join him; the excitement of the trip would pull him up out of his depression and, away from New York, he could come to grips with himself and decide what he wanted to do about this marriage of his. In Honduras he could probably find himself at last; Central America was wide open for an enterprising young man. Heartened, but still miserable and confused, Eugene agreed. A few days after his marriage, Eugene set out for Honduras and a new start. On his twenty-first birthday, October 16, 1909, he was steaming past the coast of Mexico. Behind him he left a pregnant wife.

CHAPTER FIFTEEN

Escape

Although Eugene had turned his back on the mess he had made in New York, he still suffered. Neither then nor later did he hide from himself the knowledge that he had behaved badly, nor did he try to excuse himself. Years later he would say of his son by Kathleen Jenkins, "When I survey his merits and think of the rotten mess of a life I was at his age [20] I have no fatherly superiority assumptions, believe me!"

Only one good thing had come out of this experience, the re-establishment of his bond with Mama and Papa. He had turned to them like a frightened child, and they had responded with all the protective warmth he had received in childhood. Yet, for all his sophistication, Eugene never fully understood what his father had done for him. He remained naïvely under the impression that Earl Stevens had really needed him and had hired him independently, for that was the way Papa had put the job to him. Only after several months had passed with no mention of a salary, did he write to Papa anxiously asking what Stevens intended to pay, and indignantly hoping that he wasn't working for "love." Even then it didn't occur to him that Papa had arranged the whole thing.

All James O'Neill's good friends, including Tyler, knew that he had acted fast to save his boy. Tyler's assistant, Toohey, would pick up a garbled version of the story from Tyler years later when Eugene had become famous, and would hand it on, further garbled, to Alexander Woollcott. Woollcott would then come out with the story that Eugene O'Neill had not run away to sea, but had been shanghaied by his father to get him out of the way of a scrape. At the time, Tyler, Connor, and, indeed, everyone but Eugene knew that his father had arranged a rescue.

Of course, Eugene did know that his father hoped that he would finally find himself on this trip, and, with renewed love, he tried to pull himself together and make good. He even intended to study Spanish on the boat to Honduras, but he was still too emotionally exhausted and decided he would study it "seriously" at the camp. He was full of good intentions, and in the first letter he wrote his parents on November 9, from Tegucigalpa, he tried to confirm all his father's hopes. He said he liked the country, liked the people, and thought that "there is every chance in the world for making good." He told Papa about the mining properties in Honduras he might pick up for a song, and soberly suggested they would make a good investment for the future.

But this letter, in its description of the hundred-mile journey by mule from Amapala to Tegucigalpa gave signs that Honduras was not the place where Eugene O'Neill was going to make good. He had jounced miserably on the back of his mule as it jogged along, sinking heavily into the muddy trail over the mountains. Long before the three-day mule trip was over, he was stiff and sore, and he could hardly move for two days afterward.

All along the way swarms of mosquitoes had whined about him, stinging viciously. Clouds of gnats had crawled into his nostrils and eyes. He had been bitten by flies in the native huts where they stopped, and ticks had burrowed under his skin, making nasty little sores. Always he would think of Honduras as a "hell" of insects. "I never knew there could be such a variety of creeping, crawling, flying, stinging things—some of them rank poison—in the world," he would say later. Every inch of his skin had been stung by something; he itched all over. Besides, he was appalled at the native huts, where the filth was beyond belief—children, dogs, pigs, chickens, all scrambling about on the dirt floor with swarms of flies buzzing everywhere.

Still, he liked Stevens and he admired Mrs. Stevens for her quiet endurance. He was amused by the "3-cent Western melo-drama" appearance everyone had, and which he quickly took on, becoming bronzed from the sun, cultivating a mustache, carrying a string of cartridges around his belt and over his shoulder, a .30-.30 Winchester in his hand, and a machete suspended from his middle.

By Christmas Day, when he was again able to write to his parents, he showed clearly that he wasn't going to "find himself" or "make good" in Honduras. The letter was subtly invested with the loneliness of the little boy he had been years ago, left behind at boarding school on Christmas Day. He hoped Mama and Papa were having a "Merry Christmas," but he wanted them to know that he was having a miserable one. He was wretchedly sick with fever and bilious from the greasy food: the leathery grease-soaked fried salt meat, the heavy tortillas, greasy fried rice. He was miserable from insect bites and his liking for the country and the people alternated with flashes of murderous hate. He decided that the natives were "the lowest, laziest, most ignorant bunch of brainless bipeds that ever polluted a land and retarded its future." Until fate exterminated these "human maggots" or the universe shook "these human lice from its sides," Honduras, he thought, would be nothing but "a Siberia of the tropics." Eugene would stay, he told his parents, until June, when the rainy season started and most Americans fled the malignant malarial fever. Only an American brought up in a stable could stay in Honduras, he thought, and no one was going to be fool enough to invest capital in the country as long as it went tumbling through its yearly revolutions. Eugene was miserably homesick—not for his years of wild independence in New York, but for the protective love of his parents. "I never realized how much home and

Father and Mother meant until I got so far away from them," he wrote.

A month and a half of bitter hardship—from the time they had left Tegucigalpa on November 11 until Christmas Day, 1909—had shattered Eugene's intentions to take hold of his life and make good in Honduras. They had stayed only a short while at the camp on the Upper Seale because Stevens found the gold there too fine for prospecting. They had then traveled muleback to the point where Stevens had worked the year before, where the gold was coarser. En route, they found a "Dago" who told them of gold in the Geneio River in country which was marked "inexplorada" on the map. So Eugene, Stevens, "the Dago," and two natives poled their way in a dugout for four days down the Patuca River, which flowed through the Mosquitia district. They camped at night on grounds alive with lizards (Eugene shot one), and usually, Eugene said, there was "a jaguar up on the hillside yowling you to sleep." When they reached the Geneio, they poled along it for five miles, and then tried to hack their way through the jungle to reach the upper part of the river. They realized at once that cutting through that solid jungle would take months. Their provisions wouldn't last. They couldn't go on, and Stevens said they couldn't prospect where they were, for the current was so swift it would have buried the gold too deep to get at.

So the whole exhausting trip had gone for nothing, and now they were back at Guahuiniquil preparing to make permanent camp on the Seale. The hardship had killed all the romance in the trip for Eugene. He looked forward miserably to June, when he could leave.

Actually he left long before June. His fever got worse. He wasn't any good to Stevens sick. So, miserably ill, with only a native guide to accompany him, he set out on muleback to Tegucigalpa. The trip took him ten days, and when he arrived there sick and exhausted, he found the only hotel full because the next day was a fiesta. He presented himself, shaking with malarial chills, at the American consulate for advice. The consul took one look at him, put him to bed, and called a doctor. He stayed in bed there three weeks, the consul supplementing the blankets on freezing nights in that high altitude with several faded American flags. "I looked just like George M. Cohan," said Eugene later.

As soon as he was well enough, he made the arduous trip to the coast over the mountains by muleback and took the first ship to San Francisco. It was March by the time he landed. He found, by checking his father's route, that he could join his parents in St. Louis, where on March 14 the *White Sister* would open at the Olympic. Papa was playing the role of Monsignore Saracinesca for his old friend Tyler. Eugene thought it quite a comedown for the Old Man to support such "actor-yokels" as William Farnum and Viola Allen. Privately, James O'Neill thought so, too, though he was outwardly the same charming, unpretentious gentleman as ever. "There is many a star who ought to be shovelling coal and many a staress who ought to be over a washtub," he declared.

Eugene had seen Papa open in the *White Sister* at Daly's in New York back in September, and hadn't thought the play would last. One critic called it very "gloomiferous," and said that it beat "a trip to the morgue all hollow." Eugene could see that the play was just a setup for emotional acting, with its conflict between love and religion in the heart of a nun, but Papa certainly was a natural for a Catholic priest.

Eugene enjoyed the first days of reunion with his parents. He was sorry Jamie wasn't with them. All Eugene had heard from Jamie was a scattering of postcards dropped along his one-night stands in *The Traveling Salesman.* But Eugene soon realized that he had returned to all the unresolved problems he had fled in the trip to Honduras. Papa was disappointed that he hadn't made good in Honduras and was after him at once to find some kind of work and get himself settled. After all, he was twenty-one; he had a wife in New York and soon would have a child, too. At the Old Man's urging, Eugene did a little work with the company as "assistant" to the manager—such skilled jobs as watching the gallery ticket-taker to see that he let no one in free.

Under the increased pressure from his father, Eugene's rebellion rose again, and a persistent undercurrent of anxiety mounted in him as the weeks brought him closer to the end of the tour, the question

of what next, and the birth of the child he had so carelessly be-gotten.

On April 11, 1910, less than a month after Eugene had rejoined his parents, the *White Sister* opened in Boston. One day Eugene wandered down to Mystic Wharf, and without fully grasping what he was doing, signed on a sailing ship bound for Buenos Aires. "It happened quite naturally—that voyage—as a consequence of what was really inside of me—what I really wanted, I suppose," he would say. "I struck up one day by the wharf in Boston with a bunch of sailors, mostly Norwegians and Swedes. I wanted to ship with some-body and they took me that afternoon to the captain. Signed up, and the next thing we were off."

CHAPTER SIXTEEN

At Sea

WHY had Eugene chosen a sailor's life "quite naturally"? He had been fascinated by ships ever since childhood, when he had sat on the rocks in New London and sketched the ships sailing up the Thames River into the harbor. Then, at college, he had discovered Joseph Conrad, particularly *The Nigger of the Narcissus*.

Eugene had at once seized upon Conrad's vision of human beings creating their own nobility against the backdrop of a vast and inscrutable mystery, symbolized by the immensities of sky and sea. Eugene had always felt that mystery. From Conrad, he learned to see in old-time sailors the best of human loyalty, courage, and strength. "They had been strong," wrote Conrad, "as those are strong who know neither doubts nor hopes. They had been impatient and enduring, turbulent and devoted, unruly and faithful. Well-meaning people had tried to represent these men as whining

over every mouthful of their food; as going about their work in fear
of their lives. But in truth they had been men who knew toil, privation, violence, debauchery—but knew not fear, and had no desire
of spite in their hearts. Men hard to manage, but easy to inspire;
voiceless men—but men enough to scorn in their hearts the sentimental voices that bewailed the hardness of their fate. It was a fate
unique and their own; the capacity to bear it appeared to them the
privilege of the chosen! Their generation lived inarticulate and
indispensable, without knowing the sweetness of affection or the
refuge of a home—and died free from the dark menace of a narrow
grave. They were the everlasting children of the mysterious sea."

Eugene kept this vision of the sailor for the rest of his life, and it
would impregnate every one of the sea plays he wrote. When Mary
Mullett asked him in 1922 why he had wanted to associate with
sailors, Eugene answered, "I guess it was because I liked them better than I did men of my own kind. They were sincere, loyal,
generous. You have heard people use the expression: 'He would
give away his shirt.' I've known men who actually did give away
their shirts [as had the men in *The Nigger of the Narcissus*]. I've
seen them give their own clothes to stowaways.

"I hated a life ruled by the conventions and traditions of society.
Sailors' lives, too, were ruled by conventions and traditions; but
they were of a sort I liked and that had a meaning which appealed
to me.

"You might think, for instance, that I would have rebelled at the
discipline aboard ship. But 'discipline' on a sailing vessel was not a
thing that was imposed on the crew by superior authority. It was
essentially voluntary. The motive behind it was loyalty to the ship!
Among seamen, at that time, this love of the ship was what really
controlled them."

Eugene went to sea among sailors whom he had already invested
with the inarticulate nobility of the crew of the *Narcissus*. He observed his fellow sailors with sympathetic fascination. "One of the
crew, a jovial Norwegian, was an interesting study," he would say
later. "He was constantly boasting that he had been in jail in every
seaport in the world of any importance. He said the worst one was
in India. But he was always saying when ashore, 'I know an old

boiler down by the docks we can crawl into.'" Eugene put the words, years later, into the mouth of Yank in *The Hairy Ape.*

Eugene went to sea prepared to love the forecastle and all within it, so, of course, he did. "You're musical," he remarked to Olin Downes years later. "Well, let me ask you: did you ever hear chanties sung on the sea? You never did? It's not surprising. There are even fewer sailing vessels now than there were ten short years ago when I pulled out for the open. They don't humor a privileged devil who has a fine voice and hell inside of him, as he chants that wonderful stuff and they pull to the rhythm of the song and the waves. Ah, but I wish you might hear that, and feel the roll of the ship, and I wish you might listen to the accordion going in the forecastle, through the soughing of the winds and the wash of the sea."

Eugene O'Neill felt a tremendous exhilaration as the *Charles Racine* left the shore behind. He took pencil and paper and expressed his feeling in a poem called "Free." The poem would later seem to be only an echo of Masefield and Kipling. But Eugene, writing on the moving deck of the *Charles Racine,* was putting into words not only his shame at his marriage ("I have had my dance with Folly, nor do I shirk the blame") and his inability to formulate a future for himself, but also his joyous feeling that somehow he was now "clean," free of the shambles he had made of his life.

> *Then it's ho! for the plunging deck of a bark, the*
> *hoarse song of the crew,*
> *With never a thought of those we left or what we are*
> *going to do;*
> *Nor heed the old ship's burning, but break the shackles*
> *of care*
> *And at last be free, on the open sea, with the trade wind*
> *in our hair.*

In *Long Day's Journey Into Night* he describes a moment of mystical ecstasy aboard the "Squarehead square rigger, bound for Buenos Aires": "I lay on the bowsprit, facing astern, with the water foaming into spume under me, the masts with every sail white in the moonlight, towering high above me. I became drunk with the beauty and singing rhythm of it, and for a moment I lost myself—actually lost my life. I was set free! I dissolved in the sea, became moonlight and the ship and the high dim-starred sky!"

Even the ordinary moments were beautiful to him. Although he had complained bitterly at the dried salt meat in Honduras, he now ate dried salt cod without a murmur, for through this hardship he partook of the high courage and mystical beauty of Conrad's sailors' life. In a poem he declared that the bad food, hard work, and small pay of a sailor's life were "part of the game and I loved it all."

When the ship unloaded its cargo of lumber at Buenos Aires in June, 1910, Eugene did not sign on again. Sixty-five days at sea had been enough. But he would always idealize that journey. Of his shipmates he would say, "They were fine fellows. I've never forgotten them, nor I hope, they me." The ship, too, he would keep track of for years afterward when it became the *Pass of Balmaha*. In 1915, when it had been captured and turned into a raider by the Germans, he clipped a picture of it from a newspaper and pasted it in a scrapbook.

He idealized the ship, but he couldn't stay on it. He wasn't starting a career when he signed on the *Charles Racine* at Mystic Wharf. He was as aimless as ever. "I didn't have any idea," he would say of that time. "My ambition, if you call it that, was to keep moving and do as many things as I could."

In Buenos Aires, "I just free-lanced along," he would say. "I had to do something to live, and I wanted to live." So he took a job with the Westinghouse Electric Company. "I wasn't doing much choosing," he admitted, "just grabbed whatever came along." Eugene said he was a draftsman. "Well, well, so you're a draftsman," the manager remarked satirically after the first day exposed how little Eugene remembered of his Princeton science courses. But he could trace plans neatly, so the manager kept him. "That job was probably my most dignified and best," he would say.

But Eugene, with his restless craving for experience, was soon disgusted with the monotony of Westinghouse. After six weeks he quit and wandered on to La Plata. When he ran out of money, he lied his way into a job with the Swift Meat Packing Company there by saying that he wanted to learn the packing business from the bottom up. They put him into a warehouse to sort raw hides in the midst of a "stink" he never forgot. Years later he told Hamilton Basso how that stench got into "his clothes, his mouth, his eyes, his ears, his nose, his hair." One week of it, and Eugene was already thinking of quitting, but he didn't have to. The warehouse burned down. "I didn't do it," he remarked sardonically, "but it was a good idea."

He hadn't exactly enjoyed that summer in Buenos Aires, but he still didn't want to go back to New York, where his problems had multiplied. In May, 1910, the girl he had married gave birth to a son and named him Eugene Gladstone O'Neill, Jr. It was an affirmation of love—and an appeal. Papa and Mama had seen the baby and talked of it, too, for the news got into the *Dramatic Mirror* by May 28, under "Born": "A son to Mr. and Mrs. Eugene O'Neill, and grandson to James O'Neill, in New York, May 4." They still hoped that Eugene would return and take up his responsibilities, but James O'Neill began to wonder why Kathleen should still want anything to do with her husband.

In Buenos Aires Eugene found another job to keep himself alive— and away. The Singer Sewing Machine Company hired him as an office worker. "Do you know how many models Singer makes?" the office manager asked him. "Fifty?" he guessed. "Five hundred and fifty!" the manager exclaimed. "You'll have to learn how to take each one apart and put it together again."

Meanwhile, Eugene had found another lost soul to share his life. Later, when he told Louis Kalonyme about his friend, he called him "A." "When A. left a cafe most of its liquor went along with him," Eugene said. "He was very young, about 25 at the most, and extraordinarily handsome. Blond, almost too beautiful, he was, in appearance, very like Oscar Wilde's description of Dorian Gray. Even his name was as flowery.

"He was the younger son of a traditionally noble British family. He had been through the English public schools, had acquired a university accent, and, finally down in London for good, became one of its lordly young men. He became, for example, an officer in a crack British regiment and joined the usual clubs.

"Then suddenly he messed up his life—pretty conspicuously.

Though he didn't have to leave England, he couldn't face life there, couldn't bear the thought of daily reminders of what he'd lost—a lady—and decided to try South America."

Here was a history of self-destruction to parallel his own. Eugene and his friend shared a room. They also shared the search for oblivion at the "Sailor's Opera," a saloon where they had met in the din of voices and of ragtime from a mechanical piano. "It sure was a madhouse," Eugene would say. "But somehow a regular program was in progress. Every one present was expected to contribute something. If your voice cracked your head usually did, too. Some old sailor might get up and unroll a yarn, another might do a dance, or there would be a heated discussion between, say, Yankee and British sailors as to the respective prowess of their ships. And, if nothing else promised, 'a bit of a harmless fight' usually could be depended upon as the inevitable star feature to round out the evening's entertainment."

Sometimes, seeking sensation, the two of them went to the moving pictures in the wide-open suburb of Barracas. "Those moving pictures in Barracas," Eugene would later recall, "were mighty rough stuff. Nothin' was left to the imagination. Every form of perversity was enacted, and, of course, sailors flocked to them." Then, remembering his Conradian view of sailors, he would add, "But, save for the usual exceptions, they were not vicious men. They were in the main honest, good-natured, unheroically courageous men trying to pass the time pleasantly."

And what was Eugene? Certainly a very confused young man. As usual, he was working only halfheartedly at his job. "The Singer people," he told Mary Mullett, "made about five hundred and seventy-five different types of sewing machines at that time, and I was supposed to learn every detail of every one of them. I got about as far as Number Ten, I guess, before they gave me up as hopeless. I had spent a good deal of my time down on the waterfront when I should have been studying bobbins and needles. Now I went there again, like a boy let out of school."

As his money ran out, hanging around the Paseo Colon with its gorgeous view of the harbor became less of a lark. His appearance degenerated, and the "vigilantes" began to eye him suspiciously.

"I landed in Buenos Aires a gentleman so-called," he would say, "and wound up a bum on the docks."

"On the beach," sailors called this state of homeless destitution. Eugene sank so low he actually thought of becoming a criminal. "I was then twenty-two years old," he told Hamilton Basso later, "and a real down-and-outer—sleeping on park benches, hanging around waterfront dives, and absolutely alone. I knew a fellow who used to work on a railroad down there and who had given up his job. One day, he suggested that we hold up one of those places where foreign money is exchanged. Well, I have to admit I gave the matter serious consideration. I finally decided not to do it, but since you aren't given to taking a very moral view of things when you are sleeping on park benches and haven't a dime to your name, I decided what I did because I felt that we were almost certain to be caught. A few nights later, the fellow who had propositioned me stuck the place up with somebody he'd got to take my place, and he *was* caught. He was sent to prison and, for all I know, he died there."

"Nearly everybody's life is determined to a large extent by just such accidents as these," Eugene would observe. But it was no accident that he refused. He was not desperate enough to turn bandit. He could always pick up an odd job on the docks, loading or unloading ships, and the weather was pleasantly warm. But the fact that he had listened to the suggestion seriously gave him a sharpened sense of the depths he had reached. He was lonely, wretched, lost.

Pierre Loving writes of a poet who met Eugene O'Neill in those days. The poet had just come into Buenos Aires from the pampas, and he strolled into a waterfront tavern. "The pot-bellied and exaggeratedly jovial Hollander who ran the place," the poet told Loving, "apparently recognizing a Britisher, welcomed me with a broad, 'How are you, matey?' Grateful to find myself back out of the wilds, I replied upon some wilful impulse with a line of verse from a contemporary poet. The quotation was apt. I've forgotten it now . . . but I had scarcely finished it when—imagine my amazement—a voice directly behind me, with a civilized stave in it, took it up and continued it. I slewed around and perceived a dark-haired young fellow, strong-shouldered, tanned and with a black smudge of a mustache circumflexing a fine sensitive mouth. He was clad in something that resembled a compromise between shore and sea-going clothes.

" 'You're from the States, aren't you?' I asked.

" 'Yes,' he replied with what seemed a nostalgic grin.

" 'A sailor?'

" 'Ages ago I was one, or so it seems. I've been ashore here about six months.'

"I was quite beside myself. Taking a seat opposite him, I said: 'Can you quote real poetry or . . . do you write it yourself? I've been aching to talk to someone human for weeks on end.'

" 'You haven't been any worse off than I,' he returned. 'For months I've been feeling suicidal for lack of real talk.'

"After this introduction we picked out a table farthest removed from the tin-canny piano and talked. How we talked! It was seven in the morning when we rose to leave the place. In the course of the conversation my new-found friend had said his name was O'Neill—Eugene O'Neill—and that his home was in New York."

Eugene was not exaggerating when he spoke of "feeling suicidal." He had fled New York, only to find that his guilt and his inability to take hold of life had followed him to Buenos Aires. He had achieved nothing but his own destitution. Now he fled again. At the docks he found a ship making for Portuguese East Africa, a cattle steamer loaded with mules, and signed on. When Eugene landed at Durban, he found he would need $100 to enter Africa, and so he was forced to return to Buenos Aires.

From there he had no place to go but home, and so he signed on as an ordinary seaman on a British tramp steamer bound for New York by way of Trinidad. None of the mystical beauty of Conrad's *Narcissus* invested this ship or the work of chipping rust from its decks. The food was so bad that Eugene had to subsist on marmalade and hardtack; nothing else was edible. But he was proud of his endurance. Years later, when someone suggested that he must have starved, Eugene cried, "Starve? No, never felt better in my life; weighed a hundred and sixty-five."

He became "quite good friends" with one of his fellow seamen, a

Norwegian A.B. who had been at sea twenty years without going home once. "He was a bred-in-the-bone child of the sea if there ever was one," Eugene wrote of him in a letter to the New York *Times* in 1920. "With his feet on the plunging deck he was planted like a natural growth in what was 'good clean earth' to him. If ever a man was in perfect harmony with his environment, a real part of it, this Norwegian was.

"Yet he cursed the sea and the life it had led him—affectionately. He loved to hold forth on what a fool he had been to leave the farm. There was the life for you, he used to tell the grumblers all in the fo'c'stle. A man on his own farm was his own boss. He didn't have to eat rotten grub, and battle bedbugs, and risk his life in storms on a rotten old 'limejuice' tramp.

"No, Sir, a man on his farm could get drunk every Saturday night and stay drunk all day Sunday if he wanted to! (At this point, the fo'c'stle to a man became converted to agriculture.) Then, too, a man on a farm could get married and have kids.

"Finally, the Norwegian, having got rid of his farm inhibition for the time being, would grin resignedly, and take up his self-appointed burden of making a rope mat for some 'gel' in Barracas he had promised it to the next trip down."

So Eugene landed where he had started. He was proud of the image he had of himself as a rough sailor, proud, curiously, even of the other image of the destitute "bum on the docks"—but he was still as lost, confused, and miserable as he had been when he set out. He was strangely "sick and old," as he would confess later, sick and old in his whole feeling toward life. He had been at sea figuratively as well as literally, at sea in a ship without rudder or compass or knowledge of what shore to set out for. He would continue to be ever more nightmarishly at sea in the months to come, until finally he would long to sink into the sea, to lose himself permanently.

CHAPTER SEVENTEEN

"Bottom of the Sea Rathskeller"

W HERE was he to go? What was he to do? Only a few days with his family filled him with resentful bitterness. His father was a walking accusation, his mother a silent reproach. The Old Man respected his having gone to sea; it was certainly more than Jamie had ever done for himself. But it was no great triumph for a young man with every advantage in life to end up a common sailor. Then there was the matter of the girl he had married and his child. What was he going to do about them? Eugene didn't know. The more powerfully he felt his father's disappointment in him, the more bitter against the Old Man he became.

Obviously, he couldn't stay with his family. James O'Neill, at his wit's end, arranged with Tyler to pay Eugene an allowance once a week, not more than ten dollars, and left him on his own. Eugene took the allowance with resentment at its modesty, and covered his dependency by thinking flippantly that since parents "bear" you and "bore" you, they might as well "board" you.

It was, of course, a delight to see Jamie. "What, ho!" he would call out cheerfully at sight of Gene, and the two of them would go off to get "blotto" together, sharing their bitterness against the Old Man and a need for the reinforcement of alcohol. When they ran out of money, Jamie showed his talent for obtaining credit at obscure cafés like the one under the Potter building. Or was it the Parker building? Eugene could never remember.

Jamie had toured two-and-a-half years with the road company of *The Traveling Salesman,* long enough for people to tease him about sharing his father's one-part fate. But he had never shared his father's fame. Toward the end, he had been lucky to keep the small role he had, considering how often he wavered alcoholically onto the stage. Jamie was "at liberty" now, but the Old Man was going to take him on again in his own company for a vaudeville tour.

Jimmy Byth was overjoyed to see Gene, too; beaming affectionately at him, and hiding—under a little act of briskly planning what he was going to do "tomorrow"—the hopeless impoverishment of his today. Jimmy had gone from bad to worse. His last respectable job after "the Governor" had been with Paine's Fireworks, but he had drunk his way out of that, and now he was living on little odd jobs at theatrical booking agencies. He looked "sick and old," for all his prim neatness of dress and his cheerful plans for "tomorrow."

Eugene found him a comfortable counterpart to his own sick and old soul, so he and Jimmy shared a musty, airless, roach-ridden "cell" above Jimmy the Priest's saloon on Fulton Street opposite the Washington Market. "Jimmy the Priest's certainly was a hell-hole," Gene would say. "It was awful. The house was almost coming down and the principal housewreckers were vermin." Almost with pride, he would say, "One couldn't go any lower. Gorky's Night's Lodging was an ice cream parlor in comparison." It was a refuge for broken-down telegraphers, seamen out of a job, and "lungers" who spat blood into the stove in the back room. Eugene and Jimmy shared a room barely large enough for the two beds and the rickety table that held Jimmy's dilapidated typewriter and the oil lamp, which, when they remembered to get oil for it, was the only source of light in the room other than the dingy little window looking out on a fire escape where stood an unwashed milk bottle. In the hall was a grimy sink, where everyone on the floor could wash (an infrequent practice) or get water. Through the thin walls came the coughs of the lungers and the snores of inebriates.

The back room was the social center of Jimmy the Priest's, and there the roomers congregated—in the winter as close as they could get to the stove. Here Major Adams, the remains of a British army officer long ago cashiered, sported his white military mustache. With his bright blue eyes shining in his red face, he would enthusiastically display the latest moldy secondhand volumes of obscure verse or sermons that he had picked up in his wanderings during the day. There the telegraphers gathered, including Eugene's next-door neighbor, who drank and coughed, and insisted, when some boor mentioned consumption, that he only had "bloody bronchitis."

The bar in front was livelier. There the transients gathered— sailors just released from ships and workmen from the docks—and an uproar of voices, singing, and laughter sounded all night long. There Jimmy the Priest himself presided. "With his pale, thin, clean-shaven face, mild blue eyes and white hair, a cassock would seem more suited to him than the apron he wears." So Eugene would later describe him in *Anna Christie.* "Neither his voice nor his general manner dispel this illusion which has made him a personage of the water front. They are soft and bland. But beneath his mildness one senses the man behind the mask—cynical, callous, hard as nails." In the bar "nickel-a-shot" whiskey was dispensed from a row of half-barrels, and the swinging doors opened and shut all night long on a procession of violent, noisy men, coming from nowhere, going nowhere, trying to make the present tolerable.

Why did Eugene O'Neill stay there? Years later, when someone suggested that he was seeking color, he was indignant. "Hell, no!" he exclaimed. "I was flat. The room rent at Jimmy's was $3 a month." Again and again, in later years, he would insist, "I was absolutely down, financially, those days. . . . " Why was he down? What of the weekly allowance from his father?

Actually, Eugene was "flat" by choice. As soon as he got his allowance, he would begin drinking, treating everyone at Jimmy's, including strangers. Then he would go from bar to bar on a "booze bust" that might last two full days before he returned, sick, shaken, and broke, to Jimmy the Priest's, to cadge drinks and live off the free lunch, supplemented by little windfalls of French bread and Italian cheese, until his next allowance came and he could blow it in as recklessly as he had the one before. Eugene was "flat" because he wanted to show his contempt for the "puny" amount his father gave him.

Occasionally, Eugene earned a little money on the waterfront. "There as at Buenos Aires," he would say later, "I picked up an occasional job aboard a vessel that was loading or unloading. The work was mostly cleaning ship: painting, washing the decks, and so on." "I washed enough deck area," he would add, "to cover a good-sized town."

When the hot weather came in July, he got together enough strength to sign on for one more sea voyage. On July 17, when the American Lines S.S. *New York* pulled out for Southampton, he was aboard for a salary of $25 a week, and when the *New York* was held up for repairs in Southampton, he transferred with several other members of the crew to the S.S. *Philadelphia* for the trip back to New York. When he was paid off on the docks on August 26, 1911, he had made his last trip to sea.

"An ugly, tedious job, and no place for a man who wanted to call his soul his own. I did not love it," Eugene said of this trip. "This was a steamer, you know, and what we did mainly was to swab decks and shift baggage and mail." He found as much "sea glamour" working on a passenger steamship, he told Mary Mullett, "as there would have been working in a summer hotel!"

But that last trip to sea left him with three things he valued: a navy-blue jersey pull-on sweater with "American Lines" printed on it in white letters, an able seaman's certificate, and the friendship of a very tough Irishman named Driscoll. He valued all three for the same reason; they were props for a drama he was acting out in which the central character was Eugene O'Neill, virile man of the sea. He wore the blue jersey long after that trip, and he kept a picture of himself, darkly handsome in that jersey, which hung on his wall during the later part of his life. He kept the able seaman's certificate too, pointing out with a pride he never took in Pulitzer Prizes that the term *able seaman* "means you can box the compass and do several other things which the ordinary seaman cannot."

He chummed with Driscoll for the remainder of his stay at Jimmy the Priest's, and used him, long afterward, in his sea plays. Driscoll was a Liverpool Irishman. "It seems that years ago some Irish families settled in Liverpool," Eugene explained. "Most of them followed the sea, and they were a hard lot. To sailors all over the world, a 'Liverpool Irishman' is the synonym for a tough customer." Driscoll was certainly tough. "He was a giant of a man, and absurdly strong," Eugene said of him. "He thought a whole lot of himself, was a determined individualist. He was very proud of his strength, his capacity for gruelling work. It seemed to give him mental poise to be able to dominate the stokehole, do more work than any of his mates."

Eugene had not met Driscoll on the *Philadelphia,* for Driscoll was not on board then, though he signed on as a trimmer or fireman on several voyages after that one, as the ship's records show. But even if he had been aboard, Eugene, the deck hand, would never have met him. "There is a class distinction even amongst the groups that make up the crew of an ocean liner," Eugene would point out. "But in this case, one group does not regard another as superior to it. Each has a healthy contempt for the others." In his short story "Tomorrow," Eugene indicates that he met Driscoll during a "chance adventure" in Southampton, and that seems likely, though he told Mary Mullett that he just "happened to scrape an acquaintance with" him at Jimmy the Priest's.

"The voyage after I quit going to sea," Eugene would recall, "Driscoll shipped on as usual. I stayed behind at 'Jimmy the Priest's.' . . . When the ship returned to New York Driscoll was the first to swing the saloon doors open and bellow for a drink. We could usually calculate the time of the ship's docking from the moment of Driscoll's appearance." Driscoll would bellow enthusiastically, "Gene, God blarst you for a stinkin' swine, how are ye?" and thump him on the back. Then would begin an orgy of drinking and singing of "Whiskey, Johnny" as they moved from bar to bar.

Driscoll would keep pulling off his coat to fight someone, saying he just wanted to "have a bit av fun wid him."

Other times they would wander down to the Battery together, find a bench, and watch the ships moving in and out of the harbor, exchanging stories or simply drowsing in the sun. Gene was always ready to use his allowance for a blowout with Driscoll, and Driscoll would send his ship's pay down the drain for a "bust" with Gene.

In Driscoll's company Eugene could see his drinking as a participation in the boisterous, lusty, but never mean life of the Conrad sailor. Actually, his drinking was taking on a desperate quality. His will was paralyzed. He was hounded by tensions that could be released only by frantic drinking bouts that left him exhausted, shaken, miserable, and again building the tensions and self-loathing that could be released only by another orgy of frenzied drinking.

Why, later, would he look back on those days at Jimmy the Priest's with such pride and pleasure? Why would he talk endlessly of his "sailor" days? His third wife, Carlotta Monterey, would say that his "pride seemed to be in those days." What had he accomplished to make him proud? His few trips to sea had left him with no desire to sign on another ship. At Jimmy the Priest's he found only soul sickness and drunken oblivion.

Yet he found some strange satisfaction in it all. These were the days of his final rebellion, when the "devil of hate" born in the turmoil of his adolescence had carried him as far as he could get from the obedient, code-bound "Mama's baby, Papa's pet" he had been in his childhood. He could not take pride in the Honduras episode, for that was an attempt to "make good" as his father wished. But the trip to Buenos Aires had been his own gesture of independence, and everything since then had been a defiance of his father's world.

So he drifted on at Jimmy the Priest's, but he was not entirely cut off from the habits of his former life. He was still reading, still walking, still going to the theater. When he collected his allowance from Tyler, he picked up free tickets for the Abbey Players, whom Tyler had imported for a long run at the Maxine Elliott Theatre beginning on November 20, 1911. He found these plays a revelation of what a truly poetic drama might be, a proof that the artificialities of the "well-made play" were unnecessary, that a one-act play needed no more plot than would disclose the mysterious beauty of a moment of life. He was fascinated by Yeats's *Cathleen ni Houli-han;* by Synge's *Riders to the Sea, The Well of the Saints, The Shadow of the Glen,* and *The Playboy of the Western World;* by Lady Gregory's *The Workhouse Ward, The Rising of the Moon, The Gaol Gate, Hyacinth Halvey, The Jackdaw, The Image,* and *Spreading the News.*

"You will understand why I want to go [to] Ireland if I tell you that I first saw the possibilities for dramatic realism when I witnessed a performance of the Irish players in New York," he later told Charles Merrill. "It was seeing the Irish players for the first time that gave me a glimpse of my opportunity. The first year that they came over here I went to see everything they did." Once he started writing plays, his memories of the Abbey Players gave him the courage to break with moth-eaten theatrical conventions. At the time, of course, he seemed only to be amusing himself aimlessly.

More and more, he was sinking into complete immobility and depression at Jimmy the Priest's. Sometimes Jimmy Byth tried to rouse him, saying he had only to pull himself together and his father would do anything for him, make it possible for him to complete his education, or set him up in business. But usually Jimmy Byth was too busy drowning his own self-awareness to prod Eugene's into life. Less and less frequently was Jimmy getting hold of the few dollars that, among other things, allowed him to go around to "the Chink's" and exchange his dirty shirt and collar for clean ones—he never had enough money to get all of his laundry out at once. Less and less firmly could he talk of "tomorrow."

He did pull himself together for a while, pitifully prim in his dark suit and carefully powdered shave, but Eugene at the time was on one of his "busts" and had lost track of him. When he saw Jimmy again, he had sunk back into drink. He had lost his latest job. "Nothing here," he said, forlornly tapping his forehead. Then he went up alone to his and Gene's room. Later everyone remembered hearing a heavy thud. But it was some time before he was found dead outside on the sidewalk.

Jimmy's suicide shoved Eugene further into his own life sickness —and at times appealed to him as a form of oblivion more permanent than alcohol. But he stumbled on with his own life. He shared his room now with Chris Christopherson. "He had sailed the sea until he was sick of the mention of it," Eugene would say of Chris later. "But it was the only work he knew. At the time he was my roommate he was out of work, wouldn't go to sea, and spent the time guzzling whiskey and razzing the sea."

It is hard to say how long Eugene would have drifted along at Jimmy the Priest's, depressed and emotionally paralyzed, had not something come to stir his self-loathing past bearing. But something did happen. Kathleen had kept her faith in him through the birth of her baby; but when that silent appeal in the baby's name, "Eugene Gladstone O'Neill, Jr.," was ignored, she gave up all hope of a future with Eugene O'Neill and set about getting a divorce.

Edward Ireland undertook to arrange the details between the two. There was only one ground for divorce in New York—adultery. Gene had fulfilled these grounds many times over, but there had to be proof a court would accept, sworn witnesses. And providing that proof was an ugly business.

On December 29, 1911, Eugene, who had set the date, went to Ted Ireland's apartment at 126 West 104th Street, and Ireland took him down to the Campus Restaurant at 104th Street and Columbus Avenue, where the witnesses were waiting—James C. Warren, the attorney who had been meeting with Eugene on and off since December 10, to arrange the thing; Edward Mullen, Frank Archibold, and for a while, a friend of Archibold's named Reel. Ireland left the party after a few drinks; Eugene and the others went on to the Garden Restaurant at Fiftieth Street and Broadway, where they had more drinks. After that they had drinks at a few more places along Forty-fifth Street, and finally arrived, by what seemed natural stages, at a house of prostitution at 140 West Forty-fifth Street.

Eugene had been with prostitutes many times, but now he was filled with horror. Degradation before witnesses appalled him. Always the prostitute had symbolized for him the destruction of love, and now the symbol became unendurably real. He might have been the husband of a fine girl, living like Papa and Mama in affectionate companionship, but he had destroyed that possibility, and now the spectacle of Eugene O'Neill in bed with a parlor house pig—to be witnessed and sworn to by Warren, Mullen, and Archibold—seemed to epitomize his whole life.

When he left the place, he was sick with self-loathing, and in the days that followed his sickness grew. He brooded on the senseless waste his life had been. He kept thinking of the scene with the prostitute and of Jimmy Byth's plunge from the fire escape. The image of death-peace-annihilation became increasingly alluring.

Finally, he acted. He went out and bought veronal tablets, and in the same grimy room from which the last cough of the lunger next door had been heard before he was carried off to the morgue, in the same grimy room from which Jimmy Byth had hurled himself to the sidewalk, Eugene swallowed all of the tablets in the bottle, lay down, and sank into oblivion.

CHAPTER EIGHTEEN

Afterlife

BUT he didn't die. Years later, when he finally was able to talk about this sordid episode to a few friends, he talked about it as farce. Both George Jean Nathan and Agnes Boulton, who heard the story from him, give slapstick accounts of it.

According to Nathan, Jimmy Byth's suicide and "misfortunes in an encounter with Cupid" caused Eugene to take an "overdose of veronal." When, at two in the afternoon, the hour for "whiskey breakfast," Eugene "failed to stir, failed even to respond to the brothers' nudges, pokes and peremptory kicks," they rushed him off to Bellevue in an ambulance. Three hours later, when Eugene came to, "with a whoop of joy the brothers put on their hats and moved mysteriously toward the door." They returned four hours later "magnificently drunk," having gotten fifty dollars from James O'Neill. " 'You dirty bums!' groaned O'Neill, with what vocal strength he could muster. 'How much you got left?' Thirty-two dollars, they reluctantly informed him. 'All right, divide!' he insisted. And with his sixteen dollars safe in hand, he rolled over, grinned satisfiedly, and went happily and peacefully to sleep."

Agnes Boulton, in an even more farcical account, says that Eugene's pals got so gloriously drunk while taking him to Bellevue in a taxicab that the driver brought them to the alcoholic ward, where, by an understandable error, all of them were "taken away protesting incoherently" while an intern remarked politely to Eugene, the only sober one, "Tough job you had!" Agnes Boulton turns the fifty dollars from Eugene's father into a check for "twenty-five" received in the mail, and she resurrects "Jimmy Tomorrow" for her story. Both her account and Nathan's are obviously fictionalized, but both show that Eugene himself told the story as comedy. Certainly he was laughing over it by 1919, when he wrote his comedy of suicide, *Exorcism*, in which the hero is saved by two thoroughly drunken friends who revive him in the nick of time.

Eugene was not taken to Bellevue, for the hospital has no record of receiving him. But he did try to kill himself, and he did wake up with the problem of what to do now with his life. He had followed the path of rebellion to the end. He had turned his back on love, on his parents and all they valued, and the road had led him steadily toward one destination: death. But he had escaped death, and now he fled back, back to love, back to Mama and Papa—literally as well as figuratively, because he took a train to New Orleans, where his parents were.

Later, he would deliberately try to hide the story of his flight to his parents in New Orleans. He told Mary Mullett that he just happened to wake up one morning aboard a train with a ticket to New Orleans which he didn't recall having bought, and that just "by chance" his father arrived there at the same time. He told Kyle Crichton that he had run up "five bucks" to "a thousand" playing faro and then went off to New Orleans to spend it in "two months drinking champagne and eating oysters," at which point his father "arrived in town." He told Tom Prideaux that after treating his friends to a "champagne party at the old Astor bar," he found himself on a train for New Orleans. Someone had suggested he go there, he said, and he added, "After I'd had a quart and a half of bourbon I could walk straight and talk rationally, but my brain was nuts. If anybody suggested that I climb the Woolworth Building, I'd be tickled to death to do it."

Eugene O'Neill was usually straightforward, but he was always ready to throw as much dust as possible into the eyes of a reporter threatening his real privacy. Actually, he had known that his father was opening at the Orpheum in New Orleans at the end of January, 1912.

Eugene had seen his family during the two months they spent in New York after Papa had returned from his first try at vaudeville in October, when he had toured the Middle West for the Keith circuit in a tabloid *Monte Cristo*. Papa was deeply discouraged. In Cincinnati he astonished a reporter from the *Times Star* who had known him for years by entering his dressing room sighing heavily and wondering "whether it all pays." He had been down to Sycamore Street to look at the old National Theater where he had got his start. For years it had been used as a tobacco warehouse. "I suppose I stood down there an hour," he told the reporter. "I was wondering where, had I not gone on the stage, I would be now; whether I would have been more, or less, successful; whether I would be here at all; whether I would be more happy or less happy. You can't help such thoughts, you know, at this time of life."

"Then his attitude changed," the reporter noted. "The normal cheerfulness of his nature got the upper hand. He plunged with a vim into the work of dressing for 'Monte Cristo,' describing the various processes and telling how methods had changed. Soon the door opened and a powerfully built man with keen eyes and a direct manner stepped in. 'My son, James O'Neill, Jr.,' said the veteran actor. The newcomer was a man of few words. He began peeling off his coat in order to don his costume. James O'Neill looked him over approvingly. Someone cracked a joke. Mr. O'Neill changed his 'ho, hum' to 'ha, ha,' and that sounded much more natural."

For a long time, now, Jamie had simply stopped talking in the presence of his father. The reporter thought him "a man of few words." Friends, like Tom Dorsey, Jr., realized that he "never wanted to get involved with the Old Man." Eugene knew it, too. He had heard Jamie's point of view when the family came back to New York.

Two months later, Eugene had seen Jamie off when the family left for Memphis, where Papa's Orpheum tour began. Of course, he knew his father's route. He went to New Orleans to find his family. They were glad to have him back, too. Shocked, they listened to the story of his attempt at suicide. But that disaster seemed to have brought him to his senses. For the first time in years, he was ready to accept his father's advice that he take hold of his life and do something with it. He was even willing to begin working at once, by filling out the small roles of the gaoler and the gendarme in *Monte Cristo*.

Jamie and he celebrated Eugene's return to life in a series of mad bacchanals, a final orgy of booze and what Eugene ironically called "free-not-always-love." He and Jamie would always have wild recollections of this period: of the time Eugene returned, after a night with a blonde, to the hotel where the family were staying and, irritated by the way people stared at him in the lobby, learned with a shock, on reaching his room, that he had left his trousers behind; or of the time Jamie rigged up a contraption outside their hotel window to simulate rain so that two girls in their room wouldn't leave.

At the theater, Eugene looked over the acrobats, the trained animals, and the dancers who shared the program with his father. Both he and Jamie were amused at the Old Man's horror of the "art" he was billed with. "I wonder just how long the public will tolerate and endure the fearful dances which seem to pervade our every amusement," James O'Neill said. "There is nothing graceful, nothing refining, nothing inspiring about these wriggles and trots and hugs—indeed, they do away with every semblance of art and poetry and leave one flat against the stark materialities." He was bitter about the chopped-up version of *Monte Cristo* he had to perform, too.

"That cut-down version was wonderful," Eugene would later say. "Characters came on that didn't seem to belong there and did things that made no sense and said things that sounded insane. The Old Man had been playing Cristo so long he had almost forgotten it, so he ad-libbed and improvised and never gave anybody a cue. You knew when your turn came when he stopped talking."

At the same time Eugene found it a great strain to pretend that he was only "pretending" to be an actor. "I was scared stiff on the stage, and was a very poor actor," he would later confess. "I'd never been able to keep the job as long as I did if it had not been for my father."

Although critics thought James O'Neill's support "incompetent," they still thought he turned out a magnificent performance. But one month of the vaudeville *Monte Cristo* was all he could stand. When they reached Ogden, Utah, in the middle of February, 1912, he announced that he was canceling the remainder of his tour. He still had eighteen weeks contracted for at $1,250 per week, but he didn't want the money. He found acting in this degraded version of the play that had consumed his life far too painful. He preferred not acting at all.

So Eugene's acting career lasted only a little more than three weeks. Snow held the family in Denver till the middle of March, when at last they were able to leave for New York. Early in the spring they were all back at 325 Pequot Avenue, New London.

That was not quite the end of *Monte Cristo*. Curiously, the play died in the same way that the legitimate theater died in America. First it dwindled into vaudeville. Then it was absorbed into moving pictures.

Adolph Zukor and Daniel Frohman of Famous Players had asked James O'Neill to do a long film of *Monte Cristo*, hoping to give moving pictures some of the prestige of the stage. The film would be released at a grand opening with all the great people of the theater there to do it honor. So that spring James O'Neill climbed the stairs of the old armory building on West Twenty-sixth Street to give, in fragments, his last performance of *Monte Cristo*. "In less than two weeks from the first 'shot' to the last cutting, Porter filmed a four-reel version of *Monte Cristo*," Will Irwin would later report.

Then, at the end of July—just as Zukor and Frohman were transforming *Monte Cristo* into positive prints—a rival film company, Selig Polyscope, announced that they were ready to release a three-reel version of *Monte Cristo*. (Ironically, they would do so on October 14, 1912, James O'Neill's birthday.) Quickly, Frohman and Zukor decided to substitute *The Prisoner of Zenda* with James

Hackett for *Monte Cristo* at their grand opening. So the last of *Monte Cristo* for James O'Neill was an anticlimactic entrance into films in the wake of another version and then a series of lawsuits. For the next few years, James O'Neill fought Selig Polyscope in the courts over the rights to the Fechter version of *Monte Cristo*.

From a great spiritual distance, Eugene watched *Monte Cristo* sputter out. He himself wanted only rest, a chance to recover from his attempted suicide and the orgy that he and Jamie had held to celebrate his resurrection. Now he spent hours stretched out in the pine-paneled living room reading Zola—*Germinal, L'Assommoir, La Terre*. He was profoundly impressed by Zola's vision of the large biological, economic, and hereditary forces that sweep individuals to destruction. He found himself deeply stirred by the peasants' greed for the land in *La Terre*. Later, he would portray a similar greed in *Desire Under the Elms*. From Zola he picked up a determinism that would color much of his early work. He enjoyed his reading; he even enjoyed baiting Papa, who shrank from being brought "flat against the stark materialities" by Zola, although he had known Zola long before Eugene. Way back in August, 1879, he had acted in an adaptation of Zola's *L'Assommoir* at the Baldwin Academy in San Francisco.

Gradually, Eugene's interest in life revived. He went for long walks, wearing his American Lines navy blue jersey, and swam a lot in the Sound. On July 22, 1912, he startled the whole town by swimming from Scott's wharf (a little to the side of 325 Pequot Avenue) across the broad mouth of the Thames River to the Watson estate at Eastern Point, about a mile, and later read with satisfaction the write-up in the New London *Day* of this exploit by "Eugene O'Neill, son of Actor James O'Neill." He even tried to learn a little Gaelic, to the immense joy of his father.

He still spent a lot of time with Jamie, of course. The two of them had a marvelous time with Papa's Packard, letting it out as far as it would go on the open roads, enjoying the sense of speed and power the machine gave them. Eugene saw his old friends, too. Art McGinley was working as a reporter on the New London *Morning Telegraph*, and came often to 325 Pequot Avenue. Gene went over to the McGinleys', too. Art's brothers, Tom and Wint, welcomed him warmly, but Mrs. McGinley was always nervous in his presence. Later, she confided to Art that when Eugene looked at her with his huge dark eyes, she always had the feeling that he was going to re- coil and spring at her.

Eddie Keefe was back in town, too. He had given up trying to earn a living as an artist, although Bellows was still at it, and was now working as an architect in New London. (Eugene would think of him when he wrote *The Great God Brown.*) Keefe and McGinley spent a lot of evenings at Doc Ganey's apartment at 8 Main Street, right above his office. The place was a center for bohemianism in New London. Eugene wasn't interested in the games of penny ante, but he drank with the boys, and read his way through Doc Ganey's complete de Maupassant, getting more ammunition for a war against middle-class values.

By the end of July, Eugene thought he knew what to do with him- self. He liked writing. Jamie had introduced him to Mr. Landon, a member of the Pleiades Club in New York, and Landon had decided to publish "Free" (the poem Eugene had written on the *Charles Ra- cine*) in the club's yearbook. He couldn't earn a living writing poetry, but he could write for a newspaper as Art McGinley was do- ing. Art thought they had room for another reporter on the *Tele- graph.*

So James O'Neill had a talk with his good friend Judge Latimer, publisher of the *Telegraph.* (James O'Neill knew and was liked by almost everyone in New London. A group was even trying to get him to run for mayor, but he kept refusing, saying that if he entered poli- tics he would want to aim at becoming president, and "I can't be president because I was born in Ireland, God bless it.") Judge Lati- mer was glad to give a son of James O'Neill a chance. So, in August, Eugene started work as cub reporter on the New London *Telegraph* at a salary of $20 a week.

The *Telegraph* went to press at three o'clock in the morning. Eu- gene started work at seven in the evening, pedaling his bicycle to the railroad station, the police station, or the docks on assignments; or proofreading the copy from the linotypers, counting out the let- ters for a "head," checking advertisements for accuracy, and gener- ally making himself useful about the office.

Malcolm Mollan, the city editor, tore into Eugene's first stories. Sarcastically, he told Eugene his account of a "cutting" in Bradley Street was "lovely," and added, "The smell of the rooms is made convincing; the amount of blood on the floor is precisely measured; you have drawn a nice picture of the squalor and stupidity and degradation of that household. But would you mind finding out the name of the gentleman who carved the lady and whether the lady is his wife or daughter or who? And phone the hospital for a hint as to whether she is dead or discharged or what. Then put the facts into a hundred and fifty words and send this literary batik to the picture framer's."

Art McGinley, too, liked to poke fun at Eugene's deficiencies. "He used to come to work on a bicycle and I could never understand really why he came to work at all," Art would say, "because in the months of my association with him as a fellow reporter I can't recall his ever having turned in a news story. There'd be a fire or a stout woman fainting in the public square and they'd send Eugene out on his bicycle and he would go out and come back three hours later and write 'Ode to Death.'" Later, Eugene himself would often declare, with a wry grin, that he had been "a rotten reporter."

Eugene's friends were sure he was able to hold his job on the New London *Telegraph* only because he was James O'Neill's son and Judge Latimer was a friend of James O'Neill. Years later, when Eugene O'Neill had become world-famous, his New London friends—Doc Ganey, Ed Keefe, and Art McGinley—liked to tell a story they found funny in the light of Eugene's unexpected success. Once, at two in the morning, the story ran, none of the *Telegraph*'s three reporters—Art McGinley, "Ice" Casey, or Eugene O'Neill—had appeared at the office. All three were over at the Crocker House bar, drinking. Finally, McGinley and Casey staggered over to the office, but Eugene never did show up. The next day, at a staff meeting, Mollan attacked all three reporters savagely, but Eugene in particular. "If it weren't for his father," Mollan told the assembled staff, "he'd be in the gutter where he belongs." Then Eugene arose and announced grandiloquently that he was tired of being spoken of as James O'Neill's son. "Someday," he said, "James O'Neill will be remotely remembered, if at all, as the father of Eugene O'Neill." The funny part, for the boys, was the fact that this actually came true. Back in those days it had seemed absurd.

Even if Eugene was right to call himself "a bum reporter," he was being praised for the bits of humorous, topical verse he wrote twice a week for a column called "Laconics." His father was proud of him. At last the boy seemed to have found himself. To Tyler, James O'Neill confided his joy now that Eugene was working and writing poetry. Judge Latimer had told him Eugene had talent of a very high order.

Eugene, too, felt that he was finding himself at last. Papa wasn't going on the road that year, so the household at 325 Pequot Avenue didn't break up at the end of August. Although Eugene didn't get home from work till four in the morning, he was leading a fairly regular life. The frantic drinking had stopped. He could sit for hours in a rocker on the porch with a book listening lazily to the sound of the clippers as his father cut the hedge, and he could allow himself to be pampered by Mama. He began writing verses like "A Regular Sort of a Guy" that expressed his whole childhood set of values.

His thinking had become less negative, particularly in politics. He began to see that the natives of Honduras, whom he had once thought deserved extermination, perhaps were not to blame for being stupid and lazy, but had been made that way by the malaria and bad food that had invalided him in two months. Zola taught him this, and taught him, too, in *Germinal,* that if the poor were poor, they were so because the rich were rich. Eugene became interested in socialism. Perhaps the answer for a country like Honduras was not extermination of the population, but a better social system.

For the first time, Eugene looked into basic socialist theory. He read and absorbed Karl Marx's analysis of capitalism. His social criticism took on content, became more than an instinctive rejection. He discovered that the workers create the wealth of the world, but that the owners of industry allow them only a small part of that wealth in wages. He discovered that wars are fought by rival capitalisms and that the workingmen who are made to fight in them have nothing to gain—in spite of all the flag waving of the jingoes—and everything to lose. Even his reading of Nietzsche took on richer meaning. He realized that the attacks on the "herd" were not attacks on humanity, but on conformity.

Whatever changes his political theories would undergo, whatever doubts he would later have about salvation through better social systems, he would always keep Karl Marx's explanation of what was wrong with capitalism firmly in mind, and later it would color all the social criticism in his plays, from the earliest up through *The Hairy Ape* and *Marco Millions*.

Armed with this new knowledge, he began to argue politics with everyone: his father, Art McGinley, Ice Casey, Charley Thompson, and even Judge Latimer himself. "As we used to talk together and argue our different philosophies," Judge Latimer would recall, "I thought he was the most stubborn and irreconcilable social rebel I had ever met. We appreciated each other's sympathies, but to each, in the moralities and religious thought and political notions, the other was 'all wet.' "

Eugene himself would remark with amusement later that the *Telegraph* presented strange political coverage considering the vast differences and the furious partisanship of its three reporters—he a socialist, and the other two a Democrat and a Republican. He, Art McGinley, and Ice Casey had glorious discussions. In one of the humorous verses he wrote for "Laconics," Eugene said his pipe dream was to have lots of time at the office "to sit and chatter politics."

Actually, he enjoyed working for the *Telegraph* largely because of his friendship with Charley Thompson, Art McGinley, and "Ice" Casey. All three would remain his lifelong friends. Relaxed, Eugene had much of his mother's unaffected charm. Through the summer and fall of 1912, his charm showed. Conventional girls, who were terrified of Jamie, found Eugene "sweet."

The misery he had undergone at Jimmy the Priest's seemed to have vanished without a trace. But the months there had left their mark. In October, he began to have spells of nausea. He thought they had come from something he ate. Then, by November 15, he got a dry cough. He would wake up in the night wet with perspiration. Even the sheets were soaked. He felt feverish and chilly. Clearly he needed a doctor.

He went, not to the family doctor, Sullivan, but to his own friend Doc Ganey. The diagnosis was pleurisy with effusion. He might need to have his chest tapped. Meanwhile, he was to stay in bed. He got worse, so 1000 cc. of fluid were drawn from his chest. That eased the pain in his right side for a while, but he wasn't getting better. Eugene began to feel frightened.

To James O'Neill, Ganey told the straight truth. The thing looked like tuberculosis. If that were so, Eugene would need sanitarium treatment at once. Luckily, one of the finest sanitaria in the country was in Connecticut: Gaylord Farm, over at Wallingford. James O'Neill had been planning to close the house on Pequot Avenue in December, anyway, and move to New York. Now he decided he would take Eugene with him and have him examined by a few New York specialists to make sure of the diagnosis.

In New York Eugene was examined by Dr. Livingston Farrand, an eminent tuberculosis specialist who later became president of Cornell University. His chest was tapped again and another six ounces of fluid removed. Dr. Farrand suggested they call in Dr. James Alexander Miller. From then on, events moved rapidly. On December 17, 1912, Dr. Miller wrote Dr. David R. Lyman at Gaylord Farm:

I have just seen a young man in whom Farrand is interested, who I think is a good case for your sanitarium.

His home is in New London and he has recently had a pleurisy with effusion which has been tapped. He has signs at the right apex and a few at the left base in addition to the thickened pleura at the right base. He is in excellent general condition and is, I believe, a very favorable case. He has almost no cough or expectoration and no fever and is only a few pounds below normal weight.

His name is O'Neil and he is stopping here in New York until I get him located permanently. Will you be good enough to write me immediately whether you will be able to take him?

By luck, Lyman had an opening. On December 24, 1912, Eugene O'Neill entered Gaylord Farm.

PART FIVE

REBIRTH

CHAPTER NINETEEN

Gaylord Farm

IN the measure that I love my work, and am proud to have been able to do the little I have, so much the more deep is my gratitude to you and Gaylord Farm for *saving* me for it. My blessings on the Farm 'spring eternal,' and the recollections of my stay there are, and always will be, among the most pleasant of my memories," Eugene O'Neill told Dr. Lyman. Always, he spoke of Gaylord with respect and gratitude as the place he had been "reborn in."

Yet when Eugene O'Neill entered Gaylord Farm on Christmas Eve, 1912, he was filled with bitterness at having to go there, and even his grateful affection for Dr. Lyman and the place itself never eradicated that bitterness. Jamie—so often the Mephisto of Eugene's life—started it. Looking through the literature on Gaylord Farm, he discovered that the place was partly state supported. Immediately, he told Eugene that Papa—with all his money—was sending Eugene to a "state farm" where paupers went. Eugene caught Jamie's fury and doubled it. This was the worst blow of all from the Old Man.

"It makes me want to puke!" Edmund in *Long Day's Journey Into Night* tells his father. "Not because of the rotten way you're treating me. To hell with that! I've treated you rottenly, in my way, more than once. But to think when it's a question of your son having consumption, you can show yourself up before the whole town as such a stinking old tightwad! . . . Jesus, Papa, haven't you any pride or shame? (*Bursting with rage.*) And don't think I'll let you get away with it! I won't go to any damned state farm just to save you a few lousy dollars to buy more bum property with! You stinking old miser—!"

Nor was Eugene quiet about his rage at the time, but no one could convince him that he was mistaken. His father told him he would gladly send him anywhere. Doc Ganey assured him not only then but for years afterwards, that Gaylord was one of the finest sanataria in the East. It had pioneered in the rest treatment for tuberculosis. Its reputation was brilliant. It was set up to handle cases like Eugene's that would respond quickly to treatment by rest and diet. Eugene listened, and went right on believing that he was the victim of his father's stinginess.

His bitterness appears in both *Long Day's Journey Into Night,* where Gaylord is called "Hilltown," and in *The Straw,* where it is "Hill Farm." (Gaylord Farm stood at the top of a hill, four hundred feet above the surrounding countryside.) Eugene made his tubercular heroine in *The Straw* the victim of a father unwilling to pay for her treatment. In *Long Day's Journey Into Night* he presented himself as such a victim.

What made Eugene so quick to believe the worst of his father? Then, as always, it was the ingrained expectation of rejection that he had carried with him from the time his father first banished him to Mount Saint Vincent. After his attempted suicide, Eugene had returned to the world of love, the world of his parents. But always, he lived uneasily in that world, waiting for the moment of betrayal, which had come, year after year, all through his boyhood. He expected rejection from his father, and he was always able to find it, even in what other people saw as proof of devotion. His allowance, for instance, which his father had continued to send him in the face of flagrant hostility, he took as "signal" proof that he was cruelly rejected, for he thought it should have been more. So it was with Gaylord Farm. He would always be grateful for going there, but he would never forgive his father for sending him there.

Why was he so grateful to Gaylord Farm? What happened during his six months there to make him feel "reborn"? Actually, Gaylord simply gave him time to complete a "rebirth" that was already under way. He was "reborn" the moment he awakened from his attempted suicide in Jimmy the Priest's and turned, after his long rebellion, back to love and his family. He had even analyzed the flight from love and faith that had started in his adolescence and led finally to a rejection of life in "The Lay of the Singer's Fall," a poem that the New London *Telegraph* printed on November 27, 1912.

> *A singer was born in a land of gold,*
> *In the time of long ago*
> *And the good fairies gathered from heath and wold*
> *With gracious gifts to bestow.*
> *They gave him the grace of Mirth and Song,*
> *They crowned him with Health and Joy*
> *And love for the Right and hate for the Wrong*
> *They instilled in the soul of the boy;*
>
> *But when they were gone, through the open door*
> *The Devil of Doubt crept in,*
> *And he breathed his poison in every pore*
> *Of the sleeping infant's skin,*
> *And in impish glee, said, "Remember me*
> *For I shall abide for aye with thee*
> *From the very first moment thine eyes shall see*
> *And know the meaning of sin."*
>
> *The singer became a man and he fought*
> *With might of his pen and hand*
> *To show for evil the cure long sought,*
> *And spread Truth over the land;*
> *Till the Devil mockingly said, "In sooth*
> *'T is a sorry ideal you ride,*

For the truth of truths is there is no truth!"
—And the faith of the singer died—

And the singer was sad and he turned to Love
  And the arms of his ladye faire,
He sang of her eyes as the stars above
  He sang of—and kissed—her hair;
Till the Devil whispered, "I fondly trust
  This is folly and nought beside,
For the greatest of loves is merely lust!"
—And the heart of the singer died—

So the singer turned from the world's mad strife
  And he walked in the paths untrod,
And thrilled to the dream of a future life
  As he prayed to the most high God;
Till the Devil murmured with sneering breath,
  "What think you the blind skies hide?
There is nothing sure after death but death!"
—And the soul of the singer died—

And the lips of the singer were flecked with red
  And torn with a bitter cry,
"When Truth and Love and God are dead
  It is time, full time, to die!"
And the Devil in triumph, chuckled low,
  "There is always suicide,
It's the only logical thing I know."
—And the life of the singer died.

He could write about this "devil of doubt," or, as he would later call it, "devil of hate," because he was no longer in its power, as he had been during the years of his revolt. From this time on, the devil would be under control. It would get out from time to time, but never for long.

Even Eugene's decision to become a writer was made before he went to Gaylord. "No, it isn't exactly true that my first urge to write came at the san," he would later say. "Previous to my breakdown I had done quite a lot of newspaper work in New London which included original poems, parodies, verse, etc. for the editorial page,

1.
Ellen Quinlan O'Neill
circa 1883

2.
James O'Neill
at the time
he met Ellen Quinlan

3.
James O'Neill (*seated*) and Richard M. ("Uncle Dick") Hooley
when O'Neill was a member of Hooley's Parlor Home of Comedy in Chicago

4. Eugene O'Neill as a child drawing boats on the Thames River

5. Eugene O'Neill (*left*), his brother, Jamie,
and his father, James O'Neill, on the porch of the house at New London

6.
Eugene O'Neill
circa 1911

7.
James O'Neill (*right*)
with Brandon Tynan,
his "substitute son,"
circa 1913,
when they were playing together
in *Joseph and His Brethren*

8.   Jack Reed and Louise Bryant

9.   Louise Bryant, George Cram Cook, and Eugene O'Neill
     in the Provincetown Players' production of *Thirst*, Summer 1916

10. Preparing for a production of *Bound East for Cardiff*
     in New York City, Fall 1916. Eugene O'Neill on the ladder;
     Hippolyte Havel seated; George Cram Cook far right

11.
Agnes Boulton,
Eugene O'Neill's second wife

12.
James O'Neill, Jr.,
in *Audrey,* 1902

13.
Pauline Frederick

14.
Carlotta Monterey,
Eugene O'Neill's third wife

and this experience started me, although the work itself was junk of a low order. But it was at Gaylord that my mind got the chance to establish itself, to digest and evaluate the impressions of many past years in which one experience had crowded on another with never a second's reflection. At Gaylord I really *thought about* my life for the first time, about past and future. Undoubtedly the inactivity forced upon me by the life at the san forced me to mental activity, especially as I had always been high-strung and nervous temperamentally."

From the beginning, of course, he had an easy time of it at Gaylord. He gained weight immediately, so that he was never a bed patient. After only a month and a half there, he was allowed a full hour of exercise each day. "I remember Dr. Lyman laughingly telling me I was an uninteresting case, there was so little the matter," Eugene would say. "So I can't pretend to putting up any heroic struggle myself. It was too easy." The Saturday weighing, such a tense time for the other patients, was always a triumph for him. By the time he left, he had gained over sixteen pounds and was well above normal weight. Even the slight cough disappeared quickly.

Eugene liked sleeping out on the porch of Hart Shack, his cottage, snug under a load of blankets, breathing the frosty air. He enjoyed lolling in the recliners on the porch of the "rec"—the recreation building—where the ambulatory patients ate. He liked to sit in the sun reading or writing poetry. Nothing was expected of him except that he should eat three meals a day and drink the supplementary diet, glasses of milk from Gaylord Farm's own cows that grazed on the hill.

His great pal among the patients was Bill Dwyer, who had been first baseman and captain of the Des Moines baseball team. "Last guy you'd pick as a lunger," it seemed to Eugene, as he watched Bill, big and buoyant, stride across the porch of the "rec." Bill always called Eugene "Tip"—after Tip O'Neill, president of the Western League. After a time Bill felt sure that he had recovered fully, and, in spite of Dr. Lyman's warnings, insisted on leaving the san. A little later, Eugene learned with shock that Bill had died.

With the pretty young nurses, Eugene was playfully flirtatious and with the older women, boyishly affectionate. He was a great favorite of Mary A. Clark, head nurse of the infirmary. He brought her the poems he wrote, and celebrated her birthday on May 24, 1913, with a funny poem "Ballad of the Birthday of the Most Gracious of Ladyes" about her kind use of thermometers and glasses of milk. Miss Murray, too, took a flattering interest in Eugene's writing. Eugene would always be grateful to Miss Murray, for she introduced him to Francis Thompson's "The Hound of Heaven." He read the poem with a tremendous shock of recognition. He saw in it the same flight from love that he had just recognized in his own life and had tried to express in "The Lay of the Singer's Fall." Here, in better words than his own, was the history of his wasted youth.

> *In the rash lustihead of my young powers,*
> *I shook the pillaring hours*
> *And pulled my life upon me; grimed with smears,*
> *I stand amid the dust o' the mounded years—*
> *My mangled youth lies dead beneath the heap.*
> *My days have crackled and gone up in smoke,*
> *Have puffed and burst as sun-starts on a stream.*
> *Yea, faileth now even dream*
> *The dreamer, and the lute the lutanist. . . .*

The final lines of the poem gave ecstatic voice to Eugene's own deepest perception of the wild years of revolt.

> *"Ah, fondest, blindest, weakest,*
> *I am He Whom thou seekest!*
> *Thou dravest love from thee, who dravest Me."*

So often did Eugene read this profoundly personal poem that he soon knew it by heart, and later, when drunk, he would often recite it with great feeling. When he came to write the three plays dealing with a flight from love—*Servitude, Welded,* and *Days Without End* —he designed them on the pattern of "The Hound of Heaven": a flight that led inevitably, circularly back to love and acceptance. In two of them, *Servitude* and *Days Without End,* he even quoted "The Hound of Heaven" to underline his meaning. The poem expressed his own life history, and so he made it his own.

At Gaylord Farm his body filled out, his cheeks became tanned, and his long bruised and abused consciousness healed from the wounds of his years of rebellion. Of course, he was aware that around him patients were fighting more desperately against more painful odds. From such remembrances would come the portrait of Eileen Carmody in *The Straw*. Agnes Boulton would recall his saying that Eileen was patterned on a girl at the san "he had almost forgotten." Perhaps the girl was Catherine MacKay. After her release from Gaylord, Catherine went home to care for four sisters and five brothers. Her health rapidly declined. Dr. Lyman wanted to "give the girl a chance for her life" by getting her back to Gaylord. He told Mary Gormly on February 27, 1913, "I do not think her people at all realize the necessity of sparing her in every way possible. She herself does not wish to leave home, but if she remains there the many cares that have always been hers will surely be hers yet." She died in 1915. O'Neill's Eileen Carmody would have two brothers and two sisters, and be eighteen rather than twenty-three as was Catherine MacKay, but the pattern was certainly similar. Whether or not it was Catherine's story Eugene dramatized in *The Straw*, hers was the common fate of the tubercular patient from a working-class home.

No oppressive burden would descend on Eugene O'Neill when he left Gaylord Farm. He could look forward to rest. And now he had a purpose. " . . . before I left there," he reported later, "I had made up my mind that I would rather write than do anything else." To his father in New York, he simply wrote that he would be discharged from Gaylord on June 3, 1913.

CHAPTER TWENTY

Beginnings

1912 had been a hard year for James O'Neill with both
Eugene and Ellen sick and himself idle. Then, late in the fall, Tyler
asked him, as a "favor," to play Jacob in Louis N. Parker's *Joseph
and His Brethren.* "I spent the summer at my home in New London
and got through the warm months without any trouble," James
O'Neill later told a reporter from the Rochester *Post Express,* "but
my first visit to New York made me restless. I felt like an old war
horse that had been put aside, and it was most uncomfortable, for
since I first went into stock in minor parts in 1868, the stage has
been my home. I had too much leisure. I didn't know what to do
with myself. I tired of reading and would spend hours pacing up
and down. This made my wife nervous, for she didn't understand
what was the matter. I didn't more than half know myself, but
when came this opportunity in 'Joseph and His Brethren,' I knew

it was the call of the stage. It was irresistible, and I answered it—
and I don't look unhappy, do I?"

But he was hurt that in his old age he had to be glad of a small
role. Tyler, who talked later of having persuaded "glorious old
James O'Neill to play Jacob for us," shared O'Neill's hurt. "It was a
queer feeling—and not altogether joyful either," Tyler said, "—my
first respectable job had been working for him and worshipping the
ground he walked on, and now, when he was practically retired, I
was asking him to play for me in a huge production in the biggest
theatre in New York. Almost every night during the long run of the
play I went in to catch the scenes he appeared in, because his voice
—he did have the finest voice in the world—had never ceased to
fascinate me. He had insisted on doubling in the role of Pharaoh in
addition to playing Jacob because, he said, he'd be hanged if he'd
wait in his dressing-room with nothing to do between the first and
last acts, in which Jacob made his only appearances. The courtiers
around Pharaoh's throne had to feed him his lines pretty steadily
some nights, for his memory wasn't all it had been, but you'd never
have guessed it from out front. He was a king in every sense of the
word throughout, and a king in real life as well."

In December, 1912, when James O'Neill came up to New York
for rehearsals of *Joseph and His Brethren,* he settled the immediate
future of both his sons. Jamie had been idle all fall. Now Tyler
agreed to give him a role as one of Joseph's brothers. And now
arrangements were completed for sending Eugene to Gaylord. But
James O'Neill got no gratitude from either of his sons. Jamie was
cynical about his role in *Joseph and His Brethren,* and Eugene
thought he was being sent to a "state farm."

James O'Neill's association with Brandon Tynan, star of the play,
must have been a relief to him, for from Tynan he got all the love
and admiration his sons had never given him. "To talk with Mr.
O'Neill is to realize that he is a human, sentient bridge between
two generations of playgoers and players," Tynan told a reporter
from the Chicago *News.* "His retrospect goes back beyond the
actors I worshiped as a boy to the actors of whom I have heard from
the lips of my elders. . . . Yet here he is, playing night after night,
with as much respect for an observation of the modern naturalistic

method of acting as if he had made his debut only last season after a course of Ibsen."

James O'Neill and Tynan remained great friends through all the mishaps of the play. One of them was hilarious. The coat of many colors disappeared, and the property men had to sew one together quickly and give it to Tynan when it was barely dry from the dye vats. The other actors heard Tynan and O'Neill whispering as "Jacob" invested "Joseph" with the coat of many colors.

"Jacob—Now, upon thy young shoulders I lay the robe of manhood and authority. (What's wrong with you, Tynan? Get your arms into the sleeves!) Lo, here the coat of many colors, and each color shall be for a sign—(For goodness' sake, get it on, will you?)

"Joseph, in a whisper—(It's all full of basting threads! I can't get into the blooming armholes!)

"Jacob—Azure for wisdom, and scarlet for courage; green for prayer, and white for purity. (Great Scott, the color is coming off all over us!) I clasp thee to me, flesh of my flesh, thy young heart against my old heart, whose first-born thou art. (Turn around a little, will you, so I can straighten this thing out.) I raise my hand toward the throne of God, and I cry out, God bless thee! (Are you all right now?)

"Joseph—(Yes, only I'm stepping on the front of the blamed thing. It's long enough for the statute of Liberty. There, I'm all right now.) Oh, Father! Mother! Oh, my brothers! Ye have wrapped me about with love!"

O'Neill and Tynan understood each other. In Brandon Tynan, James O'Neill saw himself as a young man, for Tynan was also an Irish lad who had risen fast as an actor. He had already written and acted in a play of his own, *Robert Emmet*. As for Tynan, he asked James O'Neill's advice, as Jamie and Eugene never had, and took it gratefully.

For the time, at least, James O'Neill no longer felt "put aside." He took part, as always, in the Lambs' Gambol, and he was the central character in the Friars' "Giggle," a take-off on the Gambol. George M. Cohan had succeeded him as prompter of the Green Room Club, but James was still on the board of directors. So the spring had been pleasantly social. Toward its end came Eugene's letter saying that he would be discharged from Gaylord Farm on June 3.

In his rooms at the Hotel Ascot, James O'Neill sighed. Thank goodness the lad was all right. If Eugene was getting out in June, they could all be together again at 325 Pequot Avenue, that is, if it was safe for the boy's mother. Ellen had been sick all year. James O'Neill decided to check with Dr. Lyman. He dashed off a note:

My son—Eugene—writes me that he was examined on Saturday, and is declared absolutely free from contagion—that is, he is so thoroughly cured that no one—not even his ailing mother can become infected with tuberculosis by living in the same house and eating at the same table with him. As the dr. in charge of him—I ask you if this is true. I do not wish to jeopardize my wife's health; and our plans for the summer will depend on your reply which I hope will be as soon as possible.

Dr. Lyman's reply, dated May 30, brought good news.

Replying to yours would say that your son's case has always been one that we call "closed tuberculosis," where there is no sputum with bacilli and in consequence no danger of contagion. At present all the evidence I can find in his chest is a slightly thickened pleura which may remain in that condition for years, and has in itself no influence or bearing on his health. I do not believe your son is absolutely cured or that any case is in less than three or four years' time. I do feel that his case is thoroughly under control, the lungs being, as far as I can see, clear; and that in his present condition he would not be a menace to any one.

So Eugene returned to his family, a bronzed, healthy-looking Eugene, who slept outdoors on the porch, rose early, drank only milk, and exercised regularly.

Above all, Eugene at last knew what he wanted to do. He had started writing a vaudeville sketch at Gaylord on May 1—so he said in his first report to Dr. Lyman. Now he was full of plans for plays and movie scripts too. (Papa knew all the General Film people.) Confidently, he mailed off his first play, the vaudeville sketch *A Wife for a Life* to Washington, and received his copyright as of August 15, 1913.

James O'Neill was pathetically proud of Eugene. To a reporter who asked him about his plans he said he might very well return to vaudeville. "In fact," he declared, "my youngest son has written a sketch which it is quite likely that I may use in the near future, but things are so uncertain in my profession, I am not planning very far. The part in this sketch, however, is not a clerical or religious one; the role that I should essay is that of a Western miner."

At the end of August, when the road tour of *Joseph and His Brethren* began, James O'Neill arranged that Eugene should stay with the Rippins, who lived just up the block on Pequot Avenue. There he could rest, get the sun, and write plays. The house at 325 Pequot Avenue was closed, and the O'Neills departed. Except for occasional visits, Eugene would not be with his family again until May.

He and Art McGinley did get up to Boston for the rehearsals and the opening of *Joseph and His Brethren* there in the middle of October. Jamie told them that there was "only one nice fellow in this cast—that's the camel on the left in the first act." But Art and Eugene knew that Jamie and Pauline Frederick, star of the play, were lovers. She had been selected by Harrison Fisher as the most beautiful woman in America—and her beauty was reminiscent of Mama's. For once, Jamie seemed really to care for a woman. But they had problems. Pauline was married to Frank Andrews, an architect. If she were to turn to Jamie, she would want him to be more than an irresponsible alcoholic playing small roles badly. She wanted him to give up drinking. Jamie thought that for her he might actually do it. Eugene observed them sympathetically.

Eugene also observed Tynan with the Old Man and was jealous. The two actors took long walks together, and Tynan pronounced the "Governor" the "best walker of the lot. A lot of us are younger, but there isn't one of us who is more virile." Eugene realized that Brandon Tynan was filling the position of son to James O'Neill. Later, in *Strange Interlude*, Eugene would have the aging Darrell find a "compensating substitute" for his hostile real son, a young man with "the rare virtue of gratitude." (How often the Old Man had accused him and Jamie of ingratitude!) Eugene would call this "substitute" son "Preston," a name very like "Brandon." Through the next few years Eugene watched his father's affection for this rival son, who would be a commercially successful playwright while he himself was still struggling for a hearing. Bitter as Eugene felt toward his father, he was deeply jealous as well.

During the summer in New London, he had spent his time reading, not writing—a case of "book-worm," he would facetiously inform Dr. Lyman. But now his reading was purposeful. He wanted to learn about drama. He had just discovered August Strindberg and was excitedly reading through his plays. Here, he felt, was a master who surpassed even Ibsen. For the rest of his life, Eugene would always be ready to declare his debt to Strindberg, and he declared it at great length when he wrote his acceptance of the Nobel Prize in 1937.

"It was reading his plays when I first started to write back in the Winter of 1913–14 that, above all else, first gave me the vision of what modern drama could be, and first inspired me with the urge to write for the theatre myself. If there is anything of lasting worth in my work, it is due to that original impulse from him, which has continued as my inspiration down all the years since then—to the ambition I received then to follow in the footsteps of his genius as worthily as my talent might permit, and with the same integrity of purpose.

"Of course, it will be no news to you in Sweden, that my work owes much to the influence of Strindberg. That influence runs clearly through more than a few of my plays and is plain for everyone to see. Neither will it be news for any one who has ever known me, for I have always stressed it myself. I have never been one of those who are so timidly uncertain of their own contribution that they feel they cannot afford to admit ever having been influenced, lest they be discovered as lacking all originality.

"No, I am only too proud of my debt to Strindberg, only too happy to have this opportunity of proclaiming it to his people. For me, he remains, as Nietzsche remains, in his sphere, the master, still to this day more modern than any of us, still our leader."

So impressed was Eugene by the relentless ending of *Miss Julie*, in which the heroine marches off to the barn to cut her throat, that he would send two characters in *Diff'rent* off to the barn to commit suicide, and would have the husband in *Before Breakfast* slit his throat. He would also follow Strindberg's picture of marriage as a hell on earth in *Bread and Butter, Before Breakfast,* and *Beyond the Horizon.* But Strindberg's most important influence was less direct. Strindberg gave him the courage to follow sequences to their logical conclusion, no matter how terrible. Strindberg showed him how to dig below the surface of human relationships to the tensions beneath, and above all, how to discard realistic means altogether in order to project the mysterious forces that determine human life.

Eugene read Wedekind, too, learning more about expressionistic techniques and stage symbolism, and appreciating more deeply the way a single large force—sex, for instance—may sweep individuals to destruction. After reading Strindberg and Wedekind, Eugene was ashamed of his first play, aimed deliberately at a vaudeville audience. Now he wished only to project truth. He wanted success, of course, but he had discovered the joy of honest creation.

"That's the year I thought I was God," Eugene would say, recalling his joy in each new play. "I'd finish them and rush down to the post office to ship them off to Washington to be copyrighted before somebody stole them." *The Web* was the first of these, copyrighted October 17, 1913. Following Zola and Strindberg, Eugene showed in it the destruction of a prostitute trying desperately to be a mother to her child, but caught in a web of overpowering circumstances, so that she is falsely accused of murder. Equally ironic was the conclusion of his next play *Thirst,* in which Eugene put a West Indian sailor, a gentleman, and a dancer adrift on a raft in order to show the basic human motives—greed, sex, thirst—in conflict. All three characters end up in the shark-infested waters.

Eugene knew he was creating a new honesty for the theater. "I had known the theatre pretty intimately, because of my father's connection with it," he would later say. "But, with me, to know it had not been to *love* it! I had always been repelled by its artificiality, its slavish clinging to old traditions. Yet, when I began to write, it was for the theatre. And my knowledge helped me, because I knew what I wanted to *avoid* doing."

Monte Cristo was exactly what he didn't want to do. "I can still see my father," Eugene would tell S. J. Woolf, "dripping with salt and sawdust, climbing on a stool behind the swinging profile of dashing waves. It was then that the calcium lights in the gallery played on his long beard and tattered clothes, as with arms out-stretched he declared that the world was his. This was the signal for the house to burst into a deafening applause that overwhelmed the noise of the storm manufactured backstage. It was an artificial age, an age ashamed of its own feelings, and the theatre reflected its thoughts. Virtue always triumphed and vice always got its just deserts. It accepted nothing half-way; a man was either a hero or a villain, and a woman was either virtuous or vile."

Long ago, Eugene had learned from Shaw's *Quintessence of Ibsenism* to scorn plays with glib happy endings. "Up to a comparatively short time ago, as late as the time when Clyde Fitch and his school were popular," he remarked, "for three acts an author would build up a thesis and then in the fourth act proceed to knock over what he had constructed. The managers felt that they knew what the public would accept and the plays had to conform to their ideas." All American playwrights had sold out, Eugene thought, even the best of them. "*The Great Divide* is a fine play for two acts and then it falls to pieces because it has to end happily. It was that way with all of them."

With his first plays, Eugene's creed of integrity solidified. He went on to apply what he had learned from Zola and Marx in *Warnings*, where he showed economic pressures forcing a telegraph operator to ship out to sea again in spite of oncoming deafness. In *Fog*, he defied realism to show the power of unselfish idealism (in the poet) over selfish materialism (in the businessman).

Soon, Eugene had enough short plays for a book—and he was very eager for publication. By March 30, 1914, he had signed an agreement with Richard G. Badger, of the Gorham Press, Boston, for the publication of *Thirst, The Web, Warnings, Fog,* and *Recklessness* in one volume. Papa put up the money: $300 when the agreement was signed, and $150 more to be paid "on receipt of complete proofs." Eugene considered this an investment, not a gift. He would pay the money back when he received his twenty-five per cent of the gross proceeds from the sale of the thousand copies in that first edition.

Joyously, Eugene looked ahead. To publish, he thought, was to achieve fame. For the first time in his life he was filled with dreams for his future. That first volume meant something. While writing it, he had formulated his creed as an artist. He had decided to communicate important ideas, regardless of their salability; to follow all problems to their logical conclusions, no matter how distasteful; and to draw characters honestly. And in writing that first book, he had also begun to learn his craft.

He turned next to a four-act play *Bread and Butter*. Even while writing it, he was telling people it would be produced "next season." The play expressed all the resentment he felt then and earlier at his father's efforts to get him to earn his own living. His chief character, John Brown of Bridgetown, Connecticut, wants to devote himself to art, but his father urges him to study law at Princeton, and only agrees to let him study art in New York in the hope that a small allowance will drive him to turn to commercial art, in which he can make big money. This dreamer is further harassed by a "sanctimonious hypocrite" of a brother, who (like James O'Neill) has been asked to run for mayor.

Into the play Eugene put pictures of his studio days with Ted Ireland, Ed Keefe, and George Bellows; his feeling of "a great sickness and lassitude of soul" during his days at Jimmy the Priest's; and his hatred of the hard labor he had done amidst the noise and smells of the dock. The play ends tragically with John relinquishing his "highest hope" in order to marry a selfish middle-class girl and accept a job in her father's store. Finding that he and his wife are "two corpses chained together," he shoots himself. Out of the materials of this play, Eugene later constructed *Beyond the Horizon*, the play that would establish him as an important playwright. He grew through everything he wrote that year.

Eugene went on to use his memories for *Abortion*, a one-act play copyrighted on May 17, 1914. Through the story of a college baseball hero who betrays a working-class girl and forces on her a fatal abortion, Eugene worked out some of his feelings toward Kathleen Jenkins: his first sense that it was "just a pleasant game we were playing," his feeling that she was "a sweet, lovely girl in spite of everything," and his sensation of having "played the scoundrel" throughout.

By September 23, 1914, Eugene had copyrighted another full-length play, *Servitude*. Here, he dealt with his own flight from love, exposing the fallacy of a playwright and follower of Nietzsche, who, far from being "the superman" and "maker of new values" he thought he was, has been "an egotist whose hands are bloody with the human sacrifices he has made—to himself!" Eugene now substituted a philosophy of "servitude in love" for the individualism of his years of revolt. He made "a superlove worthy of the superman" his new philosophy.

And he could write this with conviction, for he himself had found love. The girl was Beatrice Ash. To others, she was simply a grey-eyed "well-developed" girl with a good voice, daughter of Pete Ash, who had worked himself up to Superintendent of Street Trolleys in New London. To Eugene, she was a composite of sweetness and charm.

He confided to her his dreams, his poetry, his bitterness toward his father; and she listened sympathetically. To him she was an inspiration and a joy. He wrote love poems to her, and she wrote love poems to him. After all his tawdry affairs, at last he felt a confident trust and happiness in love.

Although she was a fairly conventional girl, not at all in sympathy with his savage attack on church and state, Eugene didn't mind. He had always associated love with his childhood values. Even in *Servitude*, he had sent his heroine—who had fled her stockbroker husband because she saw "his business in all its hideousness"—back, with her new philosophy of love, to her husband and the stock exchange.

Of course, Eugene couldn't marry Beatrice. He had no income. He had poured out some of his anger at the prudish attacks on unmarried love in his play *Abortion*, in which the hero exclaims: "Restraint? Ah, yes, everybody preaches but who practices it? And could they if they wanted to? Some impulses are stronger than we are, have proved themselves so throughout the world's history. Is it not rather our ideals of conduct, of Right and Wrong, our ethics, which are unnatural and monstrously distorted?" Certainly he and Beatrice had problems, but Eugene found happiness and strength for his creative work in his love for her.

Of all his earliest works, Eugene would later value only one, but that one, he would feel, held "the germ" of his later achievement, and it would survive, with only slight changes, among his mature works. He called the play *Children of the Sea,* after Conrad, for it expressed Conrad's view of the sailors as "men who knew toil, privation, violence, debauchery—but knew not fear." In it, Eugene pictured Driscoll, his friend from Jimmy the Priest's, and used his own memories of Buenos Aires. He had learned from the Abbey plays—Synge's in particular—that no more need happen in a one-act play than is necessary to reveal the meaning of a way of life. Now, he revealed the meaning of a sailor's life through the simple picture of a sailor facing his death bravely on a fogbound ship. Later, Eugene called the play *Bound East for Cardiff.* Out of this first year of writing, a playwright was emerging.

Meanwhile, Eugene was still writing poetry and "chattering" politics. He watched the uprising of the peons in Mexico and was horrified at the threats of intervention from the United States to protect American investments. In protest, he wrote a long poem "Fratricide," which he published in the socialist New York *Call* of May 17, 1914:

> *The call resounds on every hand*
> * The loud, exultant call to arms.*
> *With patriotic blare of band*
> * It quickens, pulses, rouses, charms;*
> *Mouthing its insolent command:*
> * "Come, let us rob our neighbor's farms."*

He showed that "the poor must fight" and attacked their "shepherds" who "bless them" and "slink off" to "polish the collection plate." Then he thought of Nietzsche and wrote:

> *"A good war haloes any cause."*
> * What war could halo this cause, pray?*
> *The wise man's words had given pause*
> * To him, were he alive today.*
> *To see by what unholy laws*
> * The plutocrats extend their sway.*
>
> *What cause could be more asinine*
> * Than yours, ye slaves of bloody toil?*

> *Is not your bravery sublime*
> *Beneath a tropic sun to broil*
> *And bleed and groan—for Guggenheim!*
> *And give your lives for—Standard Oil!*

Eugene ended with a ringing call to socialist unity:

> *Comrades, awaken to new birth!*
> *New values on the tables write!*
> *What is your vaunted courage worth*
> *Unless you rise up in your might*
> *And cry: "All workers on the earth*
> *Are brothers and WE WILL NOT FIGHT!"*

Eugene worked hard all that year. Out on the Rippins's back porch, overlooking the Thames River, he wrote for four or five hours a day. He lived carefully. He swam every day, right into the winter. Even in January he went in once a week. He startled Dr. Lyman with a picture of himself in a bathing suit standing in the snow at the edge of the water. The snapshot, he said, had been taken New Year's Day, when the water was thirty-nine degrees. He quoted from Kipling, "The uniform 'e wore / Was nothin' much before / An' rather less than 'arf of that be'ind."

All through the warm months, Eugene took the sun. He would paddle his canoe out, remove his bathing suit, and lie prone at the bottom for hours in the sun. Occasionally, boaters passing by were shocked to come upon a naked man in a canoe, but, as Doc Ganey would later recall with delight, that never troubled Gene in the least. For the first time in his life, he got through the winter without a cold or tonsilitis. He kept the enormous appetite, which, he told Dr. Lyman, he had "caught" at the san.

Mrs. Rippin mothered Eugene, although she thought the characters in his plays "'orrible," as she confided to Clayton Hamilton ("Mr. 'Am," she called him). Her daughters typed Eugene's manuscripts and sympathized with his ambitions. Judge Latimer, too, encouraged him in the long hours they spent together "on the water."

"I thought it astonishing how keen was his wit, what a complete iconoclast he was," Judge Latimer would say, "how richly he sympathized with the victims of man-made distress, how his imagination was running high as the festering skies above Ye Ancient Mariner; his descriptions strong and his spirit hot to produce something worth while for the sake of its own value and in utter scorn of its commercial value or conventional fame." Judge Latimer told Eugene he had "a very high order of genius." "He's the first one," Eugene said gratefully, "who really thought I had something to say, and believed I could say it."

Eugene met Clayton Hamilton, the drama critic, when he stayed at Mrs. Rippin's boarding house for a while that January. "When I returned to New London the next summer," Hamilton would recall, "he confessed to me with great shyness that he had been trying to write some little pieces. He hesitated to ask me to read them, for fear of imposing upon me; but he did ask me if I wouldn't teach him technically how to write a one-act play, and I answered that the technical problem was less important than the primary problem of what to write about." Later, Hamilton got the idea that he had first directed Eugene to write about the sea. Actually, Eugene had been doing so long before he asked Hamilton's advice.

Clayton Hamilton was an old friend of James O'Neill. He had first come to New London to work with Richard Mansfield on a production of Ibsen's *Peer Gynt*. Mansfield "did not consider the Irish O'Neill" sufficiently important to be invited to his parties, according to Mrs. Hamilton, so Clayton had visited James O'Neill on his own, spending many "comfortable hours" with him.

Far from being hurt, James O'Neill was always amused by Mansfield's showy mansion, his "coat of arms," and his social loftiness. With a twinkle in his eyes, he would repeat Maurice Barrymore's comment on Mansfield's snobbery. Mansfield, the rumor went, had been an illegitimate child. One night, Mansfield entered the Player's Club and stalked past James O'Neill, Maurice Barrymore, and a few others. "Isn't it a pity," Barrymore remarked caustically, "that a man who doesn't know his own father shouldn't know his own friends." James O'Neill always went on to praise Mansfield warmly for his erudition. But the man's posturing amused him.

James O'Neill had often told Hamilton of his worries over Eugene and had asked Hamilton's advice on what to do with the boy. Later,

Hamilton assumed James O'Neill still thought of his son as "a way-ward, worthless wanderer" even when Eugene had started to write. Hamilton would be influential in spreading the picture of Eugene O'Neill as a genius completely misunderstood by his father.

Of course, Eugene himself helped Hamilton to see him this way. As always, he was bitter about the size of his allowance. He had seen the bill for his 162 days at Gaylord, and knew that he had cost his father only $167.35. Now, he told Clayton Hamilton he was entirely dependent on a miserable $8 weekly allowance from his father that restricted him to New London. Hamilton got the idea that James O'Neill was doing this as "a punitive process that approached imprisonment."

Curiously, Eugene gave an entirely opposite account of his income to Dr. Lyman in his report back to Gaylord. To the question "What have you worked at?" he answered, "since May 1st, 1913— the Art of Playwriting—" and added, "also prostitution of the same by Photo-play composition." His average weekly earnings, he said, had been $30. In a long letter to Dr. Lyman, Eugene explained that he was an "Art for Art's sake" writer, yet also, although he was ashamed of it, a writer for the movies, from which he received an income that made him very rich one day and poor another. He said nothing of an allowance from his father.

Which account was true? Both, apparently. Eugene had probably written a little for the movies, but he wanted to devote himself exclusively to playwriting. He felt that the small allowance from his father—although it was quite enough to live on comfortably in those days—was meant to force him to further "prostitution." So he fretted over it, and gave Clayton Hamilton the idea that his father was punishing him through it. He never told Hamilton or Dr. Lyman that his father had put up the money to publish his plays. He had a way, then and later, of unconsciously suppressing facts that ran counter to his picture of his father as "a stinking old miser."

From Clayton Hamilton Eugene first learned the hard truth of his new profession. "It was one day I met you down at the R. R. station in New London," he told Hamilton in a letter many years later. "I had just sent off the script of what was really my first long play to some manager or other. I innocently expected an immediate personal reading and a reply within a week—possibly an acceptance. I asked you for information regarding the reading habits of managers, the chances of scripts from unknowns, etc. You handed me the desired data—with both feet! You slipped me the unvarnished truth and then sandpapered it! You wound up in words to this general effect: 'When you send off a play remember there is not one chance in a thousand it will ever be read; not one chance in a million of its ever being accepted—(and if accepted it will probably never be produced); but if it is accepted and produced, say to yourself it's a miracle which can never happen again.' I wandered off feeling a bit sick and thinking that you were hardly a fit associate for budding aspirations. But finally I reflected that you knew whereof you spoke, that I was up against a hard game and might as well realize it and hew to the line without thought of commercial stage production. Your advice gradually bred in me a gloomy and soothing fatalism which kismeted many a rebuff and helped me to take my disappointments as all an inevitable part of the game."

Certainly, Hamilton had been right about the plays he had just sent off to his father's friend George Tyler: "the two plays I sent at the station that day (to be sure they got off in the very first mail!) were never read by Tyler or anyone else," he told Hamilton. "I finally got them back two years later, from the receiver after Liebler and Company went into bankruptcy—and they were still sealed in my original envelopes! But, thanks to your warning, I was forearmed and forewarned against disappointment and I was able to accept it with a fatalistic grin."

It was Hamilton who suggested that Eugene enroll in George Pierce Baker's famous course in playwriting at Harvard, "Baker's 47." Eugene gave Hamilton the idea that his father might object, and Hamilton later reported, "Mr. James O'Neill was hesitant, because this wayward boy had run away from college once before. I put in a plea; and the matter was arranged."

Eugene wrote Baker, telling him he had been assistant manager to the *White Sister* Company and had acted in his father's vaudeville version of *Monte Cristo*. Hamilton wrote too. So Eugene became the thirteenth member of the class that Baker usually limited to twelve, and set off for Harvard in the fall of 1914.

CHAPTER TWENTY-ONE

Pan at Harvard

AT Cambridge, Eugene O'Neill clapped on his "mask of the Bad Boy Pan" on finding himself a student again at twenty-six. Clayton Hamilton had thought him a "boy," with "large and dreamy eyes, a slender, somewhat frail, and yet athletic body, a habit of silence, and an evident disease of shyness." To his classmates at Harvard, he was a sardonic man, hardened by rough living.

Underneath, of course, the boy, with his shyness and resentments, was still there. In particular he resented the fact that his father was giving him only ten dollars a week to live on. (Ten dollars in 1914 were equivalent to thirty dollars today.) His allowance was more than enough to pay for a pleasant room and excellent meals at 1105 Massachusetts Avenue, a big frame house a few blocks from the Harvard yard. His father had also paid his tuition and financed his book. But Eugene measured all this against a vision of his father's enormous wealth. Whenever he ran short of money and had to go without something, he felt deprived of love. Years later he would remember an evening in Cambridge when he didn't have streetcar fare and had to walk. He suffered over it as a son might suffer over the memory of a whipping.

None of his classmates, sitting around the seminar table on Wednesday and Friday mornings, were aware of the turmoil going on behind Eugene's handsome exterior. Everett Glass did notice that "his forehead perspired easily," and Donald Breed observed that he was "rather uneasy and inarticulate at times. You got the impression that he trembled a little, and seemed trying to keep from stuttering." But to others he was simply a "sarcastic bastard." Donald Breed could see that "he rather liked to shock us." John V. A. Weaver said he was startled when he saw Eugene's mouth. "It was the mouth of a man of forty—hard, bitter, matter-of-fact, almost cruel," he said.

Eugene did not share the "scared respect" of his classmates for "professorial admonitions," Weaver observed. "While we sat open-mouthed and earnest, he would writhe and squirm in his chair, scowling and muttering *mezza voce* fearful imprecations and protests. Of him, too, we were frightened. He kept so much to himself. He did not invite approach. For some weeks, we let him alone. Then one day Dr. Baker read aloud a scenario by an aspirant. It was lugubrious, it was flamboyant, it was very, very earnest. Several of us gave suggestions. It came O'Neill's turn. He waited some moments. Finally, he said, without a smile, 'Cut it to twenty minutes, give it a couple of tunes, and it's sure-fire burly-cue.' We howled with laughter. Dr. Baker smiled. From that time until we all parted in June there was a new ease, a refreshing relaxation in the meetings."

Soon Eugene had friends among the students of Baker's 47, particularly Felton Elkins and Malcolm Morley, a young Englishman. Morley, like Eugene, was determined to master his craft. "I was one of the hardest-working students of the lot," Eugene himself would say.

Evenings, Eugene strolled through Cambridge with his new friends. Corwin Willson would recall one of these walks. "O'Neill and I discussed politics, and he was in the same boat I was, wavering between extreme Marxian socialism on the one hand, extreme Nietzschean individualism and anarchism on the other—although he admitted to me he leaned strongest in the latter direction." They talked ardently of the magic of Nietzsche's *Thus Spake Zarathustra,* which Eugene was reading in the original German now, with the help of an English translation and a German dictionary. He wanted to learn German, he said, so that he could read more Wedekind. They talked about poetry and they talked about sex. "When he found I was married and the father of a 2-year old daughter and rather 'innocent' of the seamier side of sex," Willson recalled, "he launched into a history of his own sex life which was varied in the extreme."

Eugene talked most with Felton Elkins (or "Pinky," as he was called), to whom he told hair-raising stories of his years of rebellion. Elkins was the first to learn of Eugene's book *Thirst and Other One-Act Plays,* and he told the others. "I immediately went to the Old Corner Bookstore and bought a copy of 'Thirst,'" Everett Glass reported, "which revealed the powerful, if macabre, imagination. Elkins was enthusiastic. I have always remembered one prophecy he made *at that time:* 'O'Neill is going to be the greatest dramatist in America.'"

Eugene often joined the others on Saturday evenings. As Corwin Willson recalled, "We would go together to have 'dinner' at an upstairs Armenian restaurant where Gene warned us not to look into the kitchen which we passed at head of stairs if we wanted to enjoy our food which was delicious and cheap—all we could eat for about 25 cents. Then in a body, we'd go to the Old Howard and after the show we all went to the James Hotel to see how the burlesque gals picked up their boyfriends."

Weaver, too, had vivid recollections of evenings with O'Neill and Elkins at "one of the Shamrock bars," and told about one of them. "We drank ale," Weaver said. "We continued drinking ale until four in the morning, feet on the rail, one hand in the free lunch. It was just one of those nights. Ribald tales, anecdotes of experience, theorizing about the drama—what the collegians used to call a 'bull session.' A bull session de luxe. We piled finally into a decrepit hack. We fell into O'Neill's room some time about five. I had just purchased that day a copy of 'Spoon River Anthology.' When the dawn broke, I was sitting on a trunk, Elkins sprawled across the bed, O'Neill reading in his powerful, melancholy bass, poem after poem from that disturbing collection."

"Women were forever calling for 'Gene,'" Weaver said. "There was something apparently irresistible in his strange combination of cruelty (around the mouth), intelligence (in his eyes), and sympathy (in his voice). I would not say that he was 'good-looking.' But one girl told me she could not get his face out of her thoughts. He was hard-boiled and whimsical. He was brutal and tender, so I was told. From shop girl to 'sassiety' queen, they all seemed to develop certain tendencies in his presence. What may have resulted, deponent sayeth not. About some things 'Gene' was Sphinx-like. All I can report is the phenomena."

What of Beatrice? Eugene was still writing to her, and F. P. A. published one of his funny poems about her, "Speaking, To The Shade of Dante, of Beatrices," in his column, The Conning Tower, in the New York *Tribune* on July 5, 1915:

> *"Lo, even I am Beatrice!"*
>   *That line keeps singing in my bean.*
> *I feel the same ecstatic bliss*
>   *As did the fluent Florentine*
> *Who heard the well-known hell-flame hiss.*
>
> *Dante, your damozel was tall*
>   *And lean and sad—I've seen her face*
> *On many a best-parlor wall—*
>   *I don't think she was such an ace.*
> *She doesn't class with mine at all.*
>
> *Her eyes were not so large or grey;*
>   *She had no such heart-teasing smile,*
> *Or hair so beautiful; and say,*
>   *I hate to state it, but her style*
> *Would never get her by today.*
>
> *I'm not denying that your queen*
>   *In your eyes may have been a bear.*

> You couldn't pull the stuff I've seen
>   About her, if she wasn't there—
> That soft poetic bull, I mean.
>
> But just to call your rhythmic bluff
>   I'll say, before I ring the bell
> And kill this roundelay of fluff,
>   Like Dante, I'd go plumtoel
> For Beatrice—and that's enough!

But for all that, there was trouble between them—as Eugene showed in certain bitter comments on women that year—trouble that would pull them apart by the end of the next summer.

What did Eugene get out of his year at Harvard? "Well, not much out of the actual class-work itself," he told Barrett Clark. "Necessarily, most of what Baker had to teach the beginners about the theater as a physical medium was old stuff to me." Once, when a fellow student began to diagram the structure of a play by Augustus Thomas, Eugene, disgusted, walked out. But, as he said later, "I learned some things that were useful to me—particularly what not to do. Not to take ten lines, for instance, to say something that can be said in one line." What Baker really taught him was a method of work. Baker had his students start by writing a full scenario of their plays. Then he read the scenarios to the class and returned them for revision. "When [the] scenario seemed (to Baker) sufficiently clear and convincing," Everett Glass would recall, "the writer got the go-ahead signal and wrote his first dialogue draft, which Baker read us for criticism." Eugene adopted this method permanently. He always wrote a scenario first and revised it, then went on to the dialogue drafts, which might number as many as eight. Baker taught him a systematic approach.

The criticism in class was less helpful. For one thing, Eugene was extremely sensitive; he didn't like being the butt of class humor; indeed, his friendship with Corwin Willson cooled considerably after Willson made a joke about *The Sniper*. "Some play having to do with 'love' was read," Corwin Willson himself recalled, "and my criticism, which had an obvious sex-slant in a class of men, relative to a lack of physical action, was greeted with laughter. When

O'Neill's play [*The Sniper*] about German mutilation and rape of Belgians was read, I suggested seriously the trouble was, the play was all talk—no physical action. It was a theory of mine then that the physical acts of the main characters should tell the basic story; that words were to fill in the chinks of the action. Of course, in a play that was all about such violent things as mutilation, torture and rape, for me to complain of lack of physical action (in the theater, known as 'business') amused the class hugely. They wanted, they needed relief from the mass of God, gore, guts and guff that O'Neill's play had been concerned with for half an hour." Later Willson said, "I did not know then nor did I for months later that the play was by O'Neill and that he had taken my laughter most seriously."

Actually, of course, much of the criticism Eugene received was inept. A student who was using a play by Augustus Thomas as a model was not likely to understand a revolutionary departure in playwriting. Baker himself apparently was not able to. When Baker read Eugene's *Bound East for Cardiff* to the class, the students attacked its lack of plot. Baker agreed with them. "Though on one occasion Baker told me he didn't think *Bound East for Cardiff* (written before I entered the class) was a play at all," Eugene recalled, "I respected his judgment."

Eugene picked up and used one of Baker's favorite critical points. "I don't think any real dramatic stuff is created, to use an excellent expression of Professor Baker, 'out of the top of your head,'" Eugene would say. "That is, the roots of the drama have to be in life, however fine and delicate or symbolic or fanciful the development."

This judgment certainly applied to the plays that Eugene wrote for Baker. "The plays I wrote for him were rotten," Eugene said. They included four one-act plays—*The Dear Doctor, The Movie Man, A Knock at the Door,* and *The Sniper;* a four-act play, *The Second Engineer* (or *The Personal Equation*); and a play in six scenes, *Belshazzar,* written in collaboration with his classmate Collin Ford. "The long one [*The Second Engineer*] was a rambling thing about a seamen's and firemen's strike," Eugene recalled. "But it's funny about the one-acter [*The Dear Doctor*]. We thought it was slick enough for vaudeville, but when I began to look into the rights I found the story I'd based it on was stolen from a successful vaudeville sketch!"

For the most part, Eugene was trying to write on important subjects. In *The Sniper* he expressed his horror of the war in Europe and showed the suffering of the peasants who wanted only "to be left in peace to till our fields." In *The Movie Man,* he satirized materialism, the movies, and the bought Mexican generals of the recent war. But Baker's stress was on the commercially salable, and Eugene tried for that, too. *Belshazzar* was aimed at the current fad for Biblical pageantry. Eugene decided later that it was "worse than an Artzybasheff novel." He did not gain from Baker's immediate influence. Yet he valued Baker.

"Yes, I did get a great deal from Baker—personally," he would say. "He encouraged me, made me feel it was worth while going ahead. My personal association with him meant the devil of a lot to me at that time." In 1935, when Baker died, Eugene wrote, "Only those of us who had the privilege of membership in the drama class of George Pierce Baker back in the dark age when the American theatre was still, for playwrights, the closed shop, star system, amusement racket, can know what a profound influence Professor Baker, who died last Sunday, exerted toward the encouragement and birth of modern American drama.

"It is difficult in these days, when the native playwright can function in comparative freedom, to realize that in that benighted period a play of any imagination, originality or integrity by an American was almost automatically barred from a hearing in our theatre. To write plays of life as one saw and felt it, instead of concocting the conventional theatrical drivel of the time, seemed utterly hopeless.

"In the face of this blank wall, the bitterest need of the young playwright was for intelligent encouragement, to be helped to believe in the dawn of a new era in our theatre where he would have a chance, at least, to be heard. And of the rare few who had the unselfish faith and vision and love of the theatre to devote their life to this encouragement, Professor Baker's work stands pre-eminent. It is that encouragement which I—and I am sure all of the playwrights who knew and studied under him—will always remember with the deepest appreciation.

"Not that the technical points, the analysis of the practice of play-making taught in his class, were not of inestimable value to us in learning our trade. But the most vital thing for us, as possible future artists and creators, to learn at that time (Good God! For any one to learn anywhere at any time!) was to believe in our work and to keep on believing. And to hope. He helped us to hope—and for that we owe him all the finest we have in memory of gratitude and friendship."

Eugene needed to have hope. He knew, now, how naïve his first dreams had been. The manuscripts he had mailed so joyfully had come to nothing. His book had dropped like a stone into water. Only Clayton Hamilton finally reviewed it in April, 1915, in *The Bookman* and *The Nation*.

"Another playwright of promise," Clayton Hamilton wrote, "is Mr. Eugene G. O'Neill—a son of the noted actor, Mr. James O'Neill —who has recently published five one-act plays under the title of *Thirst*. This writer's favourite mood is that of horror. He deals with grim and ghastly situations that would become intolerable if they were protracted beyond the limits of a single sudden act. He seems to be familiar with the sea; for three of these five plays deal with terrors that attend the tragedy of ship-wreck. He shows a keen sense of the reactions of character under stress of violent emotion; and his dialogue is almost brutal in its power. More than one of these plays should be available for such an institution as the Princess Theatre in New York."

"Do you know that your review was the only one that poor volume ever received?" Eugene told Clayton Hamilton later. "And, if brief, it was favorable! You can't imagine what it meant, coming from you. It held out a hope at a very hopeless time. It did send me to the hatters. It made me believe I was arriving with a bang; and at that period I very much needed someone whose authority I respected to admit I was getting somewhere."

Few read the book; fewer bought it. (Soon, Badger offered almost the whole edition back to him at thirty cents a copy. Eugene refused, thinking it a waste of money "on my lousy drama.") Only

Hamilton and Baker gave Eugene reason to hope. Each spring Baker chose four students for his advanced class the next year. Eugene was one of the four he chose. But Eugene didn't really want another year at Harvard. He was tired of the classroom. He seemed, a friend observed, "extremely impatient with 47, and anxious to get down to live in Greenwich Village." So although Baker "was very eager that he should return for a second year of work," Eugene turned his back on Harvard.

CHAPTER TWENTY-TWO

The "Blank Wall"

Iꜰ Eugene could have broken through his bitterness to really talk with his father that summer of 1915, he would have found that they had much in common. Like his son, James O'Neill looked upon the war in Europe with dismay. He had helped the Lambs Club put on *Why?*, George V. Hobart's allegorical play about the folly of war, at the Century Theater on June 17.

He was as disturbed as Eugene by managerial opposition to serious drama, although he worried particularly over the refusal to produce Shakespeare's plays, especially *Hamlet*. "For the present day they are in the discard," he told a reporter from the St. Louis *Globe Democrat*. "It is a day of frivolity, of piffle. The serious things are lost in a souffle of skirts and suds and other light things. The moving picture, the caricature, the slang and joke, seem to be the most serious things in this world. But—mark me—the war, and poverty, and the mental, moral and financial slump are going to have a remarkable turn in this country soon. As they say in England, 'Wake up!'

"That's what we're going to do over here, some day. We're going to quit being pifflers. We're going back to the serious things of life —not so serious as to be boresome, but enough to believe that the whirl of skirts, the fluff of foam and slang and scoffing are not all of life. Then there will be a chance for serious drama."

But Eugene wasn't looking for common ground with his father. Far from it. His rage against his father increased as his love affair with Beatrice went to pieces. Papa believed that Eugene had behaved as badly in this case as he had with Kathleen Jenkins. Papa didn't understand that in this instance Eugene had been sincerely in love. People were talking—whispers ran through New London that Eugene had behaved badly.

For Eugene, the social disapproval was nothing compared to his own distress. Even Judge Latimer saw it. "He was at one time in love with a very sweet young lady quite opposed to his radical ways of looking at things," Judge Latimer would later report, "and they were in the throes of breaking apart. He was adrift in mind and spirit."

In his restless unhappiness, Eugene could not have faced another year at Harvard. Anyway, he wanted independence. He had hopes of getting a job as a drama critic at $25 a week in New York. *Joseph and His Brethren* had finally closed, so Papa would be in retirement that year. He and Mama planned to move to rooms in the Prince George Hotel for the winter. As Eugene put it, they had offered to "keep" him there, but, he told Art McGinley, he didn't want to be "kept." (Later, when the job as drama critic fell through, Eugene did accept an allowance from his father.) When his family came to New York, Eugene moved into a room at 38 Washington Square in Greenwich Village. "The garbage flat," he called it.

Eugene worked almost desperately, writing six or seven hours a day. Evenings, he slipped back into the old release from tension— alcohol. That summer Dr. Sullivan had examined his lungs and declared them "absolutely sound," so fear no longer kept him from taking refuge in drink.

His early hopes had evaporated. He might as well have spent the years drowned at the bottom of a bottle for all the notice the world had taken of his plays. He was tempted to give up. He never forgot this bitter year. He spoke of it again and again years later to a discouraged young writer, Patrick O'Neill, whom he was helping. He told Patrick that "they" would try to make him quit, try to kill his hope, but that he must keep on writing.

As always, suffering aroused his "devil of hate." As always, he fed it by a promiscuity that was almost a ritual act of degradation—sex out of hate. Art McGinley would recall his shock, one gray dawn, after he and Eugene had spent the night with two girls in Brooklyn. As they prepared to leave, the girl who had been with Gene clung to him, murmuring, "Don't you love me any more, baby?" Savagely, Eugene pushed her away. "You have a body odor like the market place in Baghdad," he said.

Yet Eugene went on writing. He tried a farce, *The G.A.M.*, and a pantomime, *Atrocity*. But his was a lonely struggle. Everywhere, still, he was faced with a "blank wall." Sardonically, in February, 1916, he watched Papa's "substitute" son, Brandon Tynan, lighting up Broadway with his Irish comedy, *Melody of Youth*. Papa himself was in the play for one week.

"I've been doing a little investigating," Papa had written Tyler, who was producing Tynan's play, "and I have discovered that there's a blind beggar in the second act of Tynan's play. I insist upon playing the part. I don't care how small it is. As one of the older generation of players I want to make a little offering to one of the most promising representatives of the younger generation." And then he added, "Besides, I've always wanted to play an Irish part."

The critics praised Papa's portrayal of the blind man. He was "an artist to his finger tips," said the critic from the New York *Star*. "This character is on the stage for perhaps five minutes, and only in one act, and yet so great is the player's artistry that the role stands out as something to be remembered. Mr. O'Neill has long been Mr. Tynan's friend and counsellor, and is said to have insisted on playing the Blind Man for a short period out of regard for his friend—than which one player could show no truer friendship for another." Jealously, Eugene watched.

Eugene himself had got no help from his father. Not that James O'Neill had not tried. Years later Irvin S. Cobb would recall, among other things, that James O'Neill had asked his advice on Eugene's plays.

"Upon his retirement he reverted to his proper and natural self," Cobb wrote of James O'Neill, "which would be another way of saying he was a simple, gracious, unassuming old gentleman. The few elocutionary flutings that he kept out of his former repertoire were as so many agreeable oddities to adorn his conversation. At the Lambs' club I spent a good deal of time in his company. One afternoon he said to me, rather diffidently, 'I wonder if I might ask a favor of you? My son Eugene—he's away now on a sea voyage—but at Harvard he studied under Professor Baker, and he has written some playlets—dramatic sketches, I suppose you might call them. Now I have read them and I confess I'm in doubt about their playability. I've brought them along with me—' he hauled some rather meager-looking folios out of his pocket—'and I'm taking the liberty of asking you to read them and give me your opinion on their possibilities. In strict confidence, of course. He knows nothing of this.'

" 'I'll be glad to give you my opinion for what it might be worth, Mr. O'Neill,' I said, 'but why not submit them to some of the regular playwrights around here—this place crawls with 'em?'

" 'You are my friend,' he said, 'and you're a writer.'

"I tried to explain to him that as between writing stories and writing plays a wide gulf intervened—that in a way of speaking it was like the distinction between laying bricks and laying eggs; both laying operations, but different functional activities were involved. He insisted, and sat near by, sipping his cocktail while I read what the young man had written.

"Before I turned the first page of the first script I could understand why this old-time melodramatic star, trained in the noisier mode of a vanished era, might be puzzled by the revolutionary technique of his junior. I read them through—there were four scripts. And then, stirred to my very marrows by the brute strength here expressed, I reread them.

" 'Mr. O'Neill,' I said, then, 'alongside some of the candy-store tripe that's being produced these days, this stuff is like a slab of fresh beef hacked with a cleaver on a butcher's block and slapped down on top of jelly beans and gumdrops. This has got raw, crude life in it—blood and muscle and guts. Worked over into short story form it might go—if you picked the magazines that would dare to print it. But as play material—well, I don't believe you'd ever find a manager to produce it or a critic who'd endorse it or a public that would go to see it.'

"'Exactly what I thought myself,' he said, resignedly."

When James O'Neill told Eugene what Cobb had said, Eugene got angry, feeling misunderstood. Long afterward, he said of his father to Barrett Clark, "He did believe in me—in a way, but as I've said, he thought I was crazy. He didn't see why I should write the kind of plays I did, and he pointed out, quite properly, that there was no market for them; but he must have thought there was something there—something he did not like or maybe quite understand. He believed I might some day amount to something—if I lived."

Before long, Eugene knew all the village saloons: The Working Girl's Home, for instance, presided over by Luke O'Connor, who had once employed John Masefield as a bartender. "He knew unerringly when the moment came for him to eject a drunken customer," Hutchins Hapgood recalled, "or caustically to interrupt a senseless conversation. I have seen him leap over the bar like a panther, grabbing a seltzer-bottle on his way, and putting out the offender by squirting the seltzer in his face till he fell over backward through the doors."

Even more alluring was the dingy Golden Swan on the southeast corner of Fourth Street and Sixth Avenue, usually called the "Hell-Hole." Behind the bar was a back room where a moth-eaten stuffed swan floated on painted lily pads; any time after five in the afternoon, tobacco smoke and whiskey fumes floated with it. The Hell-Hole, Mary Heaton Vorse thought, "was sinister." "It was as if the combined soul of New York flowed underground and this was one of its vents," she said.

Wallace, the proprietor, owned the whole building, and kept it full of down-and-outers he had adopted out of the kindness of his heart. "Every night," according to Mary Heaton Vorse, "it happened that Wallace and his aged cronies fought and got tight together.

Then, just before closing time they staggered off to bed, each man having been presented with a half pint of whiskey to sober up on the next day." Often the uproar from Wallace and his friends up front in the bar drowned out the conversation of the guests in the back room. Whereupon, the bartenders Lefty Louis or John Bull, arriving with a customer's beer, "would murmur reassuringly, 'Wallace!'"

At the Hell-Hole one evening Eugene saw, for the first time, the long, lean form of Terry Carlin, with his aesthete's face—high cheekbones, large nose, shock of white hair, and blue eyes that seemed to be looking beyond this world into another and another beyond that. Carlin was talking to some rough-looking gangsters who were listening spellbound, and his words were sheer poetry. Eugene listened, spoke to him, and ended by being completely enchanted. In Terry Carlin he found the catalyst that would bring the chaotic whirl of ideas in his mind to a focus and found also, in this penniless bum, a leader who would carry him beyond the "blank wall" into the sunshine of recognition.

PART SIX

THE "OLD FOOLOSOPHER"

CHAPTER TWENTY-THREE

Terry Carlin

H E was a splendid talker, a dreamer, a poet, a man. Wonderful Terry," Mabel Dodge would write. She was one of many who saw in Terry Carlin the wisdom and beauty of a Hindu holy man. Had he cared enough for the world to write, Terry Carlin might have been a great poet or novelist. Instead, he spread his illumination through conversation. Two writers tried to portray his amazing story: Dhan Gopal Mukerji in *Caste and Outcast* and Hutchins Hapgood in *An Anarchist Woman*. Eugene O'Neill, too, would portray him in *The Iceman Cometh*, but by that time Eugene would be too powerfully identified with Terry to keep himself out of the character of Larry Slade.

Terry's full name was Terence O'Carolan. He had started life as a skilled tanner, but two experiences had shocked him into a new way of life. First, he discovered a flaw in the process his employer

212 THE "OLD FOOLOSOPHER"

was using, gave him the valuable information and received in reward—nothing. This crystallized all his doubts about the capitalist
system, his belief that workmen were being coldly exploited. He
quit his job and determined never again to do a day's work for organized society. For the rest of his long life he carried out this determination with remarkable consistency. "It was the act of an almost impossible idealist," Hutchins Hapgood would say, "of a
dreamer, of a poet with—as Terry said of himself—a narrow but high
forehead which would never permit him to see things in the light of
the practical world."

The second experience determined his philosophy. He happened
to be at the labor meeting in the Chicago Haymarket Square in
May, 1886, when the police charged at the crowd and a bomb was
thrown. The frenzied attack on anarchists that followed and the subsequent hanging of four innocent men converted him to anarchy.
Later, when Mukerji asked him if he had had any background on
anarchism at the time, he said, "No, that explosion was my background. And now I pray to myself, 'Let it be my foreground as
well!'"

Having rejected organized society, Terry gathered to himself its
outcasts. To him the most despised became the most beautiful; he
turned to the bums, the criminals, the prostitutes, the broken ones.
"It is only in the gutter that life is truly worshipped," he would say.
"And that is why I search for my last faith there—in the gutter,
whence all faith really springs."

He gathered about him his "Rogues Gallery," as he called them,
and shared with them whatever food or shelter he could find, and
shared with them his wisdom too. He became a central figure in
Chicago anarchist circles, and with him, usually, was a girl known
only as Marie. She was, Hutchins Hapgood said, "a slight, dark,
anaemic, passionate-looking girl." Terry had found her and taught
her his anarchist ideas in time to save her from "ordinary prostitution." Hapgood, who met her at an anarchist ball, found her amazing. "When I met her at the ball," he said, "she talked to me, this
young thing did, with the utmost conviction about the conspiracy
that has existed since the birth of human society, by which strong
minorities hold the great majority in abject slavery." Her talk came,

of course, from Terry Carlin and the anarchist books they read together in their little apartment. "To me it was very significant that this girl, who naturally I think would have had no ideas of any kind," Hapgood observed, "became the passionate vehicle of the ideas in her environment." She remained a passionate anarchist long after Terry himself had broken with the movement.

Terry lived with Marie for many years, accepting her infidelities, on principle, with philosophical calm. After one of her affairs, he wrote to Hutchins Hapgood. "She is seriously ill, the result of a mad adventure. As I exist for others when they are in pain, I am her trained nurse." For three weeks, he cared for her night and day. "I feel rather worn with domestic drudgery," he confided to Hapgood, "cooking, laundering, wrestling with disease without and demons within."

Finally, her promiscuity killed his love for her. And when he broke with her, he also broke with the Anarchist Movement, which she had come to represent to him. (Eugene O'Neill would recreate her as Rosa Parritt in *The Iceman Cometh*.) Henceforth, Terry would go his way alone. "I am very 'crummy,' badly flea-bitten, overrun with bed bugs," he wrote Hapgood after his final rupture with Marie, "but, redemption of it all, I am free and always drunk."

From this time on he was the aloof, detached philosopher. Only a friend as perceptive as Eugene O'Neill would see the profound pity behind Terry's mask of detachment. Terry himself, of course, knew his detachment was illusory. "Now I am in a state of mind when I am willing to let everything go by default—everything except my last illusion, that I can never let myself out to anyone," he told Hapgood shortly after he left Marie. "To Marie—and to you— and one or two others—I have been sorely tempted to lay myself out —but not even the moon can seduce me to reveal myself. My dead and buried self is my first and last seduction. This is crazy, of course, but I am heartily sick of all the sense I know or can know." Eugene would portray this "grandstand foolosopher bunk" as Larry's (Terry's) pipedream in *The Iceman Cometh*.

After Terry left Marie, he wandered to California and fell in with a young Indian anarchist, Dhan Gopal Mukerji, whom he told immediately to go back to India. "Your ancestors found the truths you are seeking thousands of years ago; Buddha was the greatest of all anarchists." Like Mukerji, Terry slept on the floor of the I.W.W. local in return for making a few speeches a week. Soon Terry quarreled with the I.W.W. on a point of policy (he insisted that individualism would be violated if industrial control were placed in the hands of the workers). When he was asked to leave, Terry said, "All the better, I'll be rid of your vermin." "All right," came the reply. "We'll keep our vermin. You get out!" Perhaps this was the origin of the scene in *The Hairy Ape* in which Yank is thrown out of the I.W.W.

With the money Hutchins Hapgood gave him from the sale of *An Anarchist Woman,* Terry went to England. From London, he wrote Hapgood that he had been living "on a bloater a day for a year" and the diet was getting on his nerves. Hapgood was able to send him just enough money to get back. "On his arrival in New York—I was away at the time—he entered the bar at Fourth Street and Sixth Avenue, with a complete lack of coin," Hapgood recalled. "Standing before the bar, tall, gaunt and handsome, he ordered a whiskey, then another and another. The owner behind the bar finally suggested payment; but when Terry, blandly and sweetly, said he had no money, the bartender, captivated, like so many others before and since, by the beautiful ragged bum, said, 'Have another.'"

Not only was he given another, and yet another; Wallace gave him a room, and he became a permanent resident of the Hell-Hole. So it was that Eugene O'Neill found Terry Carlin, and in him the force that would resolve, in his own mind, the conflict between Marxian socialism and Nietzschean individualism in favor of individualism. Through his friendship with Terry Carlin, Eugene O'Neill became a philosophical anarchist and a confirmed mystic.

Terry, like Eugene, had been powerfully influenced by Nietzsche, and could express a blistering Nietzschean contempt for the conforming herd. "Oh, how I wish I were a fine lean satirist!—with a great black-snake whip of sarcasm to scourge the smug and genial ones!" said Terry. "How I would lash on corpulent content and fat faith with folds in its belly." Terry thought conservative morality had "an organic basis: it has its seat in those vestiges of muscles that would wag our abortive tails, and often wag our abortive tongues!"

But Terry saw no answer to bourgeois morality in socialism. "I once thought that I could help the mob to organize its own freedom. But now I see that we are all the mob, that all human beings are alike, and that all I or anyone can do is to save his own soul, to win his own freedom, and perhaps to teach others to do the same, not so much through social propaganda as by digging down to a deeper personal culture." The words might have been spoken by the later Eugene O'Neill, so perfectly did they express what he came to believe. As he would say fiercely of the American "mob" in *Days Without End*, "They explain away their spiritual cowardice by whining that the time for individualism is past, when it is their courage to possess their own souls which is dead—and stinking!"

Terry was contemptuous, too, of the vote as a political ideal. "To give a man a vote in a so-called free country is like giving a lantern to a blind man. What use is it? We are in this world to destroy our blindness and then see the light. And these fools come and want to make a ghastly mockery of blindness by giving it a vote." Again, the words might have come from the later O'Neill. As he has Yank say in *The Hairy Ape*, "Tree square a day, and cauliflowers in de front yard—ekal rights—a woman and kids—a lousy vote—and I'm all fixed for Jesus, huh? Aw, hell! What does dat get yuh? Dis ting's in your inside, but it ain't your belly."

"I call myself a philosophical anarchist," said Terry, and thirty years later Eugene would echo him. "I am a philosophical anarchist," he would say and then add, "which means, 'Go to it, but leave me out of it.' "

Terry's rejection of social answers to the human problem rested on a profound mysticism. "Let humanity alone. Humanity is the sewer through which we are all passing. We do not see why we should improve the sewer unless it clogs our passage too much," Terry told Mukerji. "If I were you, I would go back to India and sit under a tree and dream my dreams. In the West we are commercializing our dreams. Even the utopias are being made so practicable that nobody has any interest in them."

Terry was very ready to initiate others into mysticism. "I was very young in those days," Charles Hapgood (Hutchins Hapgood's son) would say of the time when Eugene O'Neill and Terry Carlin first came to Provincetown together, "but I remember Terry gave me a little book entitled *Light on the Path,* containing Hindu wisdom, and it had a great effect on me for many years." Apparently, Terry also used this book to initiate Eugene O'Neill into "the Eastern Wisdom."

Eugene was ready to absorb *Light on the Path,* for he was temperamentally a mystic. He had always been drawn by the idea of mysterious forces beyond the individual life of man. *Light on the Path* simply completed his education in mysticism. Now he would follow consciously the advice in *Light on the Path:* "Desire only that which is within you. Desire only that which is beyond you. Desire only that which is unattainable." This was the germ of Eugene's philosophy of the "hopeless hope." For the rest of his life he would search in himself for "the light," believing the mystic words: "For within you is the light of the world, the only light that can be shed upon the Path. If you are unable to perceive it within you, it is useless to look for it elsewhere. It is beyond you; because, when you reach it, you have lost yourself." In all his mature plays, Eugene would seek the answers beyond self in the struggling individual.

Terry Carlin's mysticism included a rejection of logic and reason as methods of arriving at truth. "Most of us try to think, intellectuals; fear to abandon ourselves to alarming states of feeling where reason is crowded to the wall. And yet I feel that [in] abandoning ourselves completely to mere feeling lies our only hope to find the logic of the race that no individual reason can master." The truth, Terry felt, could not be expressed in words. When Mukerji asked him, "What is the answer to all this?" he replied, "There is an answer somewhere, but he who has found it, as some of your old Indian sages have done, knows that the little chalice of the human word cannot hold it."

Eugene, too, would reject reason as a means of arriving at the truth. "Thinking explains. It eliminates the unexplainable—by which we live," he would say in *Welded,* and to Mary Mullett he would explain why the emotions are the best source of knowledge. "Our emotions are instinctive. They are the result not only of our individual experiences but of the experiences of the whole human race, back through the ages. They are the deep undercurrent, whereas our thoughts are often only the small individual surface reactions." More and more, Eugene's whole philosophy of life and of dramatic writing would rest on the premise that the emotions are better able to perceive and grasp truth than the intellect. In the theater, he would deliberately use sight, sound, and action, rather than words, to convey his meanings.

One element of Terry Carlin's mysticism was a belief in eternal recurrence—the idea symbolized for Hindus and Buddhists in the endlessly turning wheel of life and the idea Nietzsche had made his own: "Now I die and vanish and in a moment I shall be nothing. Souls are as mortal as bodies. But the knot of causes recurreth in which I am twined. It will create me again. I myself belong unto the causes of eternal recurrence. I come back not for a new life, or a better life, or an eternal life, but back eternally unto this one and same life, in the greatest and the smallest things." Terry Carlin agreed, though at times he did not welcome the prospect. "After being down-hearted for some time, I grow superstitious and imagine that some strange and fatal spell is hanging over us all. Even my own acts and thoughts take on the futility of nightmare, and Nirvana is very welcome, if I could be sure of it, but I had rather stay what I am than start life all over again in some other shape, with a possible creeping recollection of my former existence. I have at times startled intimations that I lived in vain in some former unhappy time; so I shall try to postpone the eternal recurrence as best I may."

At other times, however, Terry looked forward to eternity. "Why, to me, this world is a halting hell of hitching posts and of truculent troughs for belching swineherds. The universe has no goal that we know of unless Eternity be the aim; let us then have the modesty of the Cosmos, and no other modesty, and be content to know our course, and be sure to run it."

Eugene O'Neill, too, would become fascinated with the idea of eternal recurrence and present it often in his plays, sometimes with joy. In *The Fountain,* the idea would appear in Juan's vision: "Life is a field/ Forever growing/ Beauty a fountain/ Forever flowing." In *The Great God Brown* it would appear in Cybel's rapturous words: "Always spring comes again bearing life! Always again! Always, always forever again!" But the eternal recurrence could be terrifying, too, as it is in *Mourning Becomes Electra* where the same situations recur in generation after generation, or in *Moon for the Misbegotten* where Tyrone says, "There is no present or future—only the past happening over and over again—now."

In the Hell-Hole, talking with Terry Carlin and the Hudson Dusters, in the midst of the drinking and the smoking and the chatter, Eugene O'Neill completed his education. Terry was, in his way, a great teacher. He had a way of picking up a commonplace remark of a companion and perceiving universal wisdom in it—so that his companion could feel that Terry's wisdom was only a commentary on his own brilliant idea. Terry could listen, too. For Eugene, always hesitant in speech, Terry was the perfect companion. He never broke in on the silences that were preludes to Eugene's expression of his most intimate thoughts. He always understood what Eugene said and built upon it.

In the spring of 1916, Terry suggested they go up to Provincetown, where Hutch Hapgood always spent the summer. Eugene agreed. New York was unbearable in the summer, and he didn't want to go to New London with his family. Provincetown sounded fine. Quite without forethought, Terry led Eugene to the place where the first chink was opening in the blank wall of Broadway standards, where he would find the recognition he had dreamed of and a love beyond his wildest dreams.

CHAPTER TWENTY-FOUR

Applause in Provincetown

W<small>HEN</small> Terry and Gene arrived in Provincetown, they went at once to Hutchins Hapgood to "put the bite" on him for ten dollars, "which," Hapgood said later, "it will probably amuse Gene to know, has never been repaid." Hapgood wrote to Mabel Dodge, "Terry Carlin and O'Neill (son of James O'Neill) have taken Bayard's studio." This was a spacious room in the John Francis Apartments over John Francis's grocery store. For inspiration, Eugene painted on the rafters the rules for disciples in *Light on the Path:*

> *Before the eyes can see they must be incapable of tears.*
> *Before the ear can hear it must have lost its sensitiveness.*
> *Before the voice can speak . . . it must have lost the power*
>   *to wound.*
> *Before the soul can stand . . . its feet must be washed in the*
>   *blood of the heart.*

Terry and Eugene lived for the whole of that summer on Eugene's allowance. Eugene was working on a dramatic monologue, *Before Breakfast,* in which he expressed some of the bitterness of his dependency and of his experiences in love. The suicidal central character of the play has got a woman with child and married her. He now finds he has got another woman with child—a woman he truly loves—and is powerless to help her. Eugene was also finishing a full-length comedy *Now I Ask You,* in which he poked fun at his own "wilder revolts" when he had allowed Nietzsche and Ibsen's *Hedda Gabler* to influence him a little too directly.

While Eugene worked, Terry wandered about town, renewing old friendships among the artists and writers there and, as always, finding the outcasts. Once Terry invited some of these specimens to meet Eugene and Hutch. "You could always trust Terry to get to the bottom of things, in which he saw a significance that even I sometimes missed," Hutchins Hapgood would say. "Gene, Terry, and I had gotten to the genial stage in our drinking, when those— no, not bums, for bums are often very attractive—creatures appeared, and sat down with us around the table. Gene took one look at them and began to drink with great rapidity. Certainly within the hour he had drunk himself into a state of complete insensibility. It was clear enough to me, and also to Terry, for we afterwards compared notes. Whether consciously or not, O'Neill had acted in the spirit of self-preservation. He had a great and genuine sympathy and understanding for that type of human being, but he couldn't endure them."

Terry also introduced Gene to the artists and writers in Provincetown. Terry knew everyone, so it was not extraordinary that Susan Glaspell asked him, one day, a question that would give Eugene O'Neill his start.

The question had a history. It had begun with Susan's husband, George Cram Cook—"Jig," as his friends called him—who loved the plays of Aeschylus, Sophocles, and Euripides. He had watched a production of Aristophanes' *Lysistrata* and instead of laughing had wept at the beauty and truth of this play, alive after thousands of years, and at the loss of the great Greek theater. He and Susan wondered how anything as splendid as life could be made into anything as dull as a Broadway play. Twice, Jig Cook had glimpsed what a modern living theater might be: first, when John Reed brought two thousand embattled strikers from the Paterson Silk Mills over to Madison Square Garden and had them act out their struggle; second, when he went to the old Jewish theater on Henry Street.

Cook wanted to create a theater that would "cause" great plays to be written, as the Greek theater had. He and Susan had written a one-act satire, *Suppressed Desires,* on the craze for Freudian analysis of dreams. But no one would produce it. At Provincetown in the summer of 1915, they had found that Hapgood's wife, Neith Boyce, had written a one-act spoof on the tumultuous love affair of John Reed and Mabel Dodge called *Constancy.* For the fun of it, they decided to put on the two plays at Hapgood's house. So many people were hurt at not being invited to the delightful performance that they put on the plays again in the old fish house at the end of the wharf that Margaret Steele was renting from Mary Heaton Vorse. This production was so successful that they did two more plays, Jig Cook's *Change Your Style* and Wilbur Daniel Steele's *Contemporaries.* That was the summer of 1915.

Before Eugene O'Neill arrived in the summer of 1916, the "Provincetown Players" had put on John Reed's *Freedom* and Neith Boyce's *Winter's Night* against odds. Shortly before opening night, the fish house had caught fire. They had worked frantically with the Provincetown fire department to save the wharf. When the fire was out, they found the curtain burned and two of the walls charred black. Undaunted, they bought a new curtain, stained the other walls black to match the charred ones, and opened on schedule. More people came than the ninety they could accommodate on the hard wooden benches, and everyone enjoyed the performance. Now they were looking for new plays, and Susan Glaspell, coming upon Terry Carlin in the street, asked, "Terry, haven't you a play to read to us?"

"No, I don't write, I just think, and sometimes talk," Terry answered, smiling. "But Mr. O'Neill has got a whole trunk full of plays."

When the committee of the Provincetown Players met at Susan and Jig's house that evening, Susan told them her news. "There's a young fellow called O'Neill who says he has a trunk full of plays. Told me about one of them. Sounds a little alarming." She had invited him to come to the meeting and bring a play. At eight o'clock, Eugene came, handsome, silent, looking about him with glowing eyes. He found himself in the midst of a large group: Hutch Hapgood with his glittering glasses and the look, as Mabel Dodge would say, of a "Lutheran monk"; his wife Neith Boyce, serenely beautiful with dark red hair, a classic profile, and a satirical curl on her lips; Susan Glaspell who, Max Eastman would say, looked like "an overtired but sweetly conscientious farmer's wife"; Jig Cook, huge, white-haired, enthusiastic; John Reed, with honey-colored curls; next to Reed, a slender dark-haired girl with blue-gray eyes like Beatrice, strikingly beautiful, named Louise Bryant; and others— Freddie Burt, Edward Ballantine, Margaret and Wilbur Daniel Steele, Mary Heaton Vorse and her husband Joe O'Brien.

Eugene was too shy to read his play, so Freddie Burt did it for him while Eugene went into the dining room so that he wouldn't have to witness this test of his work. The play was *Bound East for Cardiff*. Of that evening Susan Glaspell would say, "Then we knew what we were for." Eugene suddenly found himself surrounded by admirers. Immediately he was caught up in rehearsals of *Bound East for Cardiff*. Jig Cook played the dying Yank. Eugene played the mate, although he was sick with stage fright. Susan Glaspell talked later of the beauty of that performance at the Wharf Theatre. "The sea has been good to O'Neill," she would write. "It was there for his opening. There was a fog, just as the script demanded, fog bell in the harbor. The tide was in, and it washed under us and around, spraying through the holes in the floor, giving us the rhythm and the flavor of the sea while the big dying sailor talked to his friend Drisc of the life he had always wanted deep in the land, where you'd never see a ship or smell the sea." When it was all over, "the old wharf," Susan Glaspell said, "shook with applause."

That was the beginning. A day or so later, Jig Cook rushed to Gene and told him that Adele Nathan, director of a little theater group in Baltimore, The Vagabonds, had seen his play and wanted it; she was coming to Cook's that night to meet the group. "Everybody was visibly shaken by meeting with a director." Adele Nathan would recall, "especially a director ready to pay cold cash for one-acters." The cold cash was only fifteen dollars, but it meant certain production, for no little theater group could squander fifteen dollars on a play it wasn't going to use. Eugene had only a single tattered copy of *Bound East for Cardiff*. He offered to make Adele Nathan a clean copy, but he warned her he was a rotten typist.

"At the eleventh hour he arrived with his clean copy," she would recall. "He certainly knew his limitations. He was not a good typist. He had made innumerable corrections in ink. The stage directions and off stage noises he added almost illegibly in blue and red pencil."

Eugene was jubilant. His first sale! He didn't know that The Vagabonds had rejected the plays in his volume *Thirst* before Adele Nathan came to Provincetown, nor would he ever know that she had to fight to get The Vagabonds to put on *Bound East for Cardiff*. He also would never know that the copy he gave her for $15 would later bring her an offer of $1,000 from a collector.

Edward Ballantine thought Gene had done "really good acting" in *Bound East for Cardiff*: "Gene knew sailormen." Even Harry Kemp —who played Davis—admired Gene's performance: "He had just one line to say: 'Isn't this your watch on deck, Driscoll?' but he said it with brusqueness." So Eugene was encouraged to battle stage fright again to play the West Indian sailor in his play *Thirst*. He was so sunburned he needed no make-up. Louise Bryant, the girl with the lovely eyes, played the dancer and Jig Cook was the gentleman.

The Provincetown Players were beginning to get a reputation. City reporters came down to interview them. To everyone Jig Cook talked of Eugene O'Neill—the one "unknown" among that illustrious group of writers, artists, and actors—and told them that O'Neill was "going to be heard from in places less remote than Provincetown." Exhilarated with success, Jig was already talking of renting a stable in the Village in New York and putting on plays that winter. Everyone thought he was crazy except John Reed. Between the two of them, they swept away objections. "There's no stopping it!" said Jack Reed.

Eugene was excited and grateful, particularly to Jig Cook. "Cook," he would say later, "was the big man, the dominating and inspiring genius of the Players. Always enthusiastic, vital, impatient with everything that smacked of falsity or compromise, he represented the spirit of revolt against the old worn-out traditions, the commercial theater, the tawdry artificialities of the stage. I owe a tremendous lot to the Players—they encouraged me to write."

From Jig Cook he got the exalted idea of the theater as an arena for the ritual celebration of life as the old Greek theater had been. Later, Jig would portray his idea of the history of the theater in frescoes he painted on the walls of the dining room of his Truro farmhouse: "Theater hardening into Church. Pure Dead Church. Church giving birth to Theater. Pure Dead Theater. Theater transforming itself into Living Church." That was Jig's dream: a theater that would be a "Living Church," a religious celebration of life.

The idea of the theater as a "Living Church" appealed to Eugene. He adopted it. Years later, in "Memoranda on Masks," he wrote, "I harp on the word 'imaginative'—and with intention! But what do I mean by an 'imaginative' theatre (where I hope for it, for example, in the sub-title of 'Lazarus Laughed': 'A Play for an Imaginative Theatre')? I mean the one true theatre, the age-old theatre, the theatre of the Greeks and Elizabethans, a theatre that could dare to boast—without committing a farcical sacrilege—that it is a legitimate descendant of the first theatre that sprang, by virtue of man's imaginative interpretation of life, out of his worship of Dionysus. I mean a theatre returned to its highest and sole significant function as a Temple where the religion of a poetical interpretation and symbolical celebration of life is communicated to human beings, starved in spirit by their soul-stifling daily struggle to exist as masks among the masks of living!"

Gene found himself surrounded by colorful personalities. He became a good friend of Louis Holliday, a quiet, tense man. He enjoyed talking with Harry Weinberger, a young anarchist, who became his friend and later his lawyer. Terry introduced Eugene to an old friend from his Chicago anarchist days—a short, stocky, wild-haired man with a great expanse of forehead, and an absurdly small nose, whose thick glasses, like two bright moons, dominated his face. This was Hippolyte Havel, a little volcano of a man who perpetually seethed with excitement, and moved with breathtaking swiftness from affectionate sweetness to vituperative rage.

Havel had been editor, when Terry first met him, of a Chicago anarchist publication, the *Arbeiterzeitung*. His mother had been a gypsy, his father a native of Bohemia. The family lived in Austria. Hippolyte had been arrested in his youth for anarchist activities. In court he condemned the country and his trial so vigorously that the judge had pronounced him "criminally insane," and had him thrown into a prison madhouse. Luckily, Krafft-Ebing, the eminent psychiatrist, on a visit to the madhouse met Hippolyte and quickly realized that he was perfectly sane; he simply had unconventional ideas. As a result, Havel was transferred to an ordinary prison and finally freed. His years in prison had ruined his eyesight—hence his thick glasses—but had only strengthened his anarchism. He fled to London, where he met Emma Goldman, and it was she who brought him to America.

Later, he found Emma Goldman too conventional. Mabel Dodge remembered an incident at one of her "Evenings." Emma Goldman and Big Bill Haywood spoke. When they had finished, Hippolyte burst out. Mabel Dodge reported: " 'They talk like goddam bourgeois,' suddenly cried Hippolyte Havel in a high, peevish voice, glaring around through the thick lenses in his spectacles. 'My little sister!' he exclaimed to me later that evening, in his sweet whining voice. 'My little goddam bourgeois capitalist sister!' And tears ran over his spectacles."

Those were the days when, with Polly Holliday, Havel ran a restaurant on Washington Square, which was a center of radical and artistic life in the Village. The food was excellent and Hippolyte radiated sweetness, except for his outbursts of violent jealousy when Polly took too much interest in a male customer. Theodore Dreiser was enchanted with him. "Havel is one of those men who ought to be supported by the community," Dreiser told Hutchins Hapgood; "he is a valuable person for life, but can't take care of himself. If I ever have any money, I'll certainly settle some of it on Hippolyte."

Havel was quite ready to be supported. With unabashed sweetness, he would ask for money from those who had it (he was outraged at the thought of taking from the poor). The sum he asked for was always "a dollar," no more, no less. But he was willing to work. For a long time he was cook at Hutchins Hapgood's Dobbs Ferry home; he always joined the family for dinner. If he thought a guest was a conservative, he never hesitated to shout "Goddamned bourgeois!" and once he was so enraged by a "bourgeois" remark that he threw a fork through a windowpane.

When the routine of cooking and reading oppressed him, he would dress up—in a black suit, black flowing tie, spats, and a cane— and go to the city. After a few days, Hapgood would retrieve him— drunk, broke, disheveled, sometimes with broken glasses—and bring him back to Dobbs Ferry where he resumed his reading and his cooking until he broke out again.

Eugene spent much time with Hippolyte Havel, enjoying his talk and his personality. Years later, he would reproduce Hippolyte with loving fidelity as Hugo Kalmar in *The Iceman Cometh*. In Province-town, Hippolyte was staying with John Reed and Louise Bryant as guest and cook. The house was always full of guests. Two of Reed's friends from Harvard were usually among them: Bobby Rogers, a rotund, charming man who taught English, and Robert Edmond Jones—with red hair and a "gaunt white saintly face"—who had done the scenery for Reed's Paterson Strike Pageant. Often there, too, were David Carb and Fred Boyd, a very precise English Marxist. Everyone talked. Hippolyte Havel argued violently with Reed and called him a "Parlor Socialist!" Reed called Hippolyte a "Kitchen Anarchist!"

Gene was drawn to John Reed's house again and again by Reed's warm enthusiasm for life. Then, before he realized what had happened, he found himself involved in a fantastic triangle.

CHAPTER TWENTY-FIVE

The Eternal Triangle

Reed's joyous interest in life was infectious. After a conversation with him, a Colorado schoolteacher discovered that she had a soul. "You have knocked the earth out from under me and I'm floating in the air," she told him. "Don't think I'm in love with you, because I'm in love with life all of a sudden, and now it seems something to be lived instead of just something to be endured." Reed's exuberance was very attractive to Eugene, who often found simple living an effort. Different as they were, they had much in common besides the swimming they both loved. Both were the sons of wealthy men and both had been rebels from boyhood. Both scorned "professorial dry-rot," as Eugene called it. Reed had completed his course at Harvard, to graduate in 1910, but he had not been stifled by mathematics requirements as Eugene had been at Princeton. Like Eugene, Reed thought of himself as a poet, but he wrote plays and stories as well as poems. As a reporter he had raised journalism to the level of art and was now world-famous.

His first brilliant reporting had been of the Paterson Silk strike in the spring of 1913. Quickly, he became one with the strikers, even to being jailed with them. He taught them songs of revolt, and it was he who arranged that they should present their case in a pageant at Madison Square Garden. While he and Mabel Dodge were working together on the pageant, they fell in love.

Mabel Dodge stood at the center of everything new in American art, writing, and social theory. At the famous "Evenings" in her lower Fifth Avenue apartment, she brought together artists, writers, reformers, labor leaders, and revolutionists. Everyone felt her magnetism; she had an almost magic way of drawing people out. Reed was many years younger than she, but they were immediately attracted to one another. When the pageant was over, she whisked him and Robert Edmond Jones over to her villa in Florence, where, Reed said, he felt "like the fisherman caught up by the genie's daughter and carried to the mountain-top." Bobby Jones told Mabel, "I feel there's something wonderful and immortal between you and Jack. . . ." According to Mabel Dodge, Reed whispered to her on their first night together, "I thought your fire was crimson, but you burn blue in the dark."

But Mabel Dodge, loving him, wished to devour him. "Everything seemed to take him away from me," she complained, "and I had no single thing left in my life to rouse me save his touch." So a silent fight began between them. "Reed himself was ready for anything!" she would say. "Ready at any moment to pop off into some new enthusiasm. He always seemed to have his lungs too full, and he would draw in his round chin in an effort to quiet his excited heart. *Always* there seemed some pressure of excitement going on in him. His eyes glowed for nothing, his brown curls rushed back from his high, round forehead in a furious disorder, and the round highlights on his temples gleamed."

Finally he left her. "Good-by, my darling, I cannot live with you," Reed wrote her. "You smother me. You crush me. You want to kill my spirit. I love you better than life but I do not want to die in my spirit. I am going away to save myself. Forgive me. I love you—I love you." Both suffered agonies. He returned, haggard and frantic. "Your way, not mine," he murmured. But eventually he broke with her.

Late in 1913, he went to Mexico to report the uprising of the peons. There he entered Villa's army, and rode, fought, drank, and lived with the men. He described his experiences in articles for the *Metropolitan* magazine and in a book *Insurgent Mexico*. The articles made him famous.

Reed spent part of 1914 and 1915 in Europe, observing the war. He visited the trenches, typhus hospitals, and battlefields strewn with the rotting bodies of young men, and he came back convinced that "This is not our war!" His book *The War in Eastern Europe* tried to counteract the English propaganda that was sweeping America into a pro-Ally hysteria.

After his return from Europe, he went to Portland, Oregon, to visit his mother—in December, 1915—and there he met Louise Bryant. "I think I have found Her at last," he wrote to a friend. "She's wild, brave, and straight—and graceful and lovely to look at. In this spiritual vacuum, this unfertilized soil, she has grown (how, I can't imagine) into an artist. She is coming to New York to get a job—with me, I hope. I think she's the first person I ever loved without reservation." She was married, but unhappy in her marriage. All through the next winter when she lived with Jack in his Washington Square apartment, she was negotiating for a divorce from Dr. Trullinger. It had still not come through when she and Jack went to Provincetown in the summer of 1916. Living with Reed, Louise had discovered herself as a writer. That summer the Provincetown Players put on her play *The Game*.

Eugene saw her constantly when he went to see Reed. She had a delicate, wistful face with high cheekbones and large blue-gray eyes framed by a cloud of black hair. Tall, slender, and graceful, she moved about the room or sat and listened while Gene talked with Jack about the war.

"The real war, of which this sudden outburst of death and destruction is only an incident, began long ago," Reed had written in an article for the *Masses*. "It has been raging for tens of years, but its battles have been so little advertised that they have been hardly noted. It is a clash of traders." Reed saw that England and France had grabbed the best colonies, so that German business could not expand. Now there was an open struggle for the colonies. "We must not be duped by this editorial buncome about Liberalism going forth to Holy War against Tyranny," Reed said. "This is not Our War."

Eugene agreed with him. He talked with Reed, too, of the conflict between capital and labor. He was more savage than Reed in condemning the greed of the capitalists, but he did not share Reed's belief that the workers would rise and create a new social order. Eugene thought the workers were "cowards," and their leaders "asses," who would never do anything but talk. He showed Reed a long poem "The Louse," in which he condemned the idler who lives on the blood of the workers, but also depicted the workers as stupefied by "the braying" of their leaders and enslaved by their worship of a god created for that purpose by the louse.

Eugene showed Jack his poem "Submarine" too, which showed even more strikingly how completely anarchistic his views now were.

> My soul is a submarine
> My aspirations are torpedoes.
> I will hide unseen
> Beneath the surface of life
> Watching for ships,
> Dull, heavy-laden merchant ships,
> Rust-eaten, grimy galeons of commerce
> Wallowing with obese assurance,
> Too sluggish to fear or wonder,
> Mocked by the laughter of waves
> And the spit of disdainful spray.
>
> I will destroy them
> Because the sea is beautiful.
>
> That is why I lurk
> Menacingly
> In green depths.

Reed's view was more constructive, but he liked the poems and set to work to get them published. He had only to cross the street in Provincetown to find Max Eastman, editor of the *Masses*. To Eugene's joy, Eastman accepted "Submarine." (It appeared in February, 1917.)

Reed knew editors and how to deal with them. He was quite willing to play literary agent for Eugene till he learned to fend for himself. Meanwhile, he encouraged Eugene to write short stories. So Eugene made a story of his memories of Jimmy Byth and of the moment when Jimmy lost his faith in "tomorrow." Reed was enthusiastic over "Tomorrow" and sent it off to Carl Hovey, editor of the *Metropolitan,* telling him that O'Neill could really write.

Hovey agreed that the story was "genuine and makes a real man live before you," but he thought it lacked suspense. "With all its fine sincerity and effectiveness, there is a kind of over-emphasis and sense of repetition which makes the story drag," Hovey told Reed. Jack immediately sent the story out again. Soon Eugene learned with delight that *The Seven Arts Magazine* had accepted "Tomorrow" and would pay him $50 for it. (It appeared in June, 1917.)

So Jack Reed brought Eugene his first financial success. By the end of the summer, Eugene was relying on him entirely. He read to Jack everything he had already written and brought him each new work he completed. A deep bond grew between them. In the warmth of Jack's friendship, Gene's defenses thawed. Later, he would say that he had felt more than friendship for Reed, love really. He and Reed were constantly together and so, naturally, he saw much of Louise Bryant, too.

One evening Reed told him that Louise was going to New York. When Eugene and Terry Carlin left, Louise walked to the door with them. Just as Eugene was stepping out, she handed him a book of verse, briefly remarking that he would like it. Later, when he leafed through the pages he found a note scrawled in Louise's bold hand: "Dark eyes. What do you mean?" That was all.

The words went through him like a knife. All the resistance he had built up to the attraction he had felt for her from the beginning suddenly dropped away. Now he felt himself torn between desire for Louise and his loyalty to his friend.

All the while Louise was away, he brooded over her note. When she returned, he avoided her, until Terry brought him a note from her begging him to let her explain. He listened incredulously to what she told him. She began by telling him that Jack, for all his exuberance, was sick—he had a diseased kidney. It had started when he was a boy with a sharp pain that none of the doctors could help. Then for a long time he was free of it. But in Belgrade the year before, the pain had come back, and a British doctor told him the kidney was infected.

All that winter he had been seeing the doctors and the pain had got worse and worse. He would have to have an operation, but the operation was likely to be fatal. That summer, Jack had been facing his own death. He had seen its approach in the fog that crept in from the Provincetown Harbor:

> Death comes like this I know—
> Snow soft and gently cold;
> Impalpable battalions of thin mist,
> Light-quenching and sound-smothering and slow.

Louise Bryant had been helping him to face death. Of course, she loved Jack. Who could help loving him? But she and Jack could not be lovers, she told Eugene. They had been living together as brother and sister. She was frightened. She needed fulfillment to give her the strength to stand by Jack in his need.

It was a strange and terrible story. Eugene was torn by conflicting emotions: pity and love for Jack, desire for Louise. (He must have recalled these emotions in *Strange Interlude* at the moment when Darrell agrees to become Nina's lover because he believes that they can save her husband from insanity by giving him a healthy child. "Am I right to advise this?" Darrell thinks anxiously; " . . . yes, it is clearly the rational thing to do . . . but this advice betrays my friend! . . . no, it saves him! . . . it saves his wife . . . and if a third party should know a little happiness . . . is he any poorer, am I any less his friend because I saved him?") That was the beginning of the affair between Louise and Eugene.

John Reed was not the only person who was being deceived. Eugene was too. Louise had not told him the whole truth. She certainly was not telling the truth when she said that she and Jack had been living together as brother and sister. They had been lovers from the beginning. In their first months together, Reed—off to Florida on a reporting assignment—had written her that he was becoming "more and more gloomy and mournful to think I'm not going to sleep all over you in our scandalous and sinful voluptuous bed. All my enthusiasm begins to run out of my toes when you get farther and farther away, and I can't go rushing into your room and kiss you four or five hundred times." Even when Reed's illness became serious, they had apparently remained lovers, for Reed consulted his doctors about the danger of infecting her. But Jack was certainly very ill that summer, too ill for love-making. And Louise's terror that he was going to die was real, too.

At the same time her passion for Eugene was equally real. Sensitive as he was to the possibility of betrayal, Eugene felt secure in Louise's love. Her passions, he wrote, rose up like the "tremulous heat waves" over the sand dunes. He felt that his "gnomes of despair" would become dancing elves "under her kiss." They spent long afternoons on the dunes, and soon almost everyone but Jack Reed knew they were lovers.

Even Mabel Dodge—who felt curiously possessive toward Jack although she no longer loved him—learned quickly that Louise Bryant and Gene O'Neill—"that wide-mouthed, anguished, sunburned boy," she called him—were lovers. "People said Louise was having an affair with young 'Gene O'Neill, who lived in a shack across the street with Terry," Mabel Dodge later commented, "and I thought Reed would be glad to see me if things were like that between him and Louise—but he wasn't. Jig Cook was writing a play—or was it Susan's play? Anyway, Louise was going to be in it. Hutch came in one evening with Jig—who was large and kind and had a shiny face with unidentified brown eyes. They were both rather drunk and they were talking theater. Jig was saying sententiously: 'Louise has very kindly consented to appear nude in that scene where she has to be carried in—'" Mabel Dodge felt entirely out of things. "All these people disheartened me," she decided.

As the summer went on, Eugene felt more and more torn by love for Louise and a feeling that he was betraying, not helping Jack.

Reed was as affectionate as ever and as eager to help Eugene, who gave him all the poems he had written that summer. Among them were two love poems, "Evoë" and "On the Dunes." Jack apparently thought they were about Beatrice, for "My Beatrice," which the *Tribune* had published under a different title, was with them. So the deception went on, and Eugene suffered over it.

Such was the situation when they all returned to New York for the opening of the Provincetown Players there. Reed played Death in the production of Louise Bryant's play, *The Game*. He was already scheduled to enter Johns Hopkins hospital on November 12, 1916. Just before that, Louise and Jack went to Poughkeepsie, and at the city hall a clerk in his shirt sleeves hurried through the forms, with the help of two witnesses from an adjoining office, and declared them man and wife.

The marriage was kept secret. Only Jack's very close friend, Boardman Robinson, knew about it, but as he remarked jovially to Louise, it was a "terrible scandal" and bound to get out. Within a month, a number of people, including Lucy Huffaker, were saying that Reed and Louise were married. Eugene surely knew—if not at once, soon afterward—and the revelation was torture. He was torn with violent and contradictory feelings—love, hate, jealousy, and above all, shame. He caught himself wishing that Jack would die, only to be overwhelmed with self-loathing, for Jack had given him nothing but affection and was still helping him to get his plays published.

Louise went down to Baltimore for the operation on November 22. Reed survived. A few days later Louise came back to New York, and now began a strange time. She and Eugene were constantly together. Indeed, Eugene had taken a room at 43 Washington Square South, where Reed and Louise Bryant lived. Yet every day Louise wrote affectionately deceptive letters to Reed. "I had a lump in my throat as big as the Woolworth Tower when I left the station and it still comes back any moment. The old faithfuls Nannie and Gene are taking me to dinner. I'll weep in the middle of it if they aren't careful." When Reed first went to Baltimore, she had written, "Nannie & Gene had dinner here. I'm so *tired* of their old faces and their old chatter." Now she continued to tell Reed of tiresome times with Gene. In December, when she was spending all her time at the theater where Eugene's *Before Breakfast* was in production, she wrote Reed, "I'm prompting 'Before Breakfast' tonight. If I do it every night—well, I can think of something pleasant like Croton [where she and Reed had a country cottage]—that's the only way I'd get through."

Yet through her letters runs a real and deep concern and love. "I'm so afraid you might have a change that isn't good or are in great pain—please, please let me know!" At the height of her affair with Eugene, she was writing Reed that she had just told Nannie Bailey "that I would die without your companionship because you had something so wonderful about you that other people didn't have—one just aches for you when you are away and everyone else seems stupid." Again and again, she wrote, "Darling, I do miss you so much!"

Gene, too, was caught in a masquerade. He was taking care of Reed's mail. He wrote to him and sent him his latest plays for advice. At the same time he was more in love with Louise than ever. He shared his dreams with her. He also helped her to rewrite her play *The White Rose*. But the two roles he was playing pulled him apart. He wanted to have it out with Jack. He wanted Louise to declare her love for him openly as soon as Reed got out of the hospital. But Louise couldn't make up her mind to anything. She was torn and troubled.

She was also physically ill that fall. The nature of her illness remains a mystery, for information on it appears only in her letters to Reed, and she had to deceive Reed. She had complained in the middle of November of "crazy sick-to-my-tummy spells" which, she told Reed, came from an abscess. That condition had cleared up, but on December 7 she wrote him that she had become very ill; her "whole left insides" were "inflamed and infected"; Dr. Harry Lorber had ordered her "to bed under special care or in a hospital." She had a high temperature. Dr. Lorber thought he might have to remove the ovaries, but he would "do his *damndest* to keep from operating." She was staying, she said, at Becky's house at 72 Morningside Avenue.

Reed wrote back that he had never "heard of that being done to anybody but dogs, cats and horses." He was ready to be brought to New York "on a stretcher" to protect her. Her next letter declared that the operation wouldn't be necessary, but Reed wanted word from the doctor. On December 12, Louise wrote, "There isn't any use for the doctor to write—there's nothing to tell. I'm just the same—a little better maybe. They have to wait and watch developments. There will be no operation. When you come the doctor will talk it over with you." Reed was then about to be released from the hospital, and she wrote "Wednesday I'll look for you—be *sure* to let me know when you are coming. Surprise parties won't do for me—darling—not now. Becky will get a room for you at the hotel nearby for the first night and we can make arrangements then."

Dr. Lorber knew all about her relationship with Eugene O'Neill, for later, much later, after Jack knew too, Lorber would tell him, when Louise was in a state of distress, that perhaps her problem was that she loved "someone else better." Why did she tell Lorber? Perhaps she just needed a confidant. Or perhaps, her illness was such that she had to tell him. It is just possible that her illness was not an infection as she had told Jack. It is significant, perhaps, that Nina, in *Strange Interlude,* tells Sam that she has "some woman's sickness" in order to hide from him the fact that she has had an abortion.

Whatever the truth, for Eugene the whole affair was agonizing. The year of his first real success was embittered by his torment over Louise and Jack Reed. Later, in *Strange Interlude,* he would depict the anguish of sharing a woman with a friend.

CHAPTER TWENTY-SIX

Success and Torment

J AMES and Ellen O'Neill were in New York for the winter, staying at the Prince George Hotel. Eugene spent many afternoons there, confiding his love for Louise to Mama. Jamie also understood him; he was suffering himself—Pauline Frederick had left him because he couldn't stop drinking. So he was drinking even more heavily, and Eugene joined him.

Rarely had Eugene felt so close to his family. Even his bitterness toward his father began to melt. Papa and Mama had come to see *Bound East for Cardiff* on the opening bill at the Playwright's Theater. James O'Neill was proud, and Eugene knew it. At Eugene's invitation, he came to a rehearsal of *Before Breakfast*—"a striking figure with fur-collared coat, gold-headed cane, and a diamond ring on his finger," Hutchins Hapgood recalled. "When he went away, some of us spoke to him about Gene's gift and promise, and he said benignly, 'Yes, yes, I think the boy has something in him.' "

Eugene didn't agree with all of Papa's suggestions, but "some I thought were fine," he said, and "the actors were glad to follow." James O'Neill had not approved of "the diction or 'business' " of Mary Pyne, Hapgood said, "and he began to show her how acting was done, how points were made with the voice and gesture of Monte Cristo." Sometimes Eugene interrupted to disagree, and they argued. Although Eugene saw his father "with all imperfections on his head," Hapgood observed, there was between them "something quite close."

Again in January, Papa came down for a rehearsal of *Fog*. William Carlos Williams, who was waiting out in the "narrow, cold hall" for a rehearsal of Alfred Kreymborg's *Lima Beans,* watched O'Neill's play with fascination. "I've never forgotten it," he reported later, "—a small boat offshore, half seen before a fog improvised with a voile curtain of some sort, and men calling to each other in a dangerous situation. Out in the hall stood old man O'Neill, he of Monte Cristo fame, yelling out directions and suggestions to his son and the actors. Very moving."

James O'Neill now had his own rehearsals, for he was playing the Jewish patriarch Jesse in *The Wanderer*. "I accepted the role instantly," he explained. "I would not have returned to the stage in any other kind of play, because when one has acted on the legitimate for fifty years as I have, with such great actors as Edwin Booth and Edwin Forrest, it is impossible to be resigned to the commonplaces of the modern style of play."

Eugene went to see his father open in *The Wanderer* at the Manhattan Theatre on January 23, 1917, and appreciated the way David Belasco, Papa's old friend from his San Francisco days, managed the spectacular elements of the play: whole flocks of sheep moving across the stage and pagan girls dancing in orgiastic abandon. Years later, Eugene wanted Belasco to direct his own *Marco Millions,* knowing that no one could handle panorama the way Belasco did.

"I knew it was going to be a hit the very first time I read the script and I said so," Papa said of the play after the opening. "It has the old heart quality in it, the appeal that the public cannot resist." Eugene thought wryly that he would like to do his own version of the prodigal son story. The following winter he would write *The Rope*, and put Jesse's majestic words—"For this my son was dead, and is alive again; he was lost and is found"—into the mouth of the decrepit miser Bentley, whose gift of gold for his prodigal son is hidden at the end of a rope with which he asks his son to hang himself. Perhaps Eugene's portrait of this miser-father, with his secret love for his son, derives not only from Jesse, but from James O'Neill himself, for Eugene knew that he was his father's prodigal son, and, in a way, he had been lost and now was found. Eugene also learned from *The Wanderer*—as he had learned from *Joseph and His Brethren*—how effective Biblical language can be on stage. In his own way, he used it in *The Rope* and *Desire Under the Elms*.

Whatever his opinion of the play, Eugene was proud of the reviews Papa got. Critics were astonished to realize that "this splendid and virile actor, after 50 years on the stage still has the power to thrill and the personality to charm as in the days of old." They found him "still the same commanding figure, of a wonderful personality and magnetic voice as in the days when the Baron D'Anglars dropped dead before his sword thrust, and the veteran of the stage cried 'Three!'" And Papa was more than seventy years old.

By February, when Eugene's play *The Sniper* was produced by the Provincetown Players, his nerves were badly frayed. Louise had gone up to Croton with Jack after he came out of the hospital at Christmas, and Eugene was left in a nightmare of uncertainty about what she intended to do. He was jittery from too much drinking and irritated by other people. He felt the need of a regular schedule of work. The answer, he thought, was Provincetown.

Early in March, 1917, he and Harold de Polo—"the Mad Don," Eugene called him—landed in that quiet little fishing village. Both looked forward to writing. But they had to wait while John Francis got a flat ready for them, so they couldn't settle down to work at once. Then, on March 28, as they were having lunch at the New Central Hotel, Constable Reuben O. Kelley suddenly strode to their table and told them that they were both under arrest. He refused to tell them why, and their requests to be allowed to telephone a lawyer were ignored. They were taken to the basement of the Town Hall and locked up, each in a separate cell.

At ten o'clock that night, they were brought out to meet Fred Weyand of the United States Secret Service, and discovered that they were suspected of being German spies! Chief Mosely of the United States Radio Station at North Truro had reported that two men had been prowling around the station at night. Challenged, they had replied that their doctor had advised them to walk for their health. Eugene and Harold were the only strangers in town, and people had seen them walking over the dunes, so Constable Kelley had decided that they must be the culprits. The police had notified Weyand in Boston and searched Eugene's and Harold's luggage. Two tire punctures held Weyand up, hence his late arrival. He cleared up the absurd suspicions against O'Neill and de Polo with a few questions, but Eugene and Harold were told they would have to spend the night in jail anyway and appear in court to face the official charge of vagrancy. The next morning they were brought before Judge Welsh and declared not guilty.

Meanwhile, in Provincetown, rumors spread. The spies had drawn revolvers; plans of the radio station and harbor had been found upon them. Among Eugene's friends, over the years the story became a tall tale. Jack Johnson would tell it with funny details of "a little black box" (a typewriter, of course!) that O'Neill carried out to the dunes and that Constable Kelley thought was a "wireless gadget." Mary Heaton Vorse would say that the secret service kept an agent in Provincetown to read Eugene's letters, and that he told Gene every morning, over a friendly breakfast, what to expect in the mail each day.

Finally, Eugene was able to get down to work. He wanted to develop the characters of *Bound East for Cardiff* in three more one-act plays, for he thought that play was the best of his work so far. Later, he said it held "the germ of the spirit, life-attitude, etc., of all my more important future work." Now the war hysteria shown in his arrest gave him the idea for the first of these one-act plays, *In the Zone*. In it Eugene added a central character "Smitty the Duke" to the characters of *Bound East for Cardiff*, modeling him on the blighted young Englishman he had roomed with in Buenos Aires, and giving him a sorrow similar to Jamie's at the loss of Pauline Frederick.

In the next of these one-act plays, *The Long Voyage Home,* Eugene showed the shanghaiing of a sailor bound home after years at sea. The sailor came from Eugene's memories of the Norwegian A.B. on the British tramp steamer who wished he had stayed on the farm. In the last of these plays, *The Moon of the Caribbees,* Eugene drew on his memory of a moonlit night off Trinidad on the same British tramp steamer bound for New York. Music, floating over the water to him from the island, had filled him with mystical wonder. It was this wonder he wished to communicate, for he felt that a one-act play could be "a fine vehicle for something poetical, for something spiritual in feeling that cannot be carried through a long play."

Later, Eugene would realize that he had come into his own as an artist when he completed *The Moon of the Caribbees* that winter of 1917 in Provincetown. "That was my first real break with theatrical traditions. Once I had taken this initial step other plays followed logically." As early as 1919, when *The Moon of the Caribbees and Six Other Plays* was published, Eugene knew which of these sea plays were good. He dismissed *In the Zone* as "theatrical sentimentalism," full of "clever theatrical tricks," but lacking in "spiritual import," having "no big feeling for life inspiring it." But *The Moon of the Caribbees,* he was sure, "works with truth."

"The spirit of the sea—a big thing—is in this latter play the hero," he told Barrett Clark in May, 1919. "While *In the Zone* might have happened just as well, if less picturesquely, in a boarding house of munition workers. Let me illustrate by a concrete example what I am trying to get at. Smitty in the stuffy, grease-paint atmosphere of *In the Zone* is magnified into a hero who attracts our sentimental sympathy. In *The Moon,* posed against a background of that beauty, sad because it is eternal, which is one of the revealing moods of the sea's truth, his silhouetted gestures of self-pity are reduced to their proper insignificance, his thin whine of weakness is lost in the silence which it was mean enough to disturb, we get the perspective to judge him—and the others—and we find his sentimental posing much more out of harmony with truth, much less in tune with beauty, than the honest vulgarity of his mates."

Eugene valued *The Moon* as "an attempt to achieve a higher plane of bigger finer values." So he wrote Barrett Clark, for he wanted Clark, and indeed all his critics, to understand "my feeling for the impelling, inscrutable forces behind life which it is my ambition to at least faintly shadow at their work in my plays." These words, written in 1919, were as clear a statement of his mature artistic purpose as he would ever give: to depict "the impelling, inscrutable forces behind life."

Eugene completed one more one-act sea play that winter, *Ile*. In this play he did not use the characters from *Bound East for Cardiff*. It was based, not on Eugene's memories, but on a story famous in Provincetown—that of Captain John Cook, a whaling skipper working out of Provincetown harbor. In 1903, Cook had kept his crew out past their term of employment, with only rotted scraps of food left, refusing to turn back until he got his usual high quota of whale "ile." His wife Viola had gone mad; the crew had mutinied, and later sued him.

Work could not absorb all of Eugene's hours. He kept thinking of Louise. Then, in May, she came to Provincetown. Joyful, Eugene began to believe that only pity had bound her to Jack and that now, inevitably, she must leave him.

Yet, when Louise finally quarreled with Jack later that spring, the issue was not Eugene at all. Jack was not jealous of her. She was jealous of him! Some time that spring, Jack had had a passing affair with another woman, and Louise, hearing of it, had become frantic with jealousy. How much Jack knew of her own affair with Gene O'Neill remains unclear. Perhaps he thought she had turned to Gene as a result of his own infidelity. Certainly he knew something, for later she would write him that she kept worrying "over something very terrible you said about getting out of my way if anything happened to you."

Far from sending her to Eugene, Jack's infidelity had made her even more aware of her love for him. In her emotional confusion, she felt that she was going out of her mind. Her instinct was to escape, to go somewhere, far away, where she could think. Boardman Robinson suggested Europe. She then told Jack that she must go to Europe; Jack at once saw Wheeler of the Wheeler Syndicate, and almost before she knew what had happened, Louise found herself, at the beginning of June, aboard a ship, bound for France on a reporting assignment.

"Please believe me Jack—I'm going to try like the devil to pull myself together over there and come back able to act like a reasonable human being," she wrote him from the ship. "I know I'm probably all wrong about everything. I know the only reason I act so crazy is because it hurts so much, that I get quite insane, that's all." But she was ready to forgive him. "If this thing ever happens again *don't don't* get despondent," she told him. "Maybe I'll understand better when I get back."

At once Jack replied. "Dearest of honies—Got here to find your pitiful little note—it isn't you who must learn, my honey, but me. In lots of ways we are very different, and we must both try to realize that—while loving each other. But of course on this last awful business, you were humanly right and I was wrong. I have always loved you my darling ever since I first met you—and I guess I always will."

He went on to tell Louise that he had met an old friend, Betty Eyre, looking "shockingly old and sick," found she was on the verge of suicide, and taken her to see Dr. Lorber. "I just tell you all this stupid history, my honey," he added, "so you may know all that I've been doing, and that you may believe that nevermore is there going to be any chance of any girl coming between me and my honey, and that I'm perfectly tranquil about how I shall be, waiting for you, old lover."

This effort to help a sick girl brought Jack himself to Dr. Lorber. They talked about Jack's difficulties with Louise; they talked also of Gene O'Neill, for Reed wrote Louise, "Sweetheart, I do hope you're going to get all over your awul feelings by the time you come back. I had a long talk with Lorber about you, which I'll tell you sometime. Think about you and me a good deal, will you? It is not worth keeping going if you love someone else better."

"Now, honey dearest," Louise answered, "I am feeling *very calm* as I write this. Nothing matters so much as my love for you—I don't know what you have said to Lorber or he has said to you—I *don't* love any one *else*. I'm *dead sure* of that. I just love you."

What was she telling Eugene? Certainly not that she loved only Reed. That spring Eugene and everyone who knew him felt sure Louise would come to him at last. Certainly he thought so when he went back to New London late in the spring to visit Mama, Papa, and Jamie—although he showed his tension by drinking heavily. Eugene had invited his old friend from Baker's 47, Malcolm Morley, to stay with him at 325 Pequot Avenue. Like Eugene, Morley had begun to have some success as a playwright, could be spoken of as "famous," but now he was caught by the war, and was returning to England to enter the Royal Aviation Corps. Morley, Jamie, and Eugene had wild times with the "corrupt herd" of New London friends—Ice Casey, Art McGinley, Eddie Keefe, Doc Ganey, and the rest.

The air was heavy all that spring with talk of the war, now that America was in it. Eugene was faced with the draft. As an anarchist, how was he to react to the patriotic hysteria all about him? He had agreed with Reed that the war was a clash of traders; he had declared in the poem "Fratricide," "All workers on the earth / Are brothers and WE WILL NOT FIGHT." What was he to do now? What he did was to claim exemption from the draft as an arrested case of tuberculosis. But writing to Dr. Lyman at Gaylord Farm to ask whether he needed a certificate to prove his T.B., Eugene said that he didn't want to "dodge service" but that he had heard that the army camps were deadly for men susceptible to T.B. "I want to serve my country," he told Dr. Lyman, "but it seems silly to commit suicide for it."

Was he simply paying lip service to Dr. Lyman's prejudices? If so, why did he also tell Dr. Lyman that he had "tried to enlist in the Navy," but had been rejected for "minor defects" that wouldn't bar him from the draft? Why did this anarchist try to enlist? A few months later, he would be regaling Agnes Boulton with a demonstration of how—come the revolution—he would train a machine gun from the top of a Greenwich Village office building onto the soldiers below.

Perhaps there was a genuine split in his feelings. Or perhaps he had been frightened by his arrest. An incident that Agnes Boulton reports suggests this. One evening at the Hell-Hole that autumn, two uniformed officers entered the place to inspect draft cards. From what Eugene had said of the war, she expected him to rise and denounce the officers. Instead, he suddenly became "overfriendly" to them. Soon after they left, he was again the anarchist, making wild plans for joining the Hudson Dusters and becoming their leader. Eugene declared, according to Maxwell Bodenheim, "that the under-world and the creative upper-world would have to unite before the earth could become a safe and unhampered place for intelligent people—an aristocracy of swift brawn and equally quick mind ruling the more sluggish, hypocritical, and unimaginative men and women in all walks of life."

Certainly, Eugene had not been so outspoken against the war when he was in New London as he was later that summer in Provincetown, for Art McGinley, who went back with him, was astonished to find himself in a colony "preaching Internationalism," with Eugene one of the most outspoken of them all.

Art was also astonished at Eugene's prestige among the artists and writers in Provincetown. Art felt too "unlettered" for their gatherings, but Eugene, he found, was deferred to by all in a discussion "so far above my level that it might well have been in another tongue." Eugene told him, "We're all pretenders."

Art was surprised too by the change in Eugene's appearance. Eugene had always dressed elegantly—even during his wildest years. Now he wore seamen's jerseys, old slacks, and sneakers, so that he looked as if he had spent his life bumming on the waterfront. If Art hadn't known he was a rich man's son, he would have believed, like many others, that Eugene was a common sailor turned writer.

Gene and Art had arrived in Provincetown on a wave of alcohol. Three times during the boat trip from Boston, Art would later report, the captain had threatened to put them in irons. Jig Cook took one look at Art, and told him he was a "natural" for the drunken Russian in *The Long Voyage Home,* which they had just finished casting. But Eugene quickly got down to an austere schedule of work. On his door from nine to one o'clock hung a sign reading,

"May wild jackasses desecrate the grave of your grandmother, if you disturb me."

He was working on a short story about the death of his friend Driscoll, the tough Liverpool Irishman. Driscoll had jumped overboard in mid-ocean. No one knew why. "Driscoll's curious death puzzled me," Eugene told Louis Kalonyme. "I concluded something must have shaken his hard-boiled poise, for he wasn't the type who just give up, and he loved life. Anyway it was his death that inspired the idea for the Yank of 'The Hairy Ape.'" The story didn't come out right, but a few years later when he wrote it as a play, it simply poured out of him.

In the middle of August, Eugene learned that Louise had returned from France only to sail at once for Russia with John Reed. Jack had decided the Russian masses would establish "a new human society upon the earth," and he wanted to see it happen. He and Louise would get to Moscow just in time to watch the Bolshevik Revolution. Eugene was stunned.

The success he had dreamed of was beginning to come. *Before Breakfast* had been sold to the Theatre Workshop (how he had longed to have Holbrook Blinn produce one of his plays back in 1914!). The Washington Square Players were going to put on *Bound East for Cardiff* and *In the Zone*. He had received $50 each for "Tomorrow" and *In the Zone* from *The Seven Arts Magazine*. *Smart Set* had given him $75 for *The Long Voyage Home*. And his plays had been published in *Provincetown Plays* edited by Frank Shay. Everyone talked of him as the most "promising" young American dramatist. But instead of joy, he felt only torment over Louise Byrant.

He was back in New York in the fall, and in November the Provincetown Players put on *The Long Voyage Home* and the Washington Square Players did *In the Zone*, along with three other one-act plays. The reviews were enthusiastic. "Washington Square Players Present James O'Neill's Son as a New Playwright" ran a headline in the New York *Mail*, and its critic declared that the best play of the four was "a sea tale told by Eugene O'Neill, son of James O'Neill, the venerable and venerated actor, a genius, a new playwright who seems certain to be heard from again, and most impressively heard from eventually." Papa liked *The Long Voyage Home* and was delighted to have his boy described as a genius. But Eugene's triumph was poisoned by his pain.

"There was no such darkness as Gene's," Mary Heaton Vorse would say later. "He would sit silent and suffering and in darkness." He had taken a room over the Hell-Hole, and spent his evenings there drinking with his friends, the Hudson Dusters. He liked their mindless masculinity. One of them, seeing him shivering in a light jacket on a chill fall evening, asked him his size, and offered to "lift" an overcoat for him from a store. Gene assured him he already had a good one, but had just neglected to wear it.

Gene knew all the gangsters. Scotty MacDonald was his particular friend. Once Eugene talked the Hudson Dusters out of attacking Scotty, who had cheated them in a furniture deal. Maxwell Bodenheim was present and recalled later that Eugene talked to them "with a curious mixture of restrained profanity, mild contempt, and blunt camaraderie which showed that he shared the spirit of these roughnecks and yet failed to share it." And once when Mary Heaton Vorse's dog disappeared from the Provincetown Players during a performance, Gene knew what to do. "Gene took me immediately to the Hell-Hole," Mary Vorse recalled, "to seek help from the boss of the Negro underworld. The boss was a man noted for his tenderness, a small man, yet with the conscious dignity of a chieftain. For did he not command Cornelia Street and in Minetta Lane, better known in those days as Cocaine Alley, was not his word law? And was not his woman a shining blond white woman, Miss Viola? He was a chieftain though a small man and shabby." She got her dog back, too.

It was from this "boss" that Gene first heard of a Negro gangster called "Dreamy." The name struck him, and later he derived from it the idea for his play *The Dreamy Kid.* The boss, too, gave him some of the characteristics of the Emperor Jones, and still later, of Joe Mott in *The Iceman Cometh.*

But Gene could not throw off his misery, and often in the Hell-Hole, when he was drunk, he would recite the poem that expressed his fear of love—"The Hound of Heaven." "It was on these cold bitter evenings that I first heard 'The Hound of Heaven,' in an

atmosphere of drink and smoke," Dorothy Day wrote in her autobiography. "Gene could recite all of Francis Thompson's poem, and
would sit there, black and dour, his head sunk as he intoned, 'And
now my heart is as a broken fount, wherein tear-drippings stagnate.' "

It was in the Hell-Hole, on an evening in November, 1917, that
Eugene O'Neill saw a girl seated alone at a table—a slender girl with
light hair and large blue-green eyes. Her face, like Louise's, was
delicately formed with high cheekbones. The girl was Agnes
Boulton.

PART SEVEN

HARVEST

CHAPTER TWENTY-SEVEN

Agnes

E︎UGENE stared at Agnes until Louis Ell came in, looking jealously for his wife Christine. After he left, Christine herself swept in. She hugged Agnes and greeted Eugene exuberantly. Presently, they were all sitting at the same table. Christine talked about her troubles with Louis—she loved him, but needed at times to be free of him. Soon Jamie arrived (he had promised to split the remainder of his weekly allowance with Eugene, who had already spent his $15). "What, ho!" cried Jamie. He had been held up, he said, looking "for a big blonde with a bad breath." Jamie and Christine began a playful conversation. Eugene listened, and several times broke into one of his rare smiles. But he looked uneasy when Jamie turned to Agnes and told her that she was a "wild Irish rose" designed to tear a man's heart out, so that he would cry out in his sleep for her.

When the evening was over, Jamie took Christine home—roaring like a lion in order, he said, to warn Louis of his approach—and Eugene walked with Agnes across Washington Square to the Brevoort, where she was staying. He had spoken little to her all evening. He said little during their walk. Then, when they reached the Brevoort, he suddenly began to speak. Agnes barely grasped what he was saying, but she heard his final words, "I want to spend every night of my life from now on with *you*. I mean this. *Every night of my life.*" Then he left her.

He awoke the next morning wanting to see her, but he could not bring himself to go to her hotel and ask for her. Instead, he went to see Christine, hoping that Agnes would be there. She wasn't, but Christine, who had seen that he was taken with Agnes, began to talk about her. Agnes had been earning money ever since she was sixteen by writing for the pulp magazines. Now she was twenty-four. She had left her family on a farm in Connecticut to get a part-time job in New York and to write. Christine pulled out an old clipping from the *World* and handed it to him. Eugene suddenly felt sick. He saw a picture of Agnes and the words, "No money in milk cows says woman dairy farmer who's made a brave fight. Down in New York to help the poor farmers win a milk strike—young widow has supported herself, a baby, and a herd of cows by her pen. . . . "

Eugene's dream was shattered. She had looked so young, and now he found that she had a child and a life of her own. His torment over Louise was still fresh in his mind. It seemed to him that with Agnes, too, he would have only a precarious share in a woman with a separate life. His instinctive fear of love and his expectation of betrayal came to the fore. Suddenly he hated Agnes. And when Christine told him that she would be at the party of the Provincetown Players on Saturday night, he resolved not to go. He spent the first part of Saturday evening drinking at the Hell-Hole, but later, when he had drunk enough to convince himself that Agnes meant nothing to him, he went. He saw her almost at once in the crowded room, but he pretended not to see her, and when she came up to him, he deliberately cut her and went to talk to Nina Moise, who was directing the Provincetown Players that season.

Eugene was shy, but he was capable, under the influence of alcohol and fury, of astonishingly theatrical gestures. Now he was both drunk and angry, and determined to hurt the girl who had stirred his feelings so deeply. Jumping up on a chair, which he had pulled under a clock on the wall, he chanted to the hushed crowd,

> *Turn back the universe,*
> *And give me yesterday.*
> *Turn back—*

Then he opened the clock and pushed back the hands. Everyone in the room knew about him and Louise Bryant; he felt sure that someone would tell Agnes. And, of course, someone did. At that moment Agnes happened to be standing with Susan Glaspell and Mary Pyne, and Mary had just told Agnes she looked like Louise Bryant. "I believe *Gene* is the one who sees your little friend's resemblance to Louise," said Susan Glaspell to Mary. "Maybe that's what's wrong with him tonight!"

In the tight little community of the Village, Gene came upon Agnes again and again. Soon his attraction to her overcame his fear. But the fear persisted, and occasionally the devil of hate would suddenly rise. One night, when they were visiting Hutch Collins at an apartment belonging to a friend of his, Agnes went into another room with Hutch. Eugene, who had been talking with the friend, followed them and brought her back roughly. Later Hutch went home and the friend prepared to sleep on the couch. Eugene, who was in the bedroom, called her to him. He had a dim wish, he later told her, to possess her then and there in the atmosphere of drink and cold on somebody else's unmade bed, sex as a consummation of hate, to destroy his feeling for her. But he didn't touch her. They both slept. When he awoke in the morning and saw her at the door, ready to leave, he burst into a flood of savage insults. She walked out.

At once, he was miserable. He went home, put a copy of his play *The Moon of the Caribbees* into an envelope, and left it for her at the Brevoort. She came to him later in the Hell-Hole, full of admiration for him and his play and with no trace of resentment at his outburst that morning. He was reassured, and began to accept his love for her. Later he inscribed *Beyond the Horizon* to her "in memory of the wonderful moment when first in your eyes I saw the promise of a land more beautiful than any I had ever known, a land of which I had dreamed only hopelessly, a land beyond my horizon."

At last Eugene began to feel the security of an answering love, to which he could turn in moments of anguish. It was to Agnes he turned when his friend Louis Holliday killed himself. At a party to celebrate his return from the West, Louis learned that the girl he loved and expected to marry had found another man. Louis started drinking heavily—with Gene, Terry Carlin, and Charles Demuth. Agnes had gone home earlier. Presently Louis asked for heroin; Terry, who knew how to get it, brought him some; and the evening exploded into tragedy. Louis took too much—he probably knew it was too much—and the rest of them, horrified, realized that he was dying. Eugene fled to Agnes's apartment. Finding her asleep, he lay down beside her and, holding her tightly, buried his face against her shoulder. Charles Demuth stayed and watched Louis die. Then he fled, too. Hutch Hapgood saw Demuth later that night at the Brevoort. "He literally seemed a being in hell," Hapgood recalled. "I never saw such a look of complete horror on any human being's face."

Louis died in Dorothy Day's arms. When it was over, she came to tell Gene and Agnes. She had hidden the heroin. The police were at Romany Marie's. She wanted Gene and Agnes to return there with her, and they were on the way when Gene suddenly stopped. "I'm going back to the Hell-Hole!" he cried and left them to drink himself into oblivion.

How different he was from his father! James O'Neill had been able to take charge when Louise Hawthorne fell to her death, though he had just gone through the shock of finding her body. Eugene was shattered by disaster, and looked only for escape.

When he was finally able to leave New York after the productions of *Long Voyage Home, In the Zone,* and *Ile,* he asked Agnes to go with him to Provincetown, and she agreed. Their first days away from New York were filled with quiet companionship in work and love. Eugene wanted their union to be sealed by marriage. But the arrangements were difficult. Marriage by justice of the peace was impossible in Provincetown. Alice Woods Ullman came to their rescue. She found a minister to marry them, and arranged with Mr. Darrell, the drugstore proprietor, to get their license.

Alice told Mr. Darrell to go over to the studio apartment about two in the afternoon, when Gene's working hours would be over. Mr. Darrell knocked at the door at two. Getting no answer, he strode in, calling "Mr. O'Neill." He was stunned when "Mr. O'Neill" sprang naked from the couch while Agnes, as she herself reported later, "cowered abjectly" there. Then Mr. Darrell backed out, remarking that perhaps he had come too early. But he gave them the license.

On Friday evening, April 12, 1918, the ceremony was performed by "the most delightful, feeble-minded, Godhelpus, mincing Methodist minister that ever prayed through his nose." So Eugene described him to Nina Moise. All through the ceremony, Eugene had divided feelings. He thought the minister was an "old idiot," but also "lovable." He wanted to believe in the "gentle God" the minister seemed so sure of, and was impressed by the ceremony and the symbolic beauty of the traditional words. Yet he couldn't help sneering at the "feeble-minded, Godhelpus, mincing Methodist minister."

Agnes felt the beauty of the ceremony too (although she would forget the minister's denomination, thinking him "Presbyterian"). Afterward, when they were alone, Eugene talked of their future. He wanted their marriage to be as beautiful as the marriage of his parents. His father still treated his mother with tender care, never leaving her without providing for her comfort. "I am going up to New London for a few days and Mrs. O' will be alone," James would write to an old friend like William Seymour. "I wonder if you can spare three seats for Wednesday night & give her a pleasant evening during my absence." And George Tyler told Eugene later, "your dear father loved her so much that he couldn't bear to see her be anything else than an ornament." Eugene wanted his own marriage to show that kind of devotion. He wanted Papa and Mama to know, too, that he had found real love at last, a true marriage like theirs.

Long before their marriage, Agnes and Eugene had agreed that only love, not law, could bind a marriage, and agreed to dissolve their marriage the moment either of them stopped wanting it.

But their love seemed even stronger now that Agnes was Mrs. O'Neill. "Own little wife," Eugene called her, and he felt at peace with himself and the universe. Only rarely in the first years of their marriage would that peace be broken. He felt that Agnes should be able to keep him from drinking too much under the strain of a New York production. But Agnes could only watch helplessly, and Eugene would have flashes of resentment that she couldn't save him, that he had to run the whole course of the "booze bust" with its aftermath of nausea, jumping nerves, night sweats, and days of burying his consciousness in the soothing banality of the *Saturday Evening Post* until at last he could get back to work. Still later, he would quarrel with Agnes because she demanded things of him instead of surrounding him with the maternal love he needed.

For the present, however, he knew fulfillment, and from it would later write Cape's words to his wife in *Welded*: "Often I wake up in the night—in a black world, alone in a hundred million years of darkness. I feel like crying out to God for mercy because life lives! Then instinctively I seek you—my hand touches you! You are there —beside me—alive—with you I become a whole, a truth! Life guides me back through the hundred million years to you. It reveals a beginning in unity that I may have faith in the unity of the end!"

Only rarely in the first years of his marriage did the "devil of hate" take control. It appeared, Agnes would recall, in "sudden and rather dreadful outbursts of violence" or "of bitter nastiness and malevolence" when "he appeared more like a madman than anything else." The "madman" first appeared when they went to New York in November, 1918, for the production of *Where the Cross is Made*. At a drinking party Agnes got into a conversation about modern painting with Teddy Ballantine. Both of them were intensely interested and showed it. Later, when Agnes came to Gene to urge him to leave with her, he suddenly pushed her away and then slapped her hard across the face with the back of his hand. "Then he laughed, his mouth distorted with an ironic grin." She left, but he seemed blankly unaware of her going. When he returned to their hotel room, sick and miserable, she put her hand on his head. "He reached out and put his arm around me," Agnes would say, "holding me tightly and quivering."

Only one real crisis marred their first days together: the return of Louise Bryant from Russia. She wrote a long passionate letter to Eugene, asking him to come to her in New York. She seemed absolutely sure of him, and wrote as if nothing in their relationship had altered.

Gene felt a rush of pity for her. He even thought he ought to go to New York, but he couldn't. He was completing *Beyond the Horizon*. He wrote Louise a long letter explaining exactly what had happened to him. Then he showed Agnes the letter, which ended by inviting Louise to Provincetown.

More letters came from Louise, urgent, insistent letters—all demanding that Gene come to New York. Finally, Agnes suggested that Gene should agree to meet Louise in Fall River, halfway. Eugene smiled as he wrote the letter. He expected Louise to refuse, and she did. She was angry and her pride was piqued, so her reply was scalding. She also talked a great deal of the duty she and Jack Reed had to tell America about the Bolshevik Revolution, which they had seen at firsthand, for only hysterical rumors were coming through the newspapers. A few more letters passed between her and Gene, but the tie had been broken.

Agnes always thought, as did Mabel Dodge, that Louise Bryant was an artful woman who used men for her own advancement. Later, Agnes heard the story that when Louise had returned, she found Gene on her doorstep, drunk, and had to turn him away, night after night. People told Agnes that Louise herself had told the story.

Whatever her feelings toward Gene may have been, Louise and Jack Reed stood together from then on. During the next few years, when America was swept by reaction, they worked side by side to make the world aware of what was actually going on in Russia. Louise Bryant wrote a book, *Six Red Months in Russia*, and Jack wrote his famous *Ten Days That Shook the World*. In addition, they both testified before hostile congressional committees and made speeches all over the United States.

Jack Reed loved Louise Bryant till the very end. In the spring of

1920, after a second trip to Russia—this time strictly underground—
he was caught by Finnish authorities as he tried to get back to the
United States. They threw him into prison—for political reasons—
charging him officially with smuggling. In the prison he wrote a
poem for Louise.

> *White and slim my lover*
> *Birch-tree in the shade*
> *Mountain pools her fearless eyes*
> *Innocent, all-answering.*

Reed never forgot Eugene either. While he was in the Finnish
prison, he made notes for an autobiographical novel, one of which
read, "The coming of Gene O'Neill." But the novel was never
written. The Soviet authorities negotiated Reed's release and his
return to Russia. He spent a few turbulent weeks as a delegate of
the second congress of the Communist International. Then he
caught typhus. The Soviet Union had almost no medical supplies
because of the blockade, and Jack had been weakened by his imprisonment in Finland. Louise got to him just before he died. His
last words to her were, "Listen . . . I am singing a little song for
you. . . . The whole world came between us. . . . "

When John Reed died and was buried in the Kremlin in October,
1920, Eugene O'Neill had moved a long way from the old bitterness of his entanglement with Louise and Jack. With Agnes beside
him, he felt—for long intervals at least—"a whole, a truth!"

CHAPTER TWENTY-EIGHT

"Fighting, Willing—Living!"

Eugene had come to Provincetown in the spring of 1918, ready to work on *Beyond the Horizon*. "For a long time before I wrote it," he told the New York *Times* later, "I had been planning a play of the same title, but of a very different scope—a play in which in a multitude of scenes that would have appalled any producer I wished to show a series of progressive episodes, illustrating—and, I hoped, illuminating—the life story of a true Royal Tramp at his sordid but satisfying, and therefore mysterious pursuit of a drab rainbow." For this play, Eugene "dreamed," he said, "of wedding the theme for a novel to the play form in a way that would still leave the play master of the house." (The dream would come true later in *Strange Interlude*.)

Then, "in an inexplainable flash," Eugene was led, he said, to an entirely new idea for his play: "the tragedy of the man who looks over the horizon, who longs with his whole soul to depart on the quest, but whom destiny confines to a place and a task that are not his." The flash was his memory of the Norwegian A.B. on the British tramp steamer who kept saying he should have stayed on the farm. "I thought," Eugene said, " 'What if he had stayed on the farm, with his instincts? What would have happened?' But I realized at once he never would have stayed, not even if he had saddled himself with the wife and kids. . . . "

"And from that point I started to think of a more intellectual, civilized type . . . a man who would have my Norwegian's inborn craving for the sea's unrest, only in him it would be conscious, intellectually diluted into a vague, intangible, romantic wanderlust." This weaker intellectual type came straight out of Eugene's first long play *Bread and Butter*.

Eugene designed each act of *Beyond the Horizon* with two scenes. "One scene is out of doors, showing the horizon, suggesting the man's desire and dream. The other is indoors, the horizon gone, suggesting what has come between him and his dream. In that way I tried to get rhythm, the alternation of longing and loss," Eugene explained. The rhythm, he hoped, would speak directly to the emotions of his audience. "Probably very few people who saw the play knew that this was definitely planned to produce the effect," he said later. "But I am sure they all unconsciously *get* the effect."

When the play was produced, he was irritated by the stupidity of critics who attacked him for unnecessary shifts of scene. Only Barrett Clark remarked on his "interesting technical experiment." "Why is it, I wonder," Eugene wrote Clark, "that not one other critic has given me credit for a deliberate departure in form in search of greater flexibility? They have all accused me of bungling through ignorance—whereas, if I had wanted to, I could have laid the whole play in the farm interior, and made it tight as a drum à la Pinero. Then, too, I should imagine the symbolism I intended to convey by the alternating scenes would be apparent even from a glance at the program. It rather irks my professional pride, you see, to be accused of ignorance of conventional, everyday technique—I, a

This same misunderstanding would occur again and again now Baker 47 alumnus!"

that Eugene O'Neill had crystallized his mature aesthetic creed. He would be attacked for prolixity when he was deliberately employing repetition, not to pound home an intellectual concept, but to affect his audience emotionally, to speak directly to the unconscious. As he would remark later to George Jean Nathan, reason has no place in the theater or the church, for both are "either below—or above it." As a mystic, Eugene O'Neill believed that the really important truths can only be conveyed symbolically and grasped emotionally.

The only part of his original inspiration that Eugene kept for *Beyond the Horizon* was the idea of the "hopeless hope," which, even though unachieved, is in itself a victory. This idea represented his entire philosophy of life and of tragedy. As he would tell Mary Mullett in 1922, when she asked him about his philosophy, "Well, I suppose it is the idea I try to put into all my plays. People talk of the 'tragedy' in them, and call it 'sordid,' 'depressing,' 'pessimistic'— the words usually applied to anything of a tragic nature. But tragedy, I think, has the meaning the Greeks gave it. To them it brought exaltation, an urge toward life and ever more life. It roused them to deeper spiritual understandings and released them from the petty greeds of everyday existence. When they saw a tragedy on the stage they felt their own hopeless hopes ennobled in art."

"Hopeless hopes?" Mary Mullett echoed.

"Yes," Eugene answered, "because any victory we *may* win is never the one we dreamed of winning. The point is that life itself is nothing. It is the *dream* that keeps us fighting, willing—living! Achievement, in the narrow sense of possession, is a stale finale. The dreams that can be completely realized are not worth dreaming. The higher the dream, the more impossible it is to realize it fully." And, a moment later, he continued, "A man wills his own defeat when he pursues the unattainable. But his *struggle* is his success! He is an example of the spiritual significance which life attains when it aims high enough, when the individual fights all the hostile forces within and without himself to a future of nobler values."

He had learned this from Nietzsche, who said, "And if ye have failed on great things, are ye, for that reason, yourselves a failure? The higher its ken is, the seldomer doth a thing succeed." And again, "Let your love unto life be love unto your highest hope; and your highest hope the highest thought of your life." This was what Eugene meant, when he would cry, "Life is a tragedy, hurrah!" The very tragedy of life, he thought, was the means by which man attained his personal greatness—in the striving, the dreaming, the "struggle" itself. As he wrote Mary Clark, "I see life as a gorgeously-ironical, beautifully indifferent, splendidly-suffering bit of chaos the tragedy of which gives Man a tremendous significance, while without his losing fight with fate he would be a tepid, silly animal. I say 'losing fight' only symbolically for the brave individual always wins."

When he finished *Beyond the Horizon,* Eugene let out a triumphant cry, as he always did at the finish of a play. His triumph was even greater than he supposed, for he had come of age as an artist. He had matured his philosophy of tragedy and his aesthetic creed.

Triumph of another sort came, too. Almost every week brought him new assurances that he had arrived. Lewis and Gordon were producing *In the Zone* in vaudeville on the Keith and Orpheum circuits throughout the country, which meant a steady income of $35 a week in royalties. "It is true," Eugene remarked later, "rumors occasionally reached me at the time that the direction had my cockney stop the show at a crucial point to do a specialty hornpipe and sing 'The Old Kent Road,' that my Irishman had a few of Jimmy Thornton's stories arranged in his part, etc., but—well, you cannot prove it by me for I never saw it."

Eugene even got fan mail. One letter in an unsteady hand came to him at the Greenwich Village Theatre when *Ile* opened.

Dear Mr. O'Neill:

No doubt you will be surprised to receive this letter from one you do not know. But perhaps you may have heard of me. My name is Mrs. Murray, the nurse who was with you when you were born. If I haven't seen you I have thought of you many times during the last thirty years, and wondered how you and your dear mother were getting along. I carried you in my arms to the church the day you were christened, a beautiful baby. Your godmother was Miss Annie Connors and your godfather Mr. John O'Neill. So, you see, I am not such a stranger after all. In looking over my Sunday paper I was both surprised and pleased to see your name as an author. I congratulate you. I would be pleased to see you and your parents again. My best wishes to them and yourself. I am now seventy-two years old, in fairly good health, living with friends. I would be pleased to hear from you.

Mrs. Elizabeth Murray

Papa and Mama smiled when Eugene showed it to them. After all his years of being a black sheep, at last he was bringing credit to the name of O'Neill. Eugene knew his father's pride in him, and the knowledge thawed his old bitterness. The deep bond of affection between them became more and more apparent.

Eugene's success had done more than all of Papa's urging to interest Tyler in his work. Tyler wanted to see *Beyond the Horizon.* Eugene also sent a copy to George Jean Nathan at the *Smart Set*—not that *Smart Set* would print a long play, but Nathan's opinion would be valuable. Nathan liked it so much that he brought it to John D. Williams and Williams accepted it. Williams talked of a Broadway production with the Barrymore brothers!

With all this encouragement, and joy in his marriage, Eugene felt more pleasure in simply being alive than he had for a long time, enjoyed dashing down the beach and plunging into the surf or lying on the warm sand with the sun burning him an ever darker mahogany. He had only one relapse into the old sick tension. That was when he and Agnes went down to New York for the rehearsals of *The Rope* and the opening at the Playwright's Theater on April 26, 1918. Everything went all right till just before they were to leave for Provincetown. Then, frayed by friction with other personalities and depressed by the prospect of the long train trip, he joined Jamie for a drink; one drink led to another, and he wound up in another "booze bust." It went on for a full week until all the piled-up tension in him had been released. Then, sick and miserable, he was ready to return to Provincetown.

Jamie came along, in high alcoholic spirits. At the Boston station he disappeared and returned, seconds before the train left, dragging with him a mangy, flea-ridden, starved white dog. He insisted on putting "Bowser" in the baggage car to accompany them to Provincetown. After that, he kept the whole sleeping car in an uproar for a time while he looked for "a big blonde with a bad breath." But the trip was relatively peaceful.

Then followed another painful week of "tapering off," of drugging himself with the bourgeois vacuity of the *Saturday Evening Post*, before Eugene could again get back to his schedule: writing in the morning, lunch, swimming and rest, then typing and revising. When the warm weather started, he and Agnes had moved back to the studio over John Francis's grocery store, where Gene had lived ever since his first summer in Provincetown. The studio was right on the harbor. When the tide was in, the water splashed and rushed against the pilings beneath the windows; when the tide was out, they had a long view of the empty harbor floor out to where the ocean was just beginning to foam back again.

Jamie stayed with them for the summer. He was a pleasant companion, but only a thin partition separated his cot from the rest of the studio, and his presence was inhibiting. Finally, John Francis said that Jamie could have the flat next to theirs for a very small rental. So that problem was solved.

Eugene and Jamie talked often of their past and their mad escapades. Agnes, lying in the bed on the other side of the open partition, listened while they discussed sexual aberrations with astonishing thoroughness and detail. She heard Jamie tell of the time he found an amorous homosexual in his hotel room and forced him to crawl out on his hands and knees. Eugene seemed to agree that it was no more than the fellow deserved. He had only scorn for "fairies." Much later, angry at the attack of a critic who was notoriously homosexual, he remarked that "my stuff, being masculine, will always fill these 'Sisters' with rage."

He and Jamie discussed, too, the problem of Jamie's fortieth birthday. Because of his frequent indulgence, Jamie had always expected to be worn out sexually by the time he was forty. Now he actually was—although the years of heavy drinking were what had done the damage. Jamie seemed resigned to impotence.

Eugene's ideas now were too big for the one-act form, but he wanted to be on the bill of the Provincetown Players that fall, so he wrote more one-acters. One of them was *Till We Meet*. Another was *Shell Shock*, an antiwar play about a soldier who is half-mad because he thinks that he saved his friend, who lay wounded in No Man's Land, only in order to get his cigarettes, for he had thought his friend was dead. The soldier is returned to "radiant" health by the discovery, through questions by a doctor, that he had heard his friend's screams and had really gone to rescue him. Eugene also wrote *The Dreamy Kid,* whose central character was based on the Negro gangster "Dreamy." At first, he saw it as a short story, but then he thought of a way to show, in play form, the split between the hard-boiled exterior gangster and the inner gentle boy, who is ready to risk his life to come to his dying grandmother.

In the end the Players couldn't use any of these plays for their opening bill, so Eugene wrote still another one-acter based on an idea that Agnes gave him. She had been vainly trying to shape a story called "The Captain's Walk" about an old sea captain waiting for his ship to come in. Eugene saw a play in it, so Agnes gave him what she had done. In return he gave her his old farce *Now I Ask You* as something she might rework.

What Eugene had in mind was a study in obsession that called for a full-length play. "I merely took the last act situation," he told Nathan later, "and jammed it into one-act form because I wanted to be represented on the Provincetown Player opening bill two seasons ago and had nothing else in mind for them at the time." He called it *Where the Cross is Made.* And in the same letter to Nathan, he asked, "But where did you get the idea that I really valued 'Where the Cross Is Made'? It was fun to write, theatrically very thrilling, an amusing experiment in treating the audience as insane— that is all it means or ever meant to me."

The Provincetown Players didn't put on this play until November 22, 1918. Early in November, Eugene began to receive urgent pleas from Jig Cook in New York to come down for rehearsals. Some of the players didn't want to present the ghosts in the play on stage, as the script demanded. Jig needed Eugene to back him. Irritably, Eugene prepared to go. The peace of Provincetown had been destroyed anyway. The influenza epidemic had reached the town, filling the atmosphere with fear and death. Then Jamie wrote that Mama had the flu. Eugene was miserable with worry until Jamie wrote again to say that her case was light, and that she had almost recovered. Then the flu epidemic hit the vaudeville shows. The company for *In the Zone* was laid off for six weeks, and Eugene's income from royalities stopped. Now he had the ordeal of a stay in New York, and no sooner would he get back to Provincetown after that, than he would have to go to New York again for rehearsals of *Moon of the Caribbees.* Agnes decided that the answer to their problem was a house she owned, called the Old House, at Point Pleasant, New Jersey. There Gene would have quiet for work, yet be near New York.

For the present, however, they must be in New York, and the strain began as soon as they got there. Eugene couldn't bear even such simple contacts as dealing with hotel clerks. Agnes had to register for him. Then, right off, he was faced with a fight at the Provincetown Players. Ida Rauh ("the Lioness," Mabel Dodge called her) pounced upon him. She insisted that an audience would simply laugh if ghosts were presented on stage. Eugene pointed out that since everyone in the play except the girl is mad, the spectators must see the ghosts so that they will feel mad, too. He also reminded her of the idea behind the Playwright's Theater: "The author shall produce his plays without hindrance, according to his own ideas." He got his way, but the struggle rasped his nerves.

It was at this time that Eugene introduced Agnes to Mama and Papa. On the appointed day, he was too ill from drinking to go to the Prince George Hotel early in the afternoon, as they had planned, so that Agnes had to call his parents. She said that Eugene was ill from eating oysters, but that they would come in the evening. The visit was successful. Agnes was struck particularly by Eugene's mother. She thought her "quite a beautiful person" and she understood why Mama was adored by both her sons. She was beautifully dressed, of course, and that was part of her charm. Henri Bendel designed Mama's clothes, and they were simple and lovely, like her personality. She greeted Agnes affectionately, as did James O'Neill, who said, "Eugene, you've done well."

Eugene and Agnes had only a short walk back to the Garden Hotel, where they were staying. The Garden was actually Jamie's home, close to Mama and Papa at the Prince George, but separate. Eugene had joined Jamie there for a while in the fall of 1917, before he went to Provincetown with Agnes, and now he always stayed there when he came to New York. He liked its clientele of circus people, horse breeders, and poultry raisers—who stayed there because the hotel was close to Madison Square Garden. "Used to meet them all in the bar," he would say later.

Eugene, who knew all about chicken raising and horse racing, was at ease with the poultry men and horse breeders, and he liked the others too. "One of my old chums was Volo, the Volitant, a bicycle rider whose specialty was in precipitating himself down a steep incline and turning a loop or so in the air," Eugene would recall ten years later. "Volo is now a megaphone man on one of the Broadway sightseeing buses. Billy Clark is his real name."

Eugene also enjoyed chatting with Jack Croak—an old circus man who worked in the ticket wagons of the Willard Shows. Jack Croak showed Eugene many of his tricks for shortchanging the "rubes." Later, Eugene would depict him as Ed Mosher in *The Iceman Cometh* looking "like an enlarged, elderly, bald edition of the village fat boy—a sly fat boy, congenitally indolent, a practical joker, a born grafter and con merchant."

Jack Croak had traveled through the West Indies with a tent show and talked of his adventures. "He told me a story current in Hayti concerning the late President Sam," Eugene would say. "This was to the effect that Sam had said they'd never get him with a lead bullet; that he would get himself first with a silver one. My friend, by the way, gave me a coin with Sam's features on it, and I still keep it as a pocket piece. This notion about the silver bullet struck me, and I made a note of the story." So Eugene took from Jack Croak the seed of his play *The Emperor Jones.*

Eugene liked the Garden Hotel, but it was all too easy for him to slip into a "booze bust" there, especially with Jamie ready to start him. By the time he and Agnes left for Point Pleasant, Eugene had drunk himself into nervous exhaustion.

After a dusty two-hour train trip, he and Agnes arrived at the Old House. It was freezing cold, and the place seemed to be full of animals. A dog barked at them; cats miaowed; and they smelled cat mess. Only when Agnes had started a fire did Eugene begin to relax. He didn't know—and didn't find out until a casual conversation with a townsman revealed it to him some months later—that

Agnes had evicted her family from the house in order to give him the quiet he needed for work.

Usually the Old House was empty during the winter, and Agnes had neglected to tell her family that she was planning to come there with Gene. At the last minute, she learned that all of them were established there—her mother and father, her sisters, the little girl from her first marriage, and even her grandmother from England. They agreed to move to a small rented cottage, and "Teddy," her father, an impecunious artist, took a job in the town hardware store to pay for the cottage. Agnes kept the presence of her family in the town a secret from Eugene. She knew he would not have come if he had known about it. Later, he learned it accidentally, and she introduced them. Happily, he liked them and they liked him. But all that winter his privacy was kept sacred. When a chance visitor trapped him at work, he hid in the closet.

In December, when he went to New York for the rehearsals of *Moon of the Caribbees,* Eugene began drinking again, and Agnes finally had to go after him. At the last minute, he refused to take the train because there was no baggage car, and he insisted on taking along a large white dog he had picked up near the Hell-Hole. Agnes took the train without him—for the pipes would freeze without heat and the dog and cats had to be fed. Close to dawn, Eugene arrived at the Old House with the white dog and a kindly truck driver, who had driven them in. "Brooklyn Boy," Eugene called the dog—Jamie, when he felt the alcoholic jitters coming on, would say, "The boys from Brooklyn are coming over the bridge tonight." Both Eugene and Agnes loved Brooklyn Boy. They were horribly shocked one morning to find him, his throat cut from ear to ear, lying on the front lawn. They never found out who did it.

They had another visitor from the Hell-Hole, Scotty MacDonald, whom Agnes hated, but Gene liked, perhaps because he was reassured about his own masculinity by this rough friend, as he had been by Driscoll earlier. Agnes would always believe that Scotty had deliberately killed Trixie, the family's dog, by calling him, on one of their walks, so that the dog ran in front of a truck.

That had happened after the terrible trip to New York when Hutch Collins caught his fatal illness. After a rainy night spent with

Eugene, Hutch Collins went home wet and chilled, came down with pneumonia, and died. The irony, for Eugene, was that Hutch had gone "on the wagon" and the sudden absence of alcohol was probably what weakened his resistance and killed him.

But all of those events were somehow outside of the real current of Eugene's life, his unbroken months of steady work. He wrote all morning and sometimes into the afternoon. Then he took a long walk, thinking out the problems of his play. After that, he typed and revised what he had written, then laid out his materials for the next morning's writing. In the evening he relaxed. Often he and Agnes would read in bed, side by side, propped up with pillows.

Eugene was working on a play called *Chris Christophersen* about his sea-captain roommate at Jimmy the Priest's. After his days with Gene of "razzing the sea," Chris had gotten a barge to captain. "One Christmas Eve he got terribly drunk," Eugene said, "and tottered away about 2 o'clock in the morning for his barge. The next morning he was found frozen on a cake of ice between the piles and the dock. In trying to board the barge he stumbled on the plank and fell over." This play, Eugene said, was a "character sketch." He saw in Chris man's eternal struggle with a chaotic world, for "dat ole davil sea" that Chris grumbled over, was life. But Eugene had invented a daughter for Chris, and she kept trying to take over the play.

He worked on *Chris* between the first and last drafts of *The Straw*, "a tragedy of human hope," as Eugene called it. Like *Beyond the Horizon*, it expressed the "hopeless hope." "My whole idea is to show the power of spiritual help, even when a case is hopeless. Human hope is the greatest power in life and the only thing that defeats death," Eugene said later. The play drew on his experience at Gaylord. Later, he told Mary Clark that there was much of "the 'me' of that period" in the character of Murray, "unintentionally," and that the nurse in the play, Miss Gilpin, represented the "continued kindness" of Miss Clark.

The Straw would later be tried out in New London. Eugene wrote to Ed Keefe afterward, "It was funny, 'The Straw' opening in N. L. when there is so much autobiographical stuff in it connected with that town. When I wrote it three years ago of course I never dreamed of that coincidence—or I would never have lazily picked

up actual names which, even if the stage folk were altogether different from the living, must have sounded rather mirthful. 'Doctor
Gaynor' for Doc Gayney, for example—and 'Doctor Stanton.'

"A propos of this, let me tell you something that I know will
tickle you: My cousins, the Brennans, are infuriated at me. They
take the old harridan step-mother as an insult direct aimed at their
mother whom [sic] they insist is a lady and not the creature of the
play at all—all because of the name, 'Brennan'! Can you beat it! I've
tried to explain that every city directory is pretty full of Brennans
but it's no use."

Eugene also wrote some one-acters for the Provincetown Players:
Exorcism, a farce on his attempted suicide, and two others, *Honor
Among the Bradleys* and *The Trumpet.* One came out of a walk he
took in Point Pleasant with Agnes, when they came on a family
consisting of an alcoholic father, a mother who took in washing,
seven beautiful blonde daughters, three of them pregnant, and a
yard full of illegitimate children. Later, Eugene sent *Honor Among
the Bradleys* to Nathan, and Nathan told him to tear it up for the
sake of his reputation. Eugene soon agreed that it was "a very false
and feeble piece of work."

Good or bad, Eugene's joy was in his work. But getting it produced was a constant strain. *In the Zone* survived the flu epidemic
only to die with the armistice, which brought, Eugene said, "Peace-
on-Earth-good-night-to-war-plays." Sherman was wrong, Eugene
decided, when he declared "War is hell." "*Peace,*" Eugene declared,
"is hell." The $35 a week no longer came in. Besides, Eugene be-
came frustrated as week after week, month after month, he waited
for a letter announcing the start of rehearsals of *Beyond the Horizon,*
and no letter came. Eugene kept hoping that as soon as John Barrymore closed in *Redemption,* Williams would start the Barrymore
brothers in *Beyond the Horizon.* Then, Eugene learned, with shock,
that Williams had just put the Barrymores into rehearsals of *The
Jest.* Eugene wondered if his play would ever see the light. He decided he needed an agent to fight the producers for him, so he
turned to Richard Madden of the American Play Company.

Bitterly, Eugene realized that if Papa hadn't continued his allowance, and raised it when he got married, he would have starved. His wife had to give him a home.

Then, in the spring of 1919, Agnes told him she was pregnant. At first, he was stunned. He hoped that the doctor was mistaken. He didn't want to be a father. He didn't like children. In his plays, to date, they had always been disagreeable whining creatures. He couldn't come to terms with the news. He couldn't turn to Agnes with affection. Instead, he became silent.

Then Happy, their cat, began to have kittens. She wanted company and miaowed piteously until Gene came to sit by her basket. Eugene became fascinated with the mystery of birth, and devotedly assisted Happy by singing her sea chanties while she labored. Each of the kittens was born to a different tune, and he named them accordingly, "Whiskey" for "Whiskey Johnny," "Blow" for "Blow the Man Down," and "Drumstick" for the line, "I put my hand upon her thigh" in "I'll Go No More A-Roving." Then he thought of his wife's pregnancy, and, as Agnes reported later, he "gave me a long and devoted kiss."

CHAPTER TWENTY-NINE

Rewards

Two miles out of Provincetown stood the abandoned coast-guard station, Peaked Hill Bar. Only seagulls, sandpipers, and horseshoe crabs disturbed its solitude. Eugene often had walked out there with Agnes to swim, sun himself, and enjoy the beauty of the spot. The Atlantic surged within a few feet of the house. A great wild rosebush clambered over the dune behind it. Sam Lewisohn, the millionaire, had turned the station into a summer house, but now it was for sale, fully furnished. Eugene had told Mama how much he would like to live there—if only he had the money to buy it.

The first person Eugene saw in Provincetown, when he returned in the spring of 1919, was John Francis. Smiling, John Francis handed him the deed to Peaked Hill Bar. Papa had bought it for him, arranging the whole thing through John Francis so that Eugene would be surprised.

"The place has come to mean a tremendous lot to me," Eugene told Pierre Loving a little later. "I feel a true kinship and harmony with life out there. Sand and sun and sea and wind—you merge into them, and become as meaningless and as full of meaning as they are. There is always the monotone of surf on the bar—a background for silence—and you *know* that you are alone—so alone you wouldn't be ashamed to do any good action. You can walk or swim along the beach for miles, and meet only the dunes—Sphinxes muffled in their yellow robes with paws deep in the sea."

Eugene loved the house itself, too. "The stairs are like companionways of a ship," he noted exultantly. "There are lockers everywhere. An immense open fireplace. The big boat room, now our living room, still has the steel fixtures in the ceiling from which one of the boats was slung. The look-out station on the roof is the same as when the coast guards spent their eternal two-hour vigils there. The exteriors of the buildings are as weather-beaten as the bulwarks of a derelict. The glass in the windows is ground frosty by the flying sands of the winter storms."

Eugene enjoyed pointing out to visitors the place in his living room where the coast guardsmen had laid out the corpses after a wreck. He liked Mary Heaton Vorse's tale of Captain William Wallace Cook, the last coast guard captain who had stayed there. He had said, "I got twenty-nine wrecks this winter and forty-eight corpses, and the station next me got only three wrecks and nary corpse." The very building imparted a sense of adventure and courageous living.

Yet life there was far from rugged. The whole interior had been beautifully finished by Mabel Dodge, who had originally planned to buy and remodel the coast guard station with $1000 she had saved. When she decided to spend her $1000 on the Elizabeth Duncan School instead, Sam Lewisohn told her to go ahead and remodel the station anyway; he would pay, and they could take turns using it. John Francis carried out the whole job from instructions in Mabel Dodge's letters. So faithfully did he work that Mabel Dodge remarked later, "I think it took at least ten years off his life!"

The most spectacular touch was the walls, which were covered with no fewer than seven coats of white paint. Each coat was allowed to dry thoroughly before the next was applied, so that they were not simply white, they were luminous. The floors were painted a deep Chinese blue and covered with blue and yellow braided rugs. In the living room were two enormous couches covered in blue linen with blue and yellow pillows, two white writing tables, two blue and white Morris chairs, a few natural pine Windsor chairs, and a high window seat on either side of the fireplace. On the walls hung great three-foot-wide Italian pottery plates with blue, yellow, brown, and red fish designs.

The dining room, lined with lockers, had two huge doors so that the whole room could be opened up to the sea and sand at one end. It had a long natural pine table with pine chairs and was decorated with white highly glazed Bassano pottery fruit bowls, contrasting with the soft white walls. The blue and white kitchen had every conceivable utensil, all of the finest, and beautiful copper pots, blue china, and blue glassware.

The upstairs, divided into bedroom and study, was also beautiful. Eugene had the whole history of the place from John Francis and liked to tell friends how Mabel Dodge and Robert Edmond Jones— "no less!"—had designed it. He did not tell people that the house was a gift from his father. But a picture of James O'Neill stood on the desk where he worked.

"O, I do nearly all my work here," Eugene would say. "I am safe from interruption in this place and can get the results I want. We come down early in June and stay until late in the fall. Not many people bother us here, I can assure you, not even the postman." Once a week, Peter Carr brought groceries out to them in his cart drawn by a big black horse, and occasionally a coast guardsman from the neighboring station dropped off some mail for them. Otherwise, they saw only the friends who were ready to clamber two miles over the shifting dunes, or those they went into Provincetown to visit, Jig and Susan, for instance. Sometimes, Terry Carlin stayed with them. He was never an obtrusive presence for Gene, but he tangled often with the Portuguese housekeeper they hired after Shane was born.

Gene smiled when he told Hutch Hapgood about it. "Gene loved Terry probably as much as he ever did any man," Hapgood said;

"but one day—Gene told me this story himself—the housekeeper came to him and said, 'Mr. O'Neill, either I or Terry must go.' Gene knew that there had been friction between them for a long time, and he was expecting something startling, but when he heard her say, 'Terry spat in the sink this morning,' he knew that the end had come. It was then that Gene smiled; but Terry went."

Over the years, relics of happy summers accumulated at Peaked Hill Bar. Gene had a huge desk made out of the paneling from wrecked ships that was swept in to shore, and he acquired too, a fifteen-foot red and white eskimo kayak in which he skimmed the high rollers along the coast, paddling far out to sea. The kayak was his pride and joy. "It's perfectly safe," Eugene would say, "when you know how to handle it. It was built for me by a man in New London who had a hobby for making such things. The material? Oh, cedar. She's perfectly tight and rides the waves like a cork. I use a double-ended paddle and very little exertion is required to propel the boat."

His adventures in the kayak were the talk of Provincetown. "Gene once made one of those trips about five miles offshore," Harry Kemp recalled. "He finally came up alongside a fishing schooner to ask if there was a spare codfish aboard. The skipper took one look at him, a mixture of amazement and concern. Then he roared, 'You git back to shore quick as you can, you crazy loon!' But Gene seemed to regard the kayak as being safe as an ocean liner. Often he'd paddle clear around the Cape and into Provincetown harbor." Gene, too, would tell of the astonishment of fishermen who came upon him three or four miles out. "They call him all sorts of things for what they think is his foolishness for taking such risks," Agnes would add.

He had to shovel the house out of the drifted sand when he and Agnes first moved out to Peaked Hill Bar, and he had to keep shoveling it out, after each wind storm. Later, Shane, as a small boy, would call it "the house where the wind blows." Gene picked up driftwood for the fireplace, too, and he and Agnes collected beautiful shells, sculptured driftwood, and bottles curiously frosted and carved by the blowing sands.

By the end of each summer, Gene was the color of mahogany. Perhaps that was one reason Mary Heaton Vorse thought of him as a South Sea Islander. "One could see him, slender and brown as an Indian, coming up the beach to plunge into the breakers," she would recall of times she walked out to Peaked Hill Bar. "He swam as no one else that I have ever seen, as though he belonged to the water, as if it were not a separate element, much as I imagined South Sea Islanders swim tirelessly with the smoothness of a seal." Indeed, once a seal did join him, swimming beside him until he came in to shore.

No more perfect gift could have been given him than Peaked Hill Bar, for it was a gift of a way of life that was precious to him. He worked well there all the first summer. In September, Agnes moved into Provincetown, so she would be close to the doctor when the baby came. Her mother was with her. Gene stayed on at Peaked Hill Bar and walked in to see her each day, after he had stopped working. But the baby didn't come. They had expected it about the first of October, but day after day went by, Agnes became bigger and bigger, and nothing happened. Finally, her mother had to leave, and Gene then moved back into town. And the days went by. It was almost like the production of *Beyond the Horizon,* expected to go on at any moment, but somehow refusing to happen.

It wasn't until three o'clock in the morning of October 30, 1919, that Agnes gave the first sharp cry of pain that told them that the baby was coming. Gene, "trembling violently" pulled on his trousers, called Dr. Heibert, and then helped Agnes across the street to another cottage they had prepared for the coming of the baby, as it had a heater. A little later, Dr. Heibert was spanking a large infant boy into the first breathing howl of life, and presently Eugene was holding his son, looking down at him with happy wonder and half afraid of carrying him. "Shane the Loud," he called him, punning on the glorious name the child was to bear: "Shane O'Neill, Shane the Proud." And as he bent over Agnes afterward, he said, "It'll be *us* still, from now on. Us—alone—but the three of us. A sort of Holy Trinity, eh, Shane?"

A few months later, *Beyond the Horizon* went into rehearsal for a series of special matinees at the Morosco Theatre. Richard Bennett had persuaded Williams to try the play out with Bennett as Robert Mayo. Also, Tyler was about to start rehearsals on *Chris.* So Eugene kissed Aggie and Shane and went down to New York to stay with his parents at the Prince George Hotel.

Beyond the Horizon opened on February 2, 1920. Mama and Papa were there in a box with Eugene. During the last act, Eugene could see tears rolling down his father's cheeks. He "wept his eyes out," Eugene later told friends. But still later, his father's pride in him somehow got mixed with the feeling of hurt and rejection he had so often had. Eugene reported to Hamilton Basso that his father had said, after the last curtain, "It's all right, if that's what you want to do, but people come to the theatre to forget their troubles, not to be reminded of them. What are you trying to do—send them home to commit suicide?"

"My father and I hadn't got along so well," Eugene explained to Basso. "We had had a running battle for a good many years, and I know there were times when he'd just about given me up. Not that I blame him. If anything, he was too patient with me. What I wonder now is why he didn't kick me out. I gave him every chance to. And yet, as sometimes happens, we were close to each other—we were a very close family. My father, somehow or other, managed to believe in me. When he read the plays in 'Thirst,' which he hadn't seen before they were published, he threw up his hands. 'My God,' he said. 'Where did you get such thoughts?' But he encouraged me to go ahead. I didn't expect him to like 'Beyond the Horizon,' which wasn't the sort of thing he *could* like, so I wasn't surprised by what he said. All the same, I think he was pleased."

At the time, he *knew* his father was pleased, for he told Nina Moise, "Yes, it was the greatest satisfaction he knew that I had made good in a way dear to his own heart." And Eugene added that he was ready, in Henley's words, to thank "whatever gods may be" that the play did not come "too late for him."

Clayton Hamilton remembered how, a little later, James O'Neill came to him "all aglow with pride," and said, "My boy—my boy Eugene; I always knew he had it in him! Remember how I always used to say that he would do something big some day? People told me he was wild and good-for-nothing; but I always knew he had it in him—didn't I?"

Eugene had been nervous at the opening. "I felt sure when I saw the woebegone faces of the audience on the opening day that it was a rank failure," he would comment later, "and no one was more surprised than was I when I saw the morning papers and came to the conclusion that the sad expressions on the playgoers' faces were caused by their feeling the tragedy I had written." The play was more than a success. Eugene was being spoken of, without qualifications, as the long-awaited "great American dramatist."

Eugene was delighted when George Middleton sent him a letter of congratulation on *Beyond the Horizon*, and wrote in reply: "You and St. John Ervine are the only playwrights who have given me a brotherly word of encouragement—and you can bet your letters are going into the the old oak chest as heirlooms in embryo! And your letters have taught me, I hope—if ever I get the authority for it—to do likewise and write to the first author whose play I respect—especially if I don't know him—to tell him so; for, through you, I have learned the things that count most of all." Eugene meant it, too. A little over a year later, he saw Arthur Richman's *Ambush* and immediately wrote the author: "It is a corking, fine, truthful piece of work from start to finish, and I sincerely envy you your having written it. All my loudest cheers for it and for you!"

It was a time of great joy for Eugene—and the victory was even sweeter because with it came the closest companionship he had had with his parents since he had been a small boy, "mama's baby, papa's pet." He and his father, he knew, were "pals." The old rebellious tensions were gone.

But the time of joy was short. Almost immediately, as if life demanded a kind of payment for success, Eugene found himself torn apart again by worry and tension. First Mama got sick, flu with a touch of pneumonia, and not a light case, as she had had the year before, but a serious illness that frightened them all. Then, while he was still worried about Mama, he caught the flu himself and found himself bedridden just at the time he needed his strength to supervise rehearsals for *Chris*. So he fretted and worried while Tyler started rehearsals without him, and he had visions of his work being massacred while he was lying helpless.

He was still weak and jittery from the flu when the final blow struck. Papa, who had always been a bulwark of health and strength until the last year, when he had been struck by an automobile, suddenly collapsed. He had a stroke, and the doctors were immediately grave and doubtful. He was examined at St. Vincent's Hospital, and then they knew—he and Mama and Jamie—that Papa had cancer. The doctors talked of an operation, but the case looked black. It was cancer of the intestine and already far along. Eugene learned the news with agony. Weak from the flu, sick with worry over his father, he turned helplessly to drink, which left him only more jittery and torn. He was just, as he said, "tottering up to my first 'Chris' rehearsals," when he had word that Agnes was ill in Provincetown. There was no one to take care of her. So, on the verge of breakdown himself, he rushed back to Provincetown to nurse a sick wife. "If this be the payment demanded of me for the big splash made by 'Beyond,'" he told George Jean Nathan, "then I am tempted to remark with Jurgen that 'it does not seem quite fair.'"

Frayed and jittery as he was, he blamed Tyler for the failure of *Chris,* which had tried out in Atlantic City on March 8, 1920, and gone on to Philadelphia, where it wasn't doing too well. "They cut it unmercifully in my enforced absence—on the strength of an adverse decision by an Atlantic City audience, at that!" he complained bitterly to Barrett Clark, "—and little play is left, I guess. It is in six scenes—another experiment—and the curtain rings down before 10:30—after the cutting. You can imagine the movie effect. I'm too disgusted to witness a performance, but my agent and friends in Philly have reported to me. The play is also miserably cast. As it is a character sketch built up bit by bit you can understand what the rough methods they used accomplished. I hope you'll be able to read this play some day soon. I know it has its faults, but I still think it doesn't deserve its present fate, and, if treated sympathetically, would find its public as *Beyond* has."

Already feeling betrayed and injured by Tyler, Eugene flew into a rage when he got one of Jamie's cynical letters describing a visit of Tyler to Papa, when Tyler had talked of the difficulties of producing *The Straw,* giving Jamie the impression, which he communicated with relish, that the play consisted of a lot of "coughing and spitting." Frantic, Eugene addressed a long, bitter letter to Tyler offering to take back his play. Tyler wrote a stern reply, telling Eugene that he had reached a "stupid conclusion," and that he ought to know better than to assume Tyler was simply a money-grubbing manager with no concern for art (Eugene knew full well that Tyler had been one of the first to produce Ibsen, Shaw, Yeats, and Synge in America). Eugene wrote again and the breach was healed. Curiously he had reacted to Tyler, Papa's close friend, as he used to react to Papa, with a readiness to see betrayal in anything he said, and an immediate infuriated retaliation.

Gradually, Eugene found himself recovering from the state of frantic nerves he had been in when he left New York. The devil of hate gradually submerged again. Eugene apologized to Tyler, telling him how "frayed and frazzled" he had been, and assuring him that he harbored no "false grievance" over the failure of *Chris,* that he blamed only himself, and that the proof for that was the rewritten version of *Chris,* which he would call *Anna Christie.*

Similarly, he responded to Nathan's sudden attack on him in the June issue of the *Smart Set.* "Your criticism of me and mine in the magazine is sure invigorating—grateful as keen salt breeze after much hot air puffing from all sides," he told Nathan. Then Eugene O'Neill gave his own estimate of where he stood.

"I rate myself as a beginner—with prospects," he told Nathan. "I acknowledge that when you write: 'He sees life too often as drama. The great dramatist is the dramatist who sees drama as life,' you are smiting the nail on the head. But I venture to promise that this will be less true with each succeeding play—that I will not 'stay put' in any comfortable niche and play the leave-well-enough alone game. God stiffen it, I am young yet and I mean to grow! And in this faith I live: That if I have the 'guts' to ignore the megaphone men and what goes with them, to follow the dream and live for that alone, then my real significant bit of truth, and the ability to express it, will be conquered in time—not tomorrow nor the next day nor any near, easily-attained period, but after the struggle has been long enough and hard enough to merit victory."

He had given Nathan the testament of faith which would guide him in everything he wrote from then on. Nietzsche had taught him to strive to surpass himself, but long before that his father had taught him to "work, *work*, WORK!" Not for nothing was he the son of James O'Neill.

In June, Eugene received the Pulitzer Prize for *Beyond the Horizon.* "I had never heard of the Pulitzer Prize," he told people, "until I received a telegram from my wife congratulating me upon winning it. I thought it must be a medal or something, and I was very pleased when I learned a thousand dollars went with it, for believe me, I needed the money." Eugene also took pleasure in what struck him as the absurd incongruity of Columbia University's conferring "one of its biggest blue ribbons" on him.

But he was especially pleased to be able to give the news to Papa. Papa needed good news, for he was dying. Dr. Erdmann's final verdict was that nothing could be done. The disease was too far along. They could barely ease the pain, and nothing lay beyond but more pain and death.

CHAPTER THIRTY

End of the Beginning

ALL the details of that hot August in New London when Papa lay dying at the Lawrence Memorial Hospital remained permanently etched in Eugene's mind. He remembered the nurses in their heat-crumpled uniforms, the odor of iodoform; and he remembered his father lying in pain, his great voice reduced to a whisper.

Eugene had brought Shane and Agnes down from Provincetown to New York in the spring, and Papa and Mama had been deeply pleased at their grandchild. Papa was particularly delighted with the boy's grand name—Shane O'Neill, Shane the Proud. That was the last moment of pleasure. After that, Eugene could only stand by helplessly, watching his father suffer.

Mama and Jamie took Papa back to New London that summer. When he became too ill for home care, he entered Lawrence Memorial Hospital. The doctors told them he couldn't live more than a few days. Eugene rushed down from Provincetown to be with him. But Papa didn't die. Day after day, he lay in agony; day after day, the doctors were sure he couldn't last, but he did last, to suffer even more intolerably, his "grand old constitution," Eugene thought, forcing him "to drain the cup of agony to the last bitter drop."

Looking down at his father's face, white with pain, Eugene thought bitterly that here lay a man whom all had envied, and who now was dying "broken, unhappy, intensely bitter." All that winter when he and Papa had at last sat down together in love and comradeship, Papa had talked of his regrets; his feeling that *Monte Cristo* had been his curse, that *Monte Cristo* had kept him from being Booth's successor, one of America's greatest actors. Instead, he had had the humiliation, in his old age, of supporting actors not worth his little finger. Looking at his father, Eugene thought he knew now "the tragedy of success." He thought his father had really been a failure.

What he didn't realize was that his father's last days, darkened by physical torture, were not really the sum of his life. Eugene had always sensed that, from a purely personal standpoint, his father's life had been a success, if a rich joy in living was any measure of success. James O'Neill's real verdict on life was not in the terrible words wrung out of him in his last agony, nor in the quieter regrets before that, but in his words ten years earlier, when he was sixty-four—sixty, the public thought—and answered a telegram of congratulations on his birthday.

"Sincere thanks for the Morning Telegraph's birthday message," he had written. "Life in 60 Middle Row has the same charms we knew at fifteen where we first sat in the gallery. I don't want to quote poetry, but you will recall the old couplet about distance lending enchantment. Must say that all my years on the stage form one grand poem of happiness to myself.

"That I am yet so graciously recalled is gratifying as warranting the belief that I must have afforded in turn some pleasure to playgoers.

"From seat 60 I can see life's stage without the aid of glasses, and the air is filled with roses and sunshine. I love life fully as well as ever, and my friends a whole lot better. It has been the best sixty years I have ever experienced, and I feel today as if I were going to live sixty more."

He had meant that as much as he meant what he said in his dying agony. Unlike Eugene, who shrank from contact with others ("It has always been such agony for me to be touched!"), James O'Neill's great pleasure was companionship. He would remember the name of a doorman at a theater he had visited two years earlier and pick up a conversation with him as easily as if he had just seen him five minutes ago. Always he loved good conversation. Right up to his last summer, he and Tom Dorsey and Supreme Court Justice Edward White got together regularly, once a week—Tom Dorsey, Jr., serving as bartender—and talked far into the night about art, psychology, government, politics, religion. Tom Dorsey, Jr., always had the feeling that had he listened, he would have learnt a lot. But all he remembered afterward was being startled when Justice White decided, "If I weren't a Catholic, I'd be a Jew."

Even when he was past seventy, James O'Neill enjoyed bowling off to a country fair anywhere in Connecticut. At a moment's notice, he and Tom Dorsey would just pile into a taxi and go. Indeed, long after his death, long after the rains came into the empty house and stained the pine ceiling, long after mischievous boys broke in and carved "MC" on the walnut banister, cards would keep coming to 325 Pequot Avenue from all over Connecticut, inviting James O'Neill to the fair.

Eugene would keep a rich memory of his father, comfortable and unself-conscious in his oldest clothes, puttering about the garden for hours or clipping the hedges, perfectly at peace with himself and the world through the summer afternoons. Later, Eugene, consciously putting himself in the role of his father, would spend hours clipping the hedges around his castle in France or his mansion in Georgia, trying to gain some of the simple pleasure in living that he had always sensed in his father. For Eugene it would always be a struggle to affirm life. He could do so in brief moments of mystical beauty. Otherwise, he had to make a conscious effort to do so, whereas his father had always affirmed life without a moment's thought, simply by enjoying it thoroughly most of the time.

But standing over his father in the Lawrence Memorial Hospital,

Eugene saw the meaning of his father's life in the ending, and the end was all pain and darkness. His last words to Eugene, when his voice was almost gone, were: "Eugene, I'm going to a better sort of life. This sort of life—here—all froth—no good—rottenness!" Eugene never forgot those words. "They were written indelibly—seared on my brain—" he would say afterward, "a warning from Beyond to remain true to the best that is in me though the heavens fall."

It was after midnight on August 10, 1920, when a call from the hospital told the family that Papa was dying. Eugene, Jamie, and Mama dressed hurriedly. They were staying at 55 Channing Street, and Tom Dorsey, Jr., drove them to the hospital. As they got into the car, Jamie said, "A hell of a time for the Old Man to pick to die," and Mama told him to keep quiet, and he did. When they got there, Papa was in a coma. They listened to his last strangled breathing— and then at 4:15 in the morning he died. At last, Eugene felt, Papa was free from his pain; death was for him "a true release—and peace."

The rest was nightmare. Eugene fretted over the whole business of the funeral. He didn't want to enter St. Joseph's Church for the mass. He chafed at their dressing Papa in the full regalia of the Knights of Columbus with baldric and sword. He fretted at the tremendous crowd of people at the funeral, half of New London and all the theater people down from New York. Then Aunt Maggie Platz arrived at the last minute from Cincinnati, and they opened the coffin for her at the grave. Then all the speeches! Postmaster Mahan blew off about how Papa "believed in the future greatness of our city and proved this by investing heavily in real estate." What a tribute to a life that was! Will Connor was better. "Everyone loved him," he said of Papa. "From the boys in the theatre up to the managers he was highly admired. It must have been a great satisfaction to him to have lived to see his son Eugene reach the position he now occupies as the foremost playwright in America." And he concluded with real feeling, for Will Connor truly loved Papa, "He was . . . a man in every sense and in the noblest interpretation of the word. I could not have a too high regard for him."

Eugene felt an enormous gap in his life. He knew that something tremendous was gone from him. For the rest of his life he would try to come to grips with what his father had really meant to him, remembering all the old pain of his rebellion, remembering the profound love. He would never really be able to see his father clearly, would always be too acutely torn by love and bitterness toward him.

But when he himself was aging, he would keep a whole cluster of pictures of his father—as Monte Cristo, as D'Artagnan, as himself, a "simple unpretentious" elderly man—up on the wall where he could see them always, aware that with all the immense differences between them, here was the source of his being. And he would never forget his father's last words, "a warning from Beyond to remain true to the best that is in me though the heavens fall."

I n the next three years, Eugene lost the rest of his family. First Mama, then Jamie. After Papa's death, Mama held up very well at first, perhaps because she was too busy to relapse into suffering. There were the hundreds of telegrams and letters of condolence to be answered and the flowers to be acknowledged. Then there were the tangled remains of the estate. Papa had always told Eugene and Jamie that the money was all tied up in property, that he had little ready cash, and the two of them had always thought this an excuse for pinching pennies. Now, with his death, they found he was right. It proved difficult to take hold of the gold buried in Monte Cristo.

But the tangled estate was Mama's salvation. She developed suddenly into an efficient businesswoman, sharply interested in gathering together the money invested in bits of property all over the country—something like a quarter of a million dollars in land, mines, businesses everywhere. As Tyler commented to Eugene, "It delights me beyond words to hear that she is taking a real interest in things. You see—she never had a chance before—your dear father loved her so much that he couldn't bear to see her be anything else than an ornament."

Jamie, too, curiously enough, revived at the loss of Papa. He had been in a really bad state during the year before Papa died, drinking steadily through the days. He had given up any attempt to continue his "career as a third-rate ham." Right at the end, Papa had tried to set him up in the real estate business, to care for the O'Neill property in New London, but Jamie would collect the rents and then disappear and spend all the money on booze. Papa had laid in a stock of good whiskey when Prohibition was in the air. When he found that Jamie was putting away more than a quart a day, he padlocked the cellar; whereupon Jamie took to picking the lock. He seemed to want nothing but whiskey.

But when the gigantic shadow of his father was removed and Mama had no one else to depend on, Jamie managed at last to stop drinking. He hadn't been able to do it for Pauline Frederick, but he did it for Mama. They were always together, he now perfectly sober, she as elegantly dressed as ever. And as fond of beautiful things. She complained bitterly, after a visit to Eugene and Agnes, at the careless way they used the beautiful linens she had given them when the household on Pequot Avenue broke up. She had always treasured lovely objects. She loved the exquisite jewels James had given her over the years.

For all her interest in straightening out the estate, Mama was fragile from several serious illnesses in the last few years. In January, 1922, she and Jamie were traveling to California to care for some of the property there. At New Orleans she complained of feeling ill. All the way to Los Angeles she kept feeling worse, and Jamie's anxiety mounted. Then—right after they reached the hotel—she had a stroke. Her whole right side was paralyzed. She was conscious only a little while; then followed coma and death. When she no longer recognized him, Jamie lost hold of himself completely and, as he had done throughout his life, turned to alcohol. He was drunk when she died of a brain tumor on February 28, 1922.

All the way back to New York on the train, he drank to dull his misery and his awareness that Mama was lying dead in the baggage car. The old song "And baby's cries can't waken her / In the baggage car ahead" ran persistently through his head. Then, when he got to New York, he realized that he had lost Mama's jewels. How, he didn't know, but he had managed to lose them. It was not merely the value—although the diamonds and pearls were very valuable— but Mama had treasured them. He felt guilt and horror, for he was partly aware that he had lost them as revenge, revenge on her for leaving him alone in the world.

He was in a drunken blur, absolutely devoid of feeling, all through the funeral mass in New York at the church opposite the Prince George Hotel, where Mama had gone to early morning mass. After Mama was buried, Jamie lost all hold on life. He simply wanted to annihilate his consciousness, so he drank steadily, drank anything good or bad that Prohibition allowed him to get until finally his body could take no more. He was put into Riverlawn Sanatorium in Paterson, New Jersey, and there he died on November 8, 1923. The death certificate read, "Arteriosclerosis. Cerebral Apoplexy." New Londoners whispered that he had been "stone blind" before he died, and some spoke of a "strait jacket." However it came, oblivion was what he wanted.

Eugene felt deeply the pain of losing Mama and Jamie before he had had a chance to recover from the loss of Papa. But he never really lost them. They lived vividly in his mind. *A Moon for the Misbegotten* is a requiem for the brother he loved, and his pity for Jamie's wasted life is expressed in Josie's words, "May you have your wish and die in your sleep soon, Jim, darling. May you rest forever in forgiveness and peace."

Eugene put his final thoughts and feelings on the whole family into *Long Day's Journey Into Night*. The play was "written in tears and blood," but also, as Eugene said, "with deep pity and understanding and forgiveness." It embodied all of his old anguish: his feeling of rejection by his father, his uncertainty in his mother's love, his realization of Jamie's destructive influence. And although he wrote with pity and forgiveness, he saw himself to the end as a victim of the father, the mother, the brother he loved. Never was he really able to lift himself out of that "old sorrow."

Later, when his love for Carlotta Monterey brought him some of the peace and security of his childhood, he thought for a while of returning to the house at 325 Pequot Avenue to live. But when he went back with her to see the house, he was shocked and pained by the changes that had destroyed his past. Where woods and fields had been, he found streets lined with identical bungalows. He lost his way. Then, when suddenly he came upon the old house, he found it deformed. The top porch had been blown away, so that the house had a lop-sided spindly look. The large stable in back had vanished. A garage had been dug under the living room. He couldn't bear to look at it, so they drove away.

But Papa and Mama and Jamie—and the house as it had been in his boyhood—lived with him always. So did Jimmy Byth and Terry Carlin (whom he supported right up to his death). The emotional experiences that went into all of his plays came from the years of his youth. So did much of the philosophy that shaped them. When his father died in August, 1920, Eugene O'Neill had reached maturity. He had in him the materials for all the plays he would write; he was at the end of his sowing and at the beginning of his reaping.

Although he was already recognized as America's foremost dramatist, he was perfectly correct when he evaluated himself in the spring of 1920 as "a beginner—with prospects." His major work lay ahead of him, and it was an astonishing achievement, for each work is unique in form and feeling: *The Emperor Jones, The Hairy Ape, All God's Chillun Got Wings, The Great God Brown, Marco Millions, Desire Under the Elms, Lazarus Laughed, Strange Interlude, Mourning Becomes Electra, The Iceman Cometh, Long Day's Journey Into Night.* And from beginning to end of the rich creative years ahead of him, he would remain absolutely faithful to his "highest hope," always working to surpass himself and everything he had done before, remaining, as he had sworn to remain, at his father's deathbed, "true to the best that is in me though the heavens fall."